# Robust Comprehension Instruction
# with Questioning the Author:
# 15 Years Smarter

# Robust Comprehension Instruction with Questioning the Author

## 15 Years Smarter

Isabel L. Beck
Margaret G. McKeown
Cheryl A. Sandora

THE GUILFORD PRESS
New York     London

**Library of Congress Cataloging-in-Publication Data**

Names: Beck, Isabel L., author. | McKeown, Margaret G., author. | Sandora,
   Cheryl, author.
Title: Robust comprehension instruction with questioning the author : 15
   years smarter / Isabel L. Beck, Margaret G. McKeown, Cheryl A. Sandora.
Description: New York : The Guilford Press, [2021] | Includes
   bibliographical references and index.
Identifiers: LCCN 2020028884 | ISBN 9781462544806 (hardcover) | ISBN
   9781462544790 (paperback)
Subjects: LCSH: Reading comprehension. | Questioning. | Discussion. |
   Constructivism (Education)
Classification: LCC LB1573.7 .B434 2021 | DDC 372.47—dc23
LC record available at *https://lccn.loc.gov/2020028884*

# *About the Authors*

**Isabel L. Beck, PhD,** is Professor Emerita of Education at the University of Pittsburgh. She has conducted extensive research and published widely on decoding, vocabulary, and comprehension. She is a recipient of the Oscar S. Causey Award from the Literacy Research Association, the William S. Gray Citation of Merit from the International Literacy Association, and the Contributing Researcher Award from the American Federation of Teachers. Dr. Beck was inducted into the Reading Hall of Fame and is an elected member of the National Academy of Education. She is coauthor of books including *Bringing Words to Life, Second Edition; Creating Robust Vocabulary; Illuminating Comprehension and Close Reading;* and *Making Sense of Phonics, Second Edition.*

**Margaret G. McKeown, PhD,** is Clinical Professor Emerita of Education at the University of Pittsburgh. Before her retirement, she was also a Senior Scientist at the University's Learning Research and Development Center. Her work addresses practical, current problems that classroom teachers and their students face. She has conducted research in the areas of learning, instruction, and teacher professional development in reading comprehension and vocabulary. Dr. McKeown is a recipient of the Outstanding Dissertation Award from the International Literacy Association, is a Fellow of the American Educational Research Association, and was inducted into the Reading Hall of Fame. She is coauthor of books including *Bringing Words to Life, Second Edition; Creating Robust Vocabulary;* and *Vocabulary Assessment to Support Instruction.*

**Cheryl A. Sandora, PhD,** is an English Language Arts Fellow at the Institute for Learning, an outreach of the University of Pittsburgh, where she designs curricular materials and works with districts throughout the country, facilitating professional development sessions and supporting classroom-based instruction. Dr. Sandora was a research associate at the University of Pittsburgh Learning Research and Development Center for over 20 years, working closely with Isabel L. Beck and Margaret G. McKeown to conduct classroom-based research on instructional practices targeting vocabulary and comprehension. She is coauthor of *Illuminating Comprehension and Close Reading.*

# Preface

As implied in the title of this book, we have learned a lot in the 15 years between our earlier book on Questioning the Author (QtA; Beck & McKeown, 2006) and the current one. What we have done and learned during that time is the main reason we have written this book.

To begin, we need to make clear that there were significant differences between our goals 15 years ago and our goals now. Our earlier goals were directly focused on changing the nature of questions to open queries and to reading with interspersed discussions of segments of text. In fact, we were driven by those two goals. Our drive came from several sources, but mostly from reading and analyzing individual students' transcripts, gathered from various studies, in which we asked students to read a text and then tell us about what they had read. Students' responses were recorded and subsequently transcribed. Too many students' transcripts showed confused and confounded responses as well as omissions of what was important. It was often not just one portion of text that was not understood; rather, the problems were cumulative—when students' recall included misunderstood material from an early portion of a text, subsequent recall was often negatively affected. We reasoned that interspersed discussion, in which teachers stop reading and discuss the portion just read, would reduce the chances that students would carry misunderstandings or a lack of understanding of important information into later portions of text. Rather than closed questions (e.g., "What did the colonists do when the British levied taxes?"), open queries such as "What's going on in the section we just read?" would require students to think about what was important and to put ideas together.

As a result of our laser-like attention to those features, we knew some things 15 years ago that we could and should have talked about and incorporated into QtA, but didn't, and we've learned some things since the publication of our earlier book. This book addresses both these things and others.

# Things We Should Have Included but Didn't

We didn't discuss vocabulary in our earlier book and were startled when we recognized our omission of the role of vocabulary in comprehension. Nor did we incorporate vocabulary in our example lesson plans. When that fact stared us in the face, we thought about why we, who had spent so much time engaging in vocabulary research and developing vocabulary instruction, had omitted vocabulary. *Why did we do that?* In retrospect, it was because of our intense preoccupation with changing the nature of questions to open queries and changing the simple answering of questions about the text to interspersed discussion.

After we published our original QtA book, our subsequent projects included the development of Text Talk, a program to enhance comprehension of read-alouds for young children (see, e.g., Beck & McKeown, 2004; McKeown & Beck, 2006). In the course of that work, we quite naturally included vocabulary and wrap-up queries in our example lessons. Perhaps by that time we took the use of interspersed reading and discussion as a given, thus making it obvious for us to include vocabulary in comprehension instruction and to provide a coda in the form of a wrap-up query that usually asked for students to give their opinions about aspects of a story. You can be sure that we have rightfully broadened our input into text-based comprehension and that we discuss vocabulary in this book. We also show how we incorporate vocabulary in our example lesson plans. As for wrap-up queries, we have included some for our example lessons, but we recognize the importance of including wrap-up activities that take students into deeper levels of the text. Thus we offer other useful and motivating after-reading activities tied to the text at hand.

# What We've Learned since Publication
# of the Earlier QtA Book

Our learning has come from two areas: the relevant research literature and observing QtA in operation in classrooms and talking with teachers and students who were using it.

## From Research

We have seen that a cognitive processing model has been reaffirmed in hundreds of articles. In fact, it is so much a given in psychological research on reading that many authors take the general model underlying their research for granted and go on to investigate very fine details of this model. Thus our attempt to make public what readers do as they read and comprehend stands on a strong foundation. Given the broad-based empirical support for the cognitive processing model, we attempt in this book to underscore the role of the model in comprehension.

From the more education-oriented research, one of our take-aways is that after-reading open discussions are useful and motivating (Kim et al., 2016). After-reading discussions are different from the interspersed discussions in our original QtA, which we continue to herald. Once again, in Text Talk we did include such prompts. In fact, we learned from teachers who used Text Talk that after-reading discussion prompts worked well with young children. A favorite example comes from *Beware of the Bears* (MacDonald, 1998), in which the three bears pay Goldilocks back by trashing her house. The prompt and responses follow:

- "What do you think about the bears trashing Goldilocks's house? Was it a good thing or not a good thing and why do you think that?"

- "It was kind of good and kind of not good because the bear did what Goldilocks had did . . . messed up the bears' house and it was bad because they should have forgot . . . I mean forgiven her."

The point is, you can be sure that after-reading prompts are discussed and examples provided in this book.

## From Teachers

Since the publication of our previous QtA book, we've observed about 3,000 classroom QtA lessons and talked with teachers and students about them. Although all three of us have been in classrooms, Cheryl has been in the majority. The 3,000 estimate is not all from different classrooms, as we have been in some classrooms multiple times. These classrooms have been in a dozen states beyond our home state of Pennsylvania, where the majority of visits took place. Also not included in the 3,000 visits were the reports and meetings with three teachers from a public school district who were on special assignment with our working group at the university for a year. Part of the three teachers' responsibilities was to observe QtA lessons, meet with teachers and provide feedback, and take note of specific problems and comments.

Those observations and discussions enriched our own thinking about QtA and how it is practiced in classrooms, including successes, challenges, and a learning process. Indeed, questions or comments that have come from teachers over time have resulted in the last five chapters of this book.

- Can we incorporate vocabulary? How should we handle vocabulary in the course of reading?

- Will students transfer what they learn from QtA to independent reading?

- The ideas used in QtA might be used in writing. Have you ever tried it?

- You've shown us teachers who are skilled at QtA, but I would like to see a teacher's progress. You know, I'd like to see someone who is just learning.

- It's hard to tell from a video how the moves are being used. Can you make that clearer?

We are grateful to the many teachers who have told us that "QtA works." And we love to hear comments such as "Both kids and I look forward to QtA time" and "I told my class that if they didn't settle down we would not do QtA." One teacher who struggled at the beginning of the year told us at the end of the year, "I would never have believed that I am so good at doing QtA." And finally, when students see one of us enter their classroom, some let the others know by saying, "Here comes the QtA lady!"

## Structure and Content

In this book, the basic QtA elements of open queries and interspersed discussion continue to be the linchpins of reading and comprehension, as in our other writings and research on the approach. But in the years that we and others have worked with QtA in classrooms, we have developed some enhanced ways to explain, exemplify, and enrich it. Below we describe the content of each of the 12 chapters.

Chapter 1, "The Building Blocks of Questioning the Author," explains the basic elements of the QtA approach to reading and discussion. This overview includes how QtA aligns with comprehension processes and how we came to develop the approach.

Chapter 2, "The Current Scene in Reading Comprehension," explores current topics and foci in reading comprehension. Topics include the knowledge that underlies reading and a review of current popular topics in literacy publications. The chapter also discusses what appear to be the two dominant approaches to comprehension instruction: strategies and discussion.

Chapters 3, 4, 5, and 6 provide the heart of the QtA approach. Chapter 3, "Planning for Questioning the Author Lessons," explains the particular planning process for QtA lessons and the rationale for each component of that process.

Chapter 4, "Specific Plans for a Narrative and an Expository Text," provides examples of full plans for both narrative and expository texts aimed at mid-elementary to middle school readers.

Chapter 5, "Digging into Initiating and Follow-Up Queries," provides elaborated discussion of Queries to deepen understanding of how they differ from other question types and to provide more specific guidance about how to develop Queries.

Chapter 6, "Specific Plans for a Narrative and an Expository Read-Aloud Text," describes how QtA can be used with young readers and provides full plans for a narrative and an expository read-aloud text. The chapter also includes discussion of particular issues in working with young children's comprehension and of our development of Text Talk, the companion approach to QtA for very young students.

Chapters 7, 8, and 9 address topics we have worked with for some time—but not written about before—within QtA. Chapter 7, "What Comes after Reading and Interspersed Discussion?," presents options for prompting final discussion and reflection following a QtA lesson. This includes Wrap-Up Queries, which review major text points, and other tasks such as interpretive questions for deeper discussion and rereading text portions for targeted discussion.

Chapter 8, "Vocabulary in the Context of Comprehension," begins with an exploration of how our robust vocabulary principles apply in planning QtA text lessons, with a focus on selecting words from texts that merit brief attention, extended attention, and after-text attention. As we discuss, introducing word meanings makes it far from certain that the words will be permanently learned, because vocabulary learning is a cumulative process. Thus we also include activities for following up the introduction of words toward developing fuller learning. The focus here is on words from texts that a teacher deems worthwhile for students to add to their permanent vocabulary repertoires.

Chapter 9, "Approaching Writing with a Questioning the Author Perspective," examines how a QtA perspective can be incorporated into teaching writing. Discussion includes the similarities between the QtA process and the writing process, embedding writing prompts in QtA lessons, and using QtA format to provide feedback on students' writing. As it turns out, we have tried to use QtA-type prompts for writing on several occasions with results that appear to be useful to students and make sense to teachers. Thus, given teachers' requests and the logical relationship between reading and writing, we share our experiences in this chapter.

Chapters 10, 11, and 12 all take us inside QtA classrooms. Chapter 10, "Moves to Keep Discussion Productive," introduces the concept of Discussion Moves that emerged from QtA implementations. The Moves are particular ways of responding to students that seemed to succeed in promoting meaningful discussion. The chapter presents examples of the use of Moves via transcripts from two QtA teachers' classrooms.

Chapter 11, "One Teacher's Journey with Questioning the Author," is based on requests we heard from teachers to see a teacher's own progress from early efforts to implement QtA to greater expertise. That request initiated some filming and transcribing, and in this chapter we show and discuss one teacher's growth. Changing patterns across the school year show how both teacher and students gain comfort and proficiency in their interactions around text.

The final chapter, Chapter 12, "Students Take the Wheel," turns to the eventual goal of QtA, having students take charge of their own comprehension. Here we address the question of transfer, the holy grail of attempts to influence behavior: Does experience with QtA lead to enhanced independent comprehension of texts? The discussion includes a sequence on how to move students from teacher-led, whole-class discussions to student-led discussions in small groups, to guiding students to use a QtA process when reading independently.

# Contents

## Background and Basics

## Questioning the Author Essentials

## Special Topics

# Inside the Classroom

# Appendix: Lesson Texts from Chapters 4 and 6

# Background and Basics

# CHAPTER 1

# The Building Blocks of Questioning the Author

Helping students deal effectively with text arose as a focus for us some decades ago. Our purpose was to develop effective comprehension instruction. Both our research work and our development of comprehension instruction were grounded in a cognitive processing perspective. An important message on comprehension today is that that view still holds. It is still the dominant explanation for how comprehension occurs (see, e.g., Byrnes & Wasik, 2019; Kim et al., 2016). So we thought it useful to start with a short description of that orientation.

As our earlier book (2006) explained, a cognitive processing view of comprehension provided the framework for Questioning the Author (QtA). That perspective views comprehension as a reader's active process of attending to information in text, making decisions about what information is important, holding that information in memory as further information is encountered, and making connections to new relevant information—all driven by the goal of making sense of the text, or in more cognitive terms, building a coherent representation of what a text is trying to communicate.

The goal of making sense of information in a text requires drawing connections between pieces of text information using two possible sources—information from preceding sentences in the text or relevant background knowledge. This perspective is mainly attributed to the work of Kintsch and van Dijk (1978), with many other researchers also explicating aspects of the theory and its implications (see, e.g., Fletcher, van den Broek, & Arthur, 1996; Graesser, Singer, & Trabasso, 1994; van den Broek, 1994; van den Broek, Young, Tzeng, & Linderholm, 1998).

The cognitive processing perspective made clear several aspects of reading not emphasized in earlier descriptions of the reading process. First, reading requires that the reader be engaged in an active mental process of dealing with information rather than being a mere recipient of a text's message. Second, as readers read they need to connect and integrate information rather than simply accumulating it (Linderholm, Virtue, Tzeng, & van den Broek, 2004; van den Broek & Kendeou, 2008).

The following is an illustration of how the process plays out on a simple text.

| Text | A reader's take | Relation to process |
|------|-----------------|---------------------|
| Mia, a 6-year old girl, wanted a puppy. | Girl wants puppy; possibly anticipating that parents don't want one. | Selection of key ideas and relating to knowledge of similar situations. |
| Her parents said that they would be happy to add a dog to the family. | Possible hurdle to getting a dog not at issue. | Revise anticipated conflict. |
| Her older brother, Mike, wanted a big dog he could run with. | New character has a desire—alert to possible problem. | Add new text info and anticipate how it may affect the story. |
| But Mia wanted a fluffy little dog that she could cuddle. | Root of problem is presented. Mia and Mike want different things; possible conflict likely. | Connect new information and anticipate how it may affect the story. |

QtA's approach to text embodies the cognitive processing orientation through its focus on the importance of students' active efforts to build meaning from what they read and the need for students to work at figuring out and grappling with ideas in a text. Next we provide a short overview of how we got started and brief descriptions of the features of QtA.

## How We Got Started

The work we have done in comprehension, as well as that in decoding and vocabulary, has kept us close to the schools. We have visited classrooms, worked with teachers, and interacted with students. Given this background, the road to developing QtA began with our observations that often young readers "went through" a text without understanding it. In our attempts to understand how students comprehend text and eventually develop ways to support students' comprehension, we conducted a number of studies to try out ideas with individual students as well as with borrowed classrooms. We developed many of the ideas we tried out based on an analysis we had conducted on the texts and lessons within the then-current basal readers, in particular the questions teachers' editions suggested asking students about the materials that they read (Beck, McKeown, McCaslin, & Burkes, 1979).

We often found questions in the basals to be inadequate in terms of their sequences and the content that was queried. In consideration of these issues we developed the construct of a "Story Map" (Beck & McKeown, 1981)—subsequently changed to a text map as it was intended to apply to both fiction and nonfiction. Our construct of a text map was that questions be developed based on a logical organization of events and ideas of central importance to the text and the interrelationships of these events and ideas—and most importantly that questions can't be evaluated in isolation. Rather, the value of a question depends on the text content that the question queried.

We then conducted several studies in which we redesigned lesson components and lesson texts in ways we believed would be effective for student understanding. We began by studying whether text map questions improved comprehension by comparing such questions to those in the basals and found that they did (Beck, Omanson, & McKeown, 1982). We also revised texts to make them more coherent and compared students' comprehension of the revised versions to basal texts. Again, there was improvement in students' comprehension (Beck, McKeown, Omanson, & Pople, 1984). We also studied adding a component of background knowledge to lessons (McKeown, Beck, Sinatra, & Loxterman, 1992) and again found benefits for students. But even though comprehension improved in those studies, it was far from optimal.

Given our results, we began to formulate what was needed to assist students' understanding of text. Our answer lay in helping in the course of reading the text. That is, intervening in what students were doing when they were casting their eyes on text and requiring them to consider—attend to, focus on—what the text offered and use that to make sense for themselves. Our first attempts to intervene in students' processing involved trying to figure out what students were thinking as they went through a text, by using a think-aloud procedure. We gave students a text to read and stopped them after each sentence to ask them to talk about what they had read. As we proceeded, we began to alter the probes we asked the students to see if we could prompt students to be more reflective about the text and to reveal more of what they were thinking. It was in that round of exploration that we discovered that when we asked open questions, especially those that referenced the author, such as "What do you think the author is trying to say?" we were more likely to get useful information or to get the students to take a further look at the text content.

## Other Approaches to Influencing Comprehension

As we completed our work on investigating and working to enhance student comprehension, we were aware that many colleagues in the reading field were also engaged in developing approaches to affect comprehension. One line of work sought to find the strategies that mature readers use as they read and then develop approaches for teaching, modeling, and practicing these strategies. A number of different strategies as well as a number of different approaches to teaching them to students were proposed, such as Reciprocal Teaching (Palincsar & Brown, 1984), Informed Strategies for Learning (Paris, Cross, & Lipson, 1984), Direct Explanation (Duffy et al., 1987), Transactional Strategies Instruction (Pressley et al., 1992), and cognitive process instruction (Gaskins, Anderson, Pressley, Cunicelli, & Satlow, 1993).

In our experience, strategy instruction has an inherent potential drawback, in that the attention of teachers and students can too easily be drawn to the mechanics of the strategies themselves rather than to the content of what is being read. Indeed, other researchers have questioned the necessity of employing specific strategies if the goal of reading as an active search for meaning could be kept in mind (see, e.g., Carver, 1987; Dole, Duffy, Roehler, & Pearson, 1991; Pearson & Fielding, 1991; McKeown, Beck, & Blake, 2009).

In the 1990s, another line of work with the goal of getting students actively involved in reading emerged from observations that discussion plays an important role. A number of different approaches to fostering collaborative discussion were developed, such as the Reflective Thinking Project (Anderson et al., 1992), the Book Club Project (McMahon, Raphael, Goately, Boyd, & Pardo, 1992), the Conversational Discussion Groups Project (O'Flahavan & Stein, 1992), Instructional Conversations (Goldenberg, 1992), and the Junior Great Books reading and discussion program (Dennis & Moldof, 1983). A major difference between discussion under these approaches and QtA is that those discussions take place after reading. Thus the ongoing process of building meaning that takes place during reading, or mentally "online," is not addressed.

A third direction of work on activating readers' engagement relates to the notion of promoting an active search for meaning. This work involves directing students to explain the information presented in their textbooks to themselves as they read. Chi and her colleagues have found that self-explanations can be elicited from students, and that when they are, students are better able to learn the material presented to them (Chi, Bassok, Lewis, Reimann, & Glaser, 1989; Chi, de Leeuw, Chiu, & LaVancher, 1994).

Questioning the Author shares features with these other approaches to learning from text. However, its uniqueness lies in combining collaboration with during-reading, explanatory responses.

## Building Understanding: An Overview of QtA

*Building understanding,* the goal of QtA, is what a reader needs to do to read successfully. Building understanding involves figuring out what text information we need to pay attention to and connecting that to other information. According to this view, learning can't happen by simply "getting" information from a source, nor can it simply be delivered to a learner. Rather a learner must actively deal with the information in a text in order to make sense of it. Such interactions with text are at the heart of the cognitive perspective that frames QtA.

An excellent example of the difference between "getting information" and understanding information was the incident in a fourth-grade class that several of us witnessed, when a student responded to a teacher's question with virtually the same words as were in the text. The teacher responded, "That's what the author said, but what did the author mean?" When students read a text in a QtA lesson, they are taught to address text ideas immediately, while they are reading. That is, they are taught to consider meaning, to develop and grapple with the ideas on a page that are at the ends of their noses. This is quite different from asking students to answer questions about a text after they have finished reading it. At that point, comprehension already has or has not occurred.

Given the importance of building meaning as one reads, how do you get students to do that? How do you get students to become actively involved as they read, to dive into even difficult information and grapple to make sense of it? Toward dealing with those questions, below we consider features of QtA.

## Text

QtA was initially designed to help students understand social studies textbooks, which at the time were notorious for less than coherent texts (Beck, McKeown, & Gromoll, 1989). But as we began to introduce the approach to teachers, we quickly recognized that QtA could be useful with other genres. Thus we made minor adjustments for various genres, and QtA has been successfully used with both expository and narrative texts. This includes social studies textbooks, science textbooks, basal reading selections, both fiction and nonfiction, novels, short stories, trade books, plays, and poems. We cannot think of a genre in which QtA, with minimal adjustment, would not work. In fact one of our former colleagues, Ms. O., a public school teacher who, for a while, was on special assignment from her district to our Working Group at the university, was a Sunday school teacher who adapted QtA. In the study of the Gospels, she asked such queries as "What did Luke mean when he said . . . ?" and even "What was God trying to say?" One of our colleagues, Dr. L., whose research included learning in museum environments, often suggested asking, "What do you think the artist wanted to communicate in this painting/sculpture/installation?"

## Interspersed Reading

We teach students that readers "take on" a text little by little, idea by idea, and try to understand, while they are reading, what ideas are there and how they might connect or relate those ideas. We do this to simulate what a competent reader does in the course of reading. While you are reading you are making sense of it as you go along, even though it may seem like one smooth, seamless process. You do not put comprehension on hold until you have completed a text, or even a section of text.

In contrast, it is a fairly typical teaching practice to assign material to be read and then to pose questions to evaluate student comprehension. This is basically an "after-the-fact" procedure. Because students are left on their own until reading is complete, this may not lead to productive reading for several reasons. First, students may have questions in their minds as they read or simply finish a text knowing only that they are lost but not sure why. Moreover, there is no way for teachers to know if some students have constructed misconceptions about the passage but think they have understood it. And even though students hear "right" answers in after-reading questioning, they may never understand what makes them right. But in QtA the goal is to assist students in understanding what a portion of text is about at the point of reading that portion for the first time, as well as to support them to see how ideas in previous text fit with current text.

### Interspersed Discussion

Building meaning in the course of reading means going back and forth between reading segments of text—be they a paragraph or two or a chapter in a novel—and giving voice to the ideas encountered in the segment. In fact, occasionally stopping after a sentence of great importance or a particularly difficult sentence is appropriate. There are several options for who reads the text and how it is read. A student or the teacher may read the text segment orally and the students follow along, or the teacher assigns the students to read a text segment silently. Thus the activity structure used for developing meaning intersperses reading with discussing what is read. The purpose for engaging students in these interspersed interactions in QtA departs from what is conventionally viewed as classroom discussion. Classroom discussions are typically characterized by students sharing opinions and ideas after they have already read a text and formulated their own thoughts and views about the text.

In QtA, the intention of interspered discussion is to assist students in the process of developing meaning from a text. Therefore, the discussion takes place in the course of reading a text for the first time as students share in the experience of learning how to build meaning from a text. Perhaps one of the ways to best understand the distinction is to remember that unlike in many kinds of discussions, the QtA teacher is actively involved as a facilitator, guide, initiator, and responder. This is different from, for example, Collaborative Reasoning (Reznitskaya, Kuo, Glina, & Anderson, 2009), in which a teacher sets a discussion in motion by providing a question or topical issue, and the students explore the issue with little teacher involvement.

### Queries

In a QtA lesson the interaction of text and discussion is accomplished through Queries. Queries are general probes the teacher uses to initiate and develop discussion. Queries *are* questions, but to emphasize their distinctive features and not get confused with other labels for types of questions in the field (e.g., literal, interpretive), we initiated the term *Queries*. We have seen that teachers adopt the term and refer to *Queries* when talking about QtA and use the term *questions* for non-QtA conversations.

The goal of Queries is to prompt students to consider meaning and develop ideas rather than to retrieve information and state facts. Queries are text based and open. By "open," we mean that a Query does not provide much directive information about what a correct response should be. As an example, two of us were observing a lesson in a middle school with a text called "The Tiger's Heart," in which a lion terrorizes a village at night. The story starts with two paragraphs: the first describes the jungle in the day, emphasizing how comfortable and familiar it is to the village inhabitants, and the second paragraph describes the jungle at night, and how the darkness makes it feel alien and forbidding. The teacher's question was "How does the author compare and contrast the jungle in the day and the night?"

The problem is that the question does too much work. The point of the two paragraphs is to portray the difference in the look and sound of the jungle in the night and the day, but the teacher's question already served up that information. In contrast, questions such as "What's going on in the first two paragraphs?" or "What has the author set up in the first two paragraphs?" would have encouraged students to develop that point themselves.

As noted earlier, Queries are frequently author oriented, and they place the responsibility for thinking and building meaning on students. Some examples of Queries are "So what is the author trying to tell us?"; "What have we learned in this section?"; and "What has the author told us here that connects with something we read earlier?" We will talk more about Queries in a subsequent chapter, but for now it is important to know that Queries are a key instructional tool in QtA discussions that assists students in building understanding from text.

## Collaboration

The point of QtA is to get students to grapple with an author's ideas and, if necessary, to challenge an author's intended meaning in an effort to build understanding. To accomplish this we need to hear student voices, encourage their contributions, and urge them to wrestle with ideas. Students need to learn the power of collaborating with their peers and teacher in constructing meaning.

Public grappling with text gives students the opportunity to hear from each other, to question and consider alternative possibilities, and to test their own ideas in a safe environment. Everyone is grappling, everyone is engaged in building meaning, and everyone understands that the author, not the teacher, has presented them with this challenge. The chance for cumulative misconceptions diminishes, and the opportunity for some authentic wrestling with ideas and meaningful discussion increases.

## A Snapshot of How QtA Plays Out

As text is read, the teacher intervenes at selected points and poses Queries to prompt students to consider information just read: "What's the author telling us here?" Students respond by contributing ideas: "I think the family is suspecting that someone was in their house when they were away." Students' responses may then be built upon, refined, or challenged by other students, or the teacher may prompt the student to elaborate: "They suspect someone has been in their house, what makes you say that?" Students and the teacher work collaboratively, interacting to grapple with ideas and build understanding. "Because the box wasn't where they left it" . . . "the box was their secret" . . . "now they are afraid someone has figured out their secret."

This back-and-forth process requires decisions about where to stop reading a text and begin discussion of ideas. It is the task of a QtA teacher to analyze and identify the important concepts of a text ahead of the students and make decisions about how much of the text needs to be read at once and why. In subsequent chapters, we will discuss in detail how to make decisions about where to segment a text.

## A Student Gets the Final Word

A QtA lesson requires students to be active. They need to work at figuring out and grappling with ideas in a text. A classroom anecdote from Gail Friedman's fifth-grade suggests that the students in Ms. Friedman's class worked. During the last week of school Ms. Friedman assigned the students to write about QtA. She told them that besides saying what QtA was, if they liked it they needed to say why, and similarly, if they didn't like it they needed to say why. Below is what one of Ms. Friedman's students wrote:

> What I like about QtA is that people let other people know what they're thinking. What I dislike is that it makes us work too hard! When we're done, it makes us feel like we're dead!

Short of being dead, we can't be more pleased that QtA makes students work hard.

### ENDING NOTES

- A cognitive processing view of comprehension provided the framework for our original QtA book, 15 years ago, and given that it is still the dominant explanation for how comprehension occurs, it remains the underlying theoretical orientation for the current work.

- The goal of comprehension is to make sense of text, or in more cognitive terms, build a coherent representation of what a text is trying to communicate.

- A cognitive processing perspective views comprehension as an active process in which a reader attends to information in text, decides what information is important, holds that information in memory as further information is encountered, and makes connections to new relevant information.

- For many years and continuing to the writing of this book, studies of students reading school texts show that they often do not develop adequate comprehension of what they read.

- Although studies in which we engaged as well as other studies show that comprehension can be improved by designing lessons that include a logical sequence of questions and provide relevant background knowledge and more coherent text, students' comprehension is still often sparse, or at least not good enough.

- QtA is an instructional approach based on supporting students' engagement with text in a way that mimics a successful comprehension process of building meaning from text.

- QtA operates by having a teacher pose Queries—open prompts to consider text context—as text is initially read. As students respond, the teacher follows up to encourage students to elaborate, connect, and collaborate toward building meaning from what they are reading.

# CHAPTER 2

# The Current Scene
# in Reading Comprehension

In this chapter we explore what's going on in reading comprehension currently, considering, first, the topics and concerns that are discussed by both researchers and practitioners. Second, the chapter explores key instructional approaches for comprehension that are garnering current attention.

In Chapter 1 we discussed the cognitive-processing perspective on comprehension that underlies QtA and indicated that this perspective is still the dominant explanation for how comprehension occurs (see, e.g., Byrnes & Wasik, 2019; Kim et al., 2016). With this understanding of comprehension generally accepted, there is currently much less ongoing work on the process of comprehension itself. Rather the current focus seems to be on knowledge and precursors that can affect comprehension processes in individuals and specific populations.

## Knowledge for Reading

A major focus of discussions of what affects comprehension is background knowledge. A reader's background, or prior knowledge, is important to comprehension because it is impossible for an author to include every piece of information a reader needs to comprehend a text. To take a simple example, consider the following two sentences: "Allen grabbed his cup of coffee from the counter, and it sloshed out onto the woman standing next to him. She cried out, and then looked down at her white dress." Now consider just a few key pieces of knowledge needed to understand the situation communicated by those sentences: Coffee is a liquid; grabbing a cup of liquid can cause it to spill; coffee is hot—thus the woman cried out; it can stain clothing—thus the horror when looking at her dress. The coffee example required what we might call everyday knowledge. But consider the degree to which lack of background knowledge could reduce a reader's comprehension of academic texts in history or science, or narrative texts that include places and topics beyond students' experiences.

Concerns about lack of background knowledge being an obstacle to student under-standing are well founded and have been acknowledged as a serious problem long before the present. Yet, the aspect of the problem that needs to be brought forward is that reading is a major way that we build a knowledge base, and learning how to learn from text is a part of becoming a good reader. Ideally, the texts students read should allow them to access the content and learn new information. However, think of the utter impossibility of having such a text for every student.

Providing relevant background knowledge before a text is read has been a com-mon part of reading lessons for decades. We did this ourselves in several of our stud-ies and found that students who received the background knowledge before reading did show better comprehension. However, a word of caution is needed here. Providing background knowledge should not replace learning information from reading. That is, if the information that the text is designed to communicate is provided before reading, then reading itself become unnecessary. If the goal is to provide reading experiences to build students' ability to comprehend, then the students need to use the text as their key information source.

So background information should be just that—background for understanding a text. If information is provided prior to reading, it should only be information essen-tial to assist understanding of and making connections to text ideas. For example, students reading a story set against the backdrop of the attack on Pearl Harbor might need some scene setting about the conflict that was going on before the attack, but they do not need to engage in a general discussion of World War II beyond those details. Certainly exploring the topic of World War II and engaging students in discus-sions around that topic could be worthwhile for extending their personal knowledge stores, but it is not necessary for immediate text comprehension.

## Knowledge of Language

Discussions of the need for prior knowledge usually feature content knowledge—knowledge of certain facts or disciplinary content that may be reflected in a text. But there are other types of knowledge that readers need as well, and this has been another recent focus in work on comprehension. A key body of knowledge here is knowledge of language and how language operates—phonological/orthographic, semantic, syntac-tic, and morphological knowledge.

### Phonological Knowledge

To allow the reading process to proceed efficiently, readers need to recognize words very quickly—what is often called "by sight"—as when a competent reader reads aloud with no apparent hesitation. But readers also need to figure out the pronun-ciation of words that they don't recognize instantly. Both cases implicate the need for readers to understand the letter–sound (or grapheme–phoneme) correspondences that enable the faithful representation of spoken English. The 26 letters in English result in 44 phonemes because some letters, particularly vowels, represent several different phonemes and some phonemes are represented by two letters; the sounds of /t/, /h/, and /th/ together are each phonemes. Thus if readers know the details of the relationship between written letters and their sounds, they can decode words that are unfamiliar.

## Orthographic Knowledge

As readers build their phonological knowledge, they also develop orthographic knowledge. Orthographic knowledge means understanding patterns of written words or subword parts, such as recognizing *tion* as a pronounceable English unit and *jksf* as not a pronounceable English unit. The orthography of a language is essentially its spelling system. Orthographic knowledge is important to reading as it allows readers to get through print with greater efficiency than phoneme-by-phoneme phonological knowledge alone.

## Syntactic Knowledge

Readers need to be familiar with the syntactic or grammatical patterns of language, which includes understanding that words have different functions (nouns, verbs, etc.) and the patterns by which words are combined into sentences. Syntactic knowledge allows you to, for example, read "John held the dog that bit Sara" and know who did what to whom!

## Semantic Knowledge

Readers need to know the meanings of words, and know them well enough to quickly bring them to mind as they are encountered in a text. Semantic knowledge is what you know about the meaning aspect of language. This includes not just what individual words mean, but how words operate in language, for example, that words take on different senses in different contexts, or that words are associated with other words that have similar meanings or that are used in similar circumstances. It is pretty obvious that semantic knowledge, or we can call it vocabulary knowledge, is strongly related to one's ability to read a text and understand it. In fact, researchers have called vocabulary knowledge the linchpin of successful comprehension (Perfetti & Stafura, 2014).

## Morphological Knowledge

Readers need to understand that words can have parts added to them and what these parts can do to their meanings: for example, *certain* is related to *uncertain,* as its opposite. The word *certain* and the prefix *un-* are both morphemes, which are the smallest meaningful units of language. Thus a word like *unhappiness* has three morphemes—the root word, *happy,* a prefix, *un-,* and a suffix, *-ness.*

Additional types of morphemes include suffixes indicating number (*-s, -es*) or tense (*-ed, -ing*) and roots that are not freestanding words. An example is the root *nov,* meaning new, which is found in the words *novice, novel,* and *renovate.* Typically such roots are part of the Latin heritage of English. Being able to take advantage of morphological relationships—such as understanding that someone "unreliable" cannot be relied upon—makes for efficient understanding of new words met in text. In fact, Anglin (1993) found that this kind of understanding accounts for a large part of vocabulary growth in second through fifth grades.

## Sources for Developing Knowledge

How do we acquire this knowledge? Prior to schooling, knowledge of language comes primarily from hearing and interacting with oral language. Being read to adds to language development, and then as children become readers, reading itself is a major source of language knowledge. These same sources, oral language and interacting with books, provide the basis for an individual's background knowledge as well, with the addition of experience—the more places you go, the more you know! You may have noticed a bit of a catch-22 here—knowledge is needed for reading, but a major source for building knowledge *is* reading. What that means is that to become even a novice reader, you need to have built enough knowledge to get started.

The relationship between reading ability and aspects of language is strong and well established, meaning that people who have greater knowledge of phonology, orthography, vocabulary, syntax, and morphology are more successful comprehenders. The extent to which specific instruction in those aspects is valuable is less clear, although the research base makes a strong argument that instruction in systematic phonics is a useful, and for many students necessary, step toward becoming a reader, and that high-quality instruction in vocabulary can boost comprehension. As far as phonics, some of the seminal work in the area is discussed in Adams (1990) and recently in Torgerson, Brooks, Gascoine, and Higgins (2019). Beck and Beck (2013) also provide a review of the literature and present evidence-based instructional procedures. But let us say a bit more about vocabulary, as that will be an aspect we include as we explore and illustrate the QtA approach.

A body of research going back nearly 80 years has shown the key role of vocabulary in understanding text (Davis, 1944; Perfetti & Stafura, 2014; Spearitt, 1972). Decades of research on how to boost comprehension by improving vocabulary have shown that instruction can reliably increase vocabulary knowledge, but those gains do not always transfer to comprehension (Elleman, Lindo, Morphy, & Compton, 2009; Stahl & Fairbanks, 1986). The research has also developed consensus on the type of vocabulary instruction that is likely to lead to comprehension gains. This instruction provides both definitional and contextual information about words, provides multiple encounters with individuals words, and engages students in interactions in which they need to, for example, make decisions about word use and generate contexts for words (National Reading Panel, 2000; Wright & Cervetti, 2017).

The aspects of knowledge discussed here serve as resources for the comprehension processes. If they are adequate, then comprehension can proceed. If they exhibit weaknesses, then they may become obstacles that cause the comprehension process to break down. But a major takeaway from this discussion should be that no matter what knowledge- or language-related issues a student may be dealing with, the comprehension process itself is essentially the same. It still requires attending to and making decisions about information in text, and connecting that information to subsequent text information as well as prior knowledge.

QtA takes account of various influences on and potential obstacles to comprehension by focusing on the comprehension process and providing relevant guidance as it unfolds. The specifics of how QtA deals with issues of language and background knowledge is embedded within the chapters that follow.

# Other Current Topics and Concerns

An array of topics related to promoting reading comprehension appears in recent journals for both researchers and practitioners, in books intended for reading professionals, and on the International Literacy Association's annual Hot Topics survey (*https:// literacyworldwide.org/get-resources/whats-hot-report*). Here we draw attention to several common topics that appear to recur with some frequency. These are *technology and online reading, culturally responsive teaching,* and an associated issue of choice in reading materials, *English learners* within the broader issue of differentiating instruction, and *text complexity.*

## Technology and Online Reading

This topic is also referred to as digital literacy. Two issues of concern that arise as reading becomes more focused on the Internet are, first, that dealing with the Internet presents a very different kind of requirement for locating texts and evaluating sources.

Second, online texts present unique challenges such as using links and navigating pages and menus. The types of information contained in online texts include embedded video, interactive graphics, and click-throughs. Digitally native texts add layers of complexity and decision making to the challenge of making sense of text. Research in this area focuses on how different modes of information complement or detract from one another to influence comprehension. The issues of interest may or may not overlap with processes of getting information from printed language—traditional reading. Clearly there are similar processes at play, but dealing with digital texts and the selection of online sources calls on many other processes as well. For exploration and discussion of issues in reading online, see Cho and Afflerbach (2015) and Coiro and Dobler (2007).

## Culturally Responsive Teaching

Culturally responsive teaching (CRT) is based on tailoring instruction to make school experiences more compatible with students' cultures and acknowledging the legitimacy of students' histories and cultures (McIntyre, 2015). The underlying motivation for CRT is that of bringing equity in education to all learners. In reading, CRT particularly relates to the kinds of participation patterns that characterize different cultures and the kinds of connections students make as they read. As examples of participation patterns, McIntyre points to the preference for group work and discussion in African American culture and overlapping speech in native Hawaiian culture. An issue is that teachers may see these as departing from classroom norms, and recognizing them as cultural practices and integrating them into classroom routines requires sensitivity and effort.

Diverse cultural histories may lead students to make quite different connections to and among text ideas than a teacher might expect. Or students might miss connections that might seem clear to students familiar with the dominant culture. It is also the case that students from other cultures and ethnicities may not recognize themselves in texts presented in school.

The situation of students' likenesses and cultures being represented in texts reflects a more general issue also prominent in literacy instruction literature, student interest in and choice of reading materials. A persistent theme in current discussions of literacy instruction is that the selection of reading materials used in school should reflect students' interests and backgrounds, and at least some of the time students should be able to select their own materials. Underlying these recommendations are the role of motivation in engaging students in reading and the ability of students' knowledge about topics of interest to propel them as readers.

Using principles of CRT includes being aware of multiple cultures within a classroom and learning to honor and integrate practices from other cultures. This approach can help students not only honor their own cultural beliefs but also gain access to other cultures and to the wider culture.

## English Learners

The concerns around English learners (ELs) are a special case of larger issues of differentiating instruction to provide appropriate support for students of differing strengths, challenges, and backgrounds, and of providing for educational equity. Students whose first language is not English make up approximately 8% of the student population in U.S. K–12 public schools. However, the EL population varies greatly across the country, ranging from 0.09% in West Virginia to just over 20% in California (*https://nces. ed.gov/programs/coe/indicator_cgf.asp*). ELs often have word-level skills that are on a par with native English speakers; however, their higher-level literacy skills, especially comprehension, tend to lag behind. Possibly the most serious issue ELs face is the need to acquire English academic vocabulary (Rueda, Unrau, & Son, 2015).

Researchers who focus on English learners emphasize that although there are some evidence-based strategies that can be integrated into the curriculum specifically for ELs, comprehension instruction that is effective for native English speakers is also effective for ELs (August & Shanahan, 2006; Goldenberg, 2006).

## Text Complexity

Concerns over text complexity arose around questions of whether students were receiving an appropriate progression of challenging texts to feed development of increasingly higher-order reading skills. Common sense would dictate that students need "just right" texts, not so hard that they cannot access them, but hard enough to offer opportunities for growth and acquisition of new vocabulary. The challenge is how to analyze texts to find that sweet spot. Text difficulty comes from a variety of factors including text structure, knowledge demands, syntactic complexity, language clarity, and cohesion. Traditional readability formulas capture a very restricted set of factors, basically sentence length and a rough measure of word difficulty. The Lexiles framework (MetaMetrics; *www.lexile.com*) mostly relies on those characteristics as well. More sophisticated measures exist that more closely map onto the comprehension process, but they are quite complex and difficult to apply (Caccamise, Friend, Littrell-Baez, & Kintch, 2015). Needless to say, work continues in this area.

## The Bottom Line

The foregoing issues all merit consideration within the larger framework of a reading program in school, to varying degrees depending on the population of students. The bottom line, however, is that these are issues that surround getting meaning from text. But no matter the students or materials, the basic process of comprehension is the same. At the core of comprehending text is the process, detailed in Chapter 1, of attending to text information, drawing connections between text ideas and between text information and background knowledge, and putting that together into an overall understanding of what a text is about.

# Instructional Approaches to Comprehension

Two general approaches to comprehension guidance have dominated the literature for at least a couple of decades now. These are strategy instruction and discussion. Their history as approaches for comprehension instruction dates from the 1980s, and both feature prominently in current recommendations for promoting effective comprehension. In fact, IES Practice Guides for reading instruction for kindergarten through third grade (Shanahan et al., 2010) and for adolescent readers (Kamil et al., 2008) include strategy instruction and discussion of text in their top five recommendations.

## Strategies Approaches to Reading Instruction

A strategies approach to interacting with text grew from research that viewed thinking and learning as inherently active and strategic. This began with Ann Brown and her colleagues, who explored the potential of strategies for general learning tasks (Brown, Bransford, Ferrara, & Campione, 1983) and for studying behaviors, such as note taking and underlining (Brown, 1981, 1982; Brown & Smiley, 1977). From this work, Brown and her colleagues surmised that strategies might be useful to improve comprehension of young or less able learners (Brown & Smiley, 1978). The eventual manifestation of this line of work in reading was Reciprocal Teaching, an approach that taught young students to apply strategies of summarizing, questioning, clarifying, and predicting (Palincsar & Brown, 1984).

An approach to strategies via thinking and problem solving is represented by Pressley and his colleagues (Symons, Snyder, Cariglia-Bull, & Pressley, 1989). This line of thinking led them to develop Transactional Strategies Instruction, an approach to facilitate comprehension in which the teacher explains and models strategies and uses strategies to guide dialogue about text (Pressley et al., 1992).

Strategies approaches generally consist of explicitly teaching students to implement individual routines for dealing with text, such as summarizing, drawing inferences, and predicting. The approach is intended to engage students with text and with processing text information, although text is engaged though the execution of strategies. For example, as a text is being read in the classroom, the teacher might stop and ask the students to summarize a portion of the text just read. Follow-up would include asking students to recall what kind of information goes into a good summary. The teacher might also ask other students if it was a good summary and why or why not. Such interactions with authentic classroom texts take place only after students have been taught how to summarize and practiced summarization on short texts.

A key question in implementing strategies is which specific strategies to employ. Hundreds of individual strategies have been identified and labeled, but most educators agree that the fewer the better! That is, choosing a limited set of strategies that have some basis in evidence of effectiveness is the best path. For example, two seminal reports on reading instruction, from the National Research Council (NRC) in 1998 (Snow, Burns, & Griffin, 1998) and from the National Reading Panel (NRP) in 2000, have highlighted specific strategies as showing positive effects. The NRC report focuses on summarizing, predicting, drawing inferences, and monitoring for coherence. The NRP report lists comprehension monitoring, summarization, question generation, question answering, cooperative learning, graphic and semantic organizers, and multiple-strategy teaching.

## Discussion Approaches to Reading Instruction

The productiveness of talk for student learning has a history going back to Socrates. Talk as part of learning and instruction in the current era has roots in socioconstructivist and cognitive text-processing frameworks. In a socioconstructivist view, talk is "thinking together," a way to make mental processes explicit and visible, such that critical reflection and elaboration are encouraged (Wilkinson, Sotor, & Murphy, 2010). From a text-processing perspective, the mental processes in reading focus on developing coherence through organizing the meaningful elements of a text. In this view, a reader moves through text identifying each new piece of text information and deciding how it relates to information already given and to background knowledge (see Kintsch & van Dijk, 1978).

As with strategies instruction, discussion approaches take many forms. Summarizing approaches that focus on meaningful talk about text, Applebee, Langer, Nystrand, and Gamoran (2003) note that the form and focus of the various approaches significantly overlap, and that the features that appear to be most effective for comprehension include open questions, student control of interpretive authority, more student than teacher talk, and teacher responses that are based on students' responses.

## Examining Strategies and Discussion Approaches Together

Underlying both strategies and discussion approaches is the tenet that learners need to be mentally active in order to process text successfully. Thus a common feature of both the discussion and strategies approaches is that they aim to promote active student engagement with reading. A major distinction between the two approaches is that strategies instruction encourages students to think about their mental processes and on that basis to execute specific strategies with which to interact with text. In contrast, instruction around discussion approaches attempts to engage students in the process of attending to text ideas and building a mental representation of the ideas, with no direction to consider specific mental processes. With this difference in mind, and cognizant that no studies had looked at both together, we undertook research to compare the two. To conduct the study, we developed sets of standardized lessons for strategies and discussion around a common set of texts, both narrative and expository, for fifth grade (McKeown et al., 2009). The study ran for 2 consecutive years.

The approach to discussion was what we labeled a content approach, whose purpose is continually striving to make sense of the content of a text as one reads. QtA exemplifies a content approach. To develop the strategies lessons, we considered strategies that had been found effective, and then considered which of those might be most naturally called on as a reader works through a text to understand the content. Our thinking was that readers tend to summarize important information as they read, to develop a sense of what may be coming next, and to draw inferences to create connections, and they may form questions to check that they are on track. Additionally, effective readers monitor their understanding and take steps to remedy the situation if they do not understand. We thus selected summarizing, predicting, drawing inferences, question generation, and comprehension monitoring as the strategies for our lessons. Lessons within both approaches featured interspersed reading and discussion, with open questions and following up of student responses characterizing the content lessons and explicit application of strategies to the text characterizing strategies lesson.

To explore outcomes, we first assessed students' recall of texts used in the lessons and found that the content approach yielded better recall in terms of length and quality for both narrative and expository. We also used a transfer task, in which students independently read texts that had not been discussed in class. Again we found differences in quality and length of recall that favored the content group. We also examined transcripts of lessons recorded during the study and found that, first, lesson discussions in the content classrooms included more information that was directly related to the text than the strategies discussions. Second, content students' contributions to discussions were on average twice as long as those in strategies classrooms.

Our findings suggest that getting students to actively build meaning while reading does not necessitate knowledge of and focus on specific strategies, but rather it may simply require attention to text content in ways that promote selecting important ideas and establishing connections between them.

## ENDING NOTES

- A cognitive processing perspective on comprehension, which underlies QtA, is still the dominant explanation for how comprehension occurs.

- Current research related to comprehension seems to focus on knowledge needed for reading and precursors that can affect comprehension processes in individuals and specific populations.

- A major topic is the effect of a reader's background, or prior, knowledge on comprehension.

- Providing background knowledge before reading should focus only on information essential to assist understanding, but should not replace learning information from reading.

- A key body of knowledge needed for reading is knowledge of language and how language operates—phonological, orthographic, semantic (vocabulary), syntactic, and morphological knowledge.

- The relationship between reading ability and aspects of language is strong and well established, meaning that people who have greater knowledge of phonology, orthography, vocabulary, syntax, and morphology are more successful comprehenders.

- Current common topics that appear with some frequency in the literature include *technology and online reading, culturally responsive teaching* and an associated issue of choice in reading materials, *English learners* within the broader issue of differentiating instruction, and *text complexity*.

- No matter the students or materials, the basic process of comprehension is the same: attending to text information, drawing connections between text ideas and between text information and background knowledge, and putting that together into a coherent understanding of a text.

- The two general approaches to comprehension guidance that have dominated the literature for at least the past couple of decades are strategy instruction and text discussion.

- Strategies approaches generally consist of explicitly teaching students to implement individual routines for dealing with text, such as summarizing, drawing inferences, and predicting.

- Features of effective discussions include open questions, student control of interpretive authority, more student than teacher talk, and teacher responses that are based on students' responses.

- A major distinction between strategies and discussion approaches is that strategies instruction encourages students to execute specific strategies with which to interact with text, while discussion approaches attempt to engage students directly in the process of dealing with text ideas.

- Findings from our study comparing strategies and discussion approaches suggest that getting students to actively build meaning while reading does not necessitate use of specific strategies, but may simply require attention to text content in ways that promote selecting important ideas and establishing connections between them.

# Questioning
# the Author Essentials

# CHAPTER 3

*Planning for Questioning
the Author Lessons*

A particular kind of planning is an essential part of the QtA approach. In this chapter, we describe the process of planning a QtA lesson, how it differs from conventional lesson-planning activities, and why we view it as instrumental to success in supporting students' comprehension.

To set the stage, we offer some thoughts that teachers shared with us after they implemented QtA in their classrooms for a year, including using the QtA planning process. At the end of that school year, we asked teachers to reflect on several topics, one of which was the planning process. One teacher, Ms. K., commented about some changes in her views:

> "Before QtA, I didn't really understand the role . . . the important role planning plays in a successful lesson. . . . Why do all that stuff ? . . . I always read the text ahead of time, and I think I kind of made a mental note about what was important, but it never occurred to me to actually write down major understandings. . . . And it never occurred to me that planning was a process. . . . I didn't think that my understanding of the major ideas would have any effect on my students. After a year of using the planning process I saw the change in the quality of my lessons. I am thrilled."

Ms. B.'s reflections focused on her students.

> "Well . . . now I see that thinking about . . . I mean thinking through the important ideas in the text, identifying potential obstacles, and then segmenting and designing queries really do make a difference . . . really, it's a big difference. I get so excited to see my kids grapple with ideas, figure out what's happening in what we are reading, and what I love . . . they make connections. After the lesson, I'm pretty confident . . . actually very confident . . . that my students have a good understanding of what they read, and I know it's because of how I planned for the lesson."

The reflections speak to the teachers' new perspective on planning and the recognition of the direct impact of that process on the success of their students. The reflections also highlight that teachers find QtA planning quite distinct from typical lesson planning approaches. So let's start by considering ways of planning that are typically seen in the field.

Some teachers rely on their teachers' manuals for the kinds of questions and activities to use. An unfortunate consequence of relying on teachers' manuals is that teachers rarely scrutinize the text material themselves. The work has already been done, and the teachers generally trust that it has been done well. Although it seems reasonable to view teachers' manuals as reliable resources for content and instructional expertise, in too many cases we have found that the suggested questions fail to tap real understanding. In addition, we have found that in some basal teachers' manuals, the questions are driven by the "skill of the week," rather than the content of the text.

Another problem, especially with manuals for older students, is that the questions sometimes go directly to analysis and interpretation, assuming that general comprehension of the text has readily occurred. Other teachers plan by looking over the text and thinking about the big ideas but not really engaging in any specific planning.

In contrast, some teachers are concerned that planning too much might interfere with students taking ownership of the discussion. So instead of planning specific questions, they allow the discussion to unfold as they are reading. However, without a solid plan, the discussion can easily wander and become unproductive. With QtA, we do want students to have ownership of the discussion, but we think that is best accomplished if teachers develop a blueprint that provides students with opportunities to construct meaning and take ownership as they become armed with understanding.

## The QtA Planning Process

There is often not enough recognition of the hard work it may take on the part of students to comprehend complex or sophisticated texts. Toward addressing these issues, QtA encourages teachers to adopt a new way of thinking about lesson planning, a way that includes teachers trying to anticipate the kinds of problems students might encounter when reading a given text and the kinds of support that can be offered. The QtA planning process consists of the following three steps:

1. Identifying the major understandings students should develop from a text and anticipating obstacles to comprehension.

2. Segmenting the text to decide where in the text to stop reading and initiate discussion.

3. Developing Initiating Queries and potential Follow-Up Queries to promote students' understanding of text ideas.

## Major Understandings and Potential Obstacles

Planning for any QtA lesson always begins with reading the text with careful attention. The purpose of a careful reading is more than just to become familiar with the content of the text, as in traditional planning. A QtA teacher reads the text carefully first, to determine the major understandings being targeted for students to develop, and second, to anticipate and plan for potential obstacles to understanding. A key feature for making this stage of planning effective is for the teacher to read the text while thinking about how the ideas in the text might be encountered by students in their classroom, especially less skilled readers.

## Identifying Major Understandings

At first, the difference between familiarizing oneself with a text and determining major understandings may not seem obvious, but there is an important distinction, which is to take into account an author's intent or meaning. Most of the time, the author is in the background while the content of a text is in the foreground. The text is considered to be a source of fixed information or, in the case of narrative, a story that has already unfolded. Teachers tend to think of text as a finished product, something past tense in nature, a place to find meaning that has been determined.

The awareness of an author that QtA emphasizes helps students and teachers alike to bring the author to the foreground. When the author is a participant in the discussion, reading becomes a more active and interactive experience, more like a conversation. When, for example, we speak to our friends, argue a point, or even tell a story, our listener can interrupt, pose a question, or ask to have something clarified. In conversation, meaning is developed in the course of the conversation, with the assistance of the person communicating the ideas.

The conversation analogy may help to capture the difference between reading to familiarize oneself with what is already there in a text and reading as if an author were there to question. In QtA, we teach students that the author is there to question. Among our favorite anecdotes of students doing just that is the student we witnessed reading on his own when, in frustration with not understanding the text, threw out his arms with his palms turned up and said, "What is this guy saying?" This student clearly is questioning the author.

One way to think about major understandings is as a kind of enhanced summary that focuses not so much on the facts of a text, but on key inferences that are needed to understand the author's points. For example, a text we frequently see included in reading programs is the story of the "War of the Worlds" radio broadcast by Orson Welles in 1938, and how it terrified many people, who believed that Martians were invading Earth. The story can cause confusion for young readers trying to keep track of what is true and not true: the broadcast was real, the invasion was not. The major understandings would include the following, which are not explicitly stated in the text:

- There was no invasion.

- The event was a program on the radio intended as entertainment, not to make people believe that Martians had landed.

- Mr. Welles was really arrested, though, for causing panic.

Another way to think about major understandings is in terms of dinner-table talk. We ask teachers to think about their students having dinner with their families and to imagine someone at the table asking their youngster what she read about in school. What would you want her to say? Likely not a list of details. Rather you'd probably be delighted if she shared a kind of synopsis of the story that hit on the big ideas and how they played out.

## Anticipating Potential Obstacles

As adult skilled readers, we don't usually have problems comprehending a text, even when the text is poorly written or complex. We are skilled at making inferences about ideas not explicitly stated, making connections to previously read or known information, and figuring out meanings of unfamiliar words through the context of the story and our morphological knowledge. We do most of these things rather automatically, which makes it all the harder for us to predict places in a text that students may find difficult or confusing. Yet, in order to anticipate and plan for problematic portions of a text, teachers need to anticipate problems the text might pose to young and less experienced readers.

We tell teachers that it can be helpful to think about potential obstacles in categories, such as unfamiliar words, unfamiliar content, transitions between paragraphs that don't make connections clear, inferences that may be hard to draw, instances where specific background knowledge may be needed.

Sometimes the sources of potential difficulties are intentional features of an author's craft. Literary techniques, such as flashback and allegory, add depth and dimension to a text, but they also cause confusion for young readers. A simple simile can trip up a young reader, let alone an abstract metaphor. Of course, we want students to appreciate authors' craft, but we must recognize that sometimes these devices are sources of potential confusion.

Relatedly, good authors use good words. They might be particularly expressive or especially meaningful in their forcefulness and eloquence—but they are not the kinds of words that are acquired through everyday language. We labeled such words Tier Two words (Beck, McKeown, & Kucan, 2002, 2013). We developed the notion of three tiers of words to identify words toward which instruction should be targeted. Tier One words—*give, sleep, walk*—are words that are most often acquired from everyday language and rarely require instruction. Tier Three words are mostly found in content-area and technical material, for instance *boycott* or *détente* might come up in history, and *obsidian* in geology. Those words should be dealt with within the appropriate subject matter.

Tier Two words are general words that occur across domains. They are most often found in written language and not used frequently in everyday language, and thus are less likely to be learned independently. Often they are the more literate versions of concepts that students already know. For example, in a text one might find *obliging* instead of *helpful, repugnant* instead of *awful, abode* instead of *house*. Tier Two words can be obstacles to comprehension, but their advantage when found in good text is that instruction can be targeted to such words.

Reading to anticipate comprehension problems for students means being aware of parts of the text that are potentially difficult. A way to develop that awareness is to read the text and consciously monitor your comprehension, trying to notice when you're doing extra work. Extra work could include having to reread a portion of text to understand a passage, or stopping to think about how the current idea follows from the previous one. Teachers who find themselves going off "automatic pilot" as they read and doing extra work can be reasonably sure that their students will also encounter difficulties and may not be able to resolve the problems without support.

## Segmenting the Text

When segmenting a text, it is the major understandings and potential obstacles that drive decisions about where to stop reading and initiate discussion, not paragraph breaks in a text or where the text ends on a page. Sometimes a single sentence needs attention because the information it presents is key. In other cases, a series of paragraphs, or when reading novels, several pages, can be dealt with all at once because they don't really move the plot or introduce new situations or concepts. Segmenting should occur after reading enough text to provide grist for discussion. A stop after too little text has been read doesn't allow for grappling with ideas and leads to restating what was just read. On the other hand, too much text in a segment, especially if it is packed with key ideas and complex content, can lead to an unfocused discussion and confusion.

As an example of the decision process and how it leads to varying segment size, consider a lesson we developed for the "War of the Worlds" text. We decided to create the first segment after just one brief, two-sentence paragraph in which the author describes people in 1938 sitting around listening to their radios. We felt it was necessary to help students establish firmly in mind that the unfolding story was happening by radio, with no visual information available. The next three segments we created are each multiple paragraphs. For example, two paragraphs of text detail the radio announcer, voice shaking, describing a monster emerging from a vehicle that had landed. It includes abundant details, but it is all focused on providing a description of the landing, so it seemed best as a single segment. The intent is to select stopping points where a reader might naturally pause for just an instant and take stock.

## Developing Queries

At the selected stopping points, the teacher initiates discussion by posing a Query, an open question that invites students to consider what they have gotten so far from the text. As we noted in Chapter 1, the wording of Queries is deliberately very general in nature, because the intent is to invite student reaction to text and not to provide too much information from the text. Answering a question that provides too much information is like "fill-in-the-blank," where a student does not have to do much thinking beyond providing a few words.

For example, in the "War of the Worlds" text, a paragraph describes people being terror-stricken as a reporter describes an alien spaceship landing. A Query at that point would simply ask, "What's going on?" Compare that to a question such as: "What have people heard on the radio that has made them so terrified?" The Query asks students to articulate the entire scene; the question merely requires a student to provide a fact from the text: "a spaceship landed."

An issue that arises in asking open questions is that students may indeed answer them in a closed way, such as simply saying that a spaceship landed in response to the Query "What's going on?" That is where Follow-Up Queries come in. A teacher might follow up by responding, "A spaceship landed? How are people getting that idea?"

In Chapter 4, we will provide two texts and the segments and Queries we developed for those texts. For now the important concept to remember in planning and implementing QtA lessons is that Queries are meant to initiate discussion. A single Query often does not suffice—it gets the ball rolling. So in Chapter 4, in addition to providing specific Initiating Queries for specific texts, we will provide and discuss Follow-Up Queries. We do find, however, that after students experience QtA in their classroom for a time, they begin to provide the whole picture when they are initially asked.

# A Perspective on the Teacher's Role

The relationship between planning and teaching is different in QtA than it is in traditional teaching. Planning a lesson in QtA might be likened to a rehearsal in a stage production. In a rehearsal for a play, performers and directors do more than prepare or plan for the performance; that is, they go a step beyond planning to playing out how the performance will unfold. They do things like block out scenes, determine what specific moves are most effective, and practice orchestrating the simultaneous demands of onstage movements and cues from each other. A director's job is to anticipate audience response and reaction, decide what will enhance the production's overall appreciation and success, and prepare for potential problems.

In the same way rehearsals are related to productions, planning a QtA lesson is related to teaching a QtA lesson. However, in a QtA lesson, the teacher is both the director and an actor. As the director, the teacher blocks out the lesson in terms of identifying important ideas to be discussed and tries to anticipate how the lesson might develop. As an actor, the teacher must be ready to improvise as the lesson develops in ways he or she may not have anticipated.

Preparing a QtA lesson, which teachers will not only direct but also participate in as actors, calls for a special approach to planning that anticipates how understanding will unfold for students. We have found that taking the role of the student helps teachers perform in their roles as facilitators for students who are engaged in building meaning from a text.

It is often said that a teacher has to be a jack-of-all-trades. As shown above, we have added two more trades!

## ENDING NOTES

- The QtA approach requires a particular kind of planning that is intended to keep discussion productive.

- Because it is easy to overlook how complex text comprehension can be for students, QtA planning emphasizes anticipating problems that students might encounter when reading a given text and the kinds of support they might need.

- There are three basic steps in the planning process:

    1. Identify major understandings and anticipate obstacles to comprehension.

    2. Segment the text, deciding where to stop reading and initiate discussion.

    3. Develop Initiating and potential Follow-Up Queries.

- Identifying major understandings means writing enhanced summaries that include key inferences needed to understand an author's points.

- Recognizing potential obstacles refers to identifying places that may interfere with comprehension (ranging from an unfamiliar word to challenging content), transitions that don't make connections clear, inferences that may be hard to draw, or concepts that may confuse students.

- Segmenting the text is the process of deciding where to stop and initiate discussion. As these stopping points are driven by the content, think about stopping at places where key ideas occur or possible confusion may arise.

- Developing Queries is the process of designing open, text-based queries that invite students to engage with and build meaning from the ideas in the text.

- Planning a QtA lesson in which teachers will not only lead but also participate calls for an approach to planning that anticipates how understanding will unfold for students.

# CHAPTER 4

# Specific Plans for a Narrative and an Expository Text

In the previous chapter we talked about planning; in this chapter we do it. That is, we go through the planning process for a narrative and then for an expository text. In each case we discuss the thinking for every decision we made within each of the three planning categories: (1) determining major understandings and identifying potential obstacles, (2) segmenting the text, and (3) developing Initiating and Follow-Up Queries.

## Planning for a Narrative Text

The narrative text that we use for planning is "The Bridge on the River Clarinette" by Pierre Gamarra (1993).[1] This text ranges broadly, and our experience with the story indicates that it can be used from fifth grade into high school, and is probably most comfortably targeted to middle school. We suggest that you read the story, which follows, initially just to get a general sense of the plot. A copy of the story formatted for ease in making multiple copies for the classroom appears in the Appendix (pp. 172–174) and also on the book's companion website (see the box at the end of the table of contents).

### The Bridge on the River Clarinette
by Pierre Gamarra

*Translated from the French by Paulette Henderson*

The inhabitants of the little town of Framboisy-sur-Clarinette were worried. The bridge that spanned the River Clarinette was about to collapse. And if

---

[1] Reprinted from Gamarra (1993) by permission of the Estate of Pierre Gamarra.

the bridge did collapse, the citizens of Framboisy would lose touch with the rest of France. There would be no more trade, no more traffic, no more tourists.

It was therefore necessary to reconstruct the bridge. But Framboisy was poor, and the town council was deeply troubled.

Just the other morning—on Framboisy's large central plaza—Monsieur Leopold, the owner of the Green Swan Inn, greeted Madame Barbette, the grocer. "How are things with you this morning, Madame Barbette?"

"Very bad, Monsieur Leopold. Business is falling off. I did not sell more than one package of macaroni last week. People just don't have money anymore."

Monsieur Leopold sighed. "As for me, I don't have customers either. The tourists don't dare cross the bridge nowadays."

"Did it split last night?"

"Yes, it did; I heard it. It's a disgrace. It could cave in at any moment."

"What's to become of us? What we need is a new bridge."

At that moment Monsieur Leopold and Madame Barbette saw the mayor and the teacher coming out of the town hall.

"Well, well, gentlemen," said Monsieur Leopold, "how are town matters going? Are we going to rebuild the bridge?"

The mayor shook his head with infinite sadness. "The council has examined various bridge plans. But it's an outrageously expensive undertaking. We'll never be able to pay for it."

"Nevertheless, you must make a decision," insisted Madame Barbette, nearly stabbing the mayor with her long, pointed nose. "Without a bridge we're ruined. No one dares to venture across our dilapidated old bridge."

The teacher shaded his eyes and gazed in the direction of the bridge. "Someone is coming!" he called.

"Stranger! Impossible! He wasn't afraid to cross," cried Monsieur Leopold.

"Amazing!" agreed the teacher. "But what an odd sort of person, all dressed in red and black and hopping from side to side. Look at his strange, uncanny smile, and the glint in his eyes."

The stranger approached the group and bowed to each of the citizens with great respect. His eyes glowed like deep red rubies. "I am very honored," he said, "to be visiting the distinguished inhabitants of Framboisy-sur-Clarinette."

"Monsieur is travelling?" the innkeeper asked politely.

"I'm going about the land on business."

"Monsieur is a businessman, then?" queried the teacher.

"Yes, I buy and I sell."

"And what is it that you sell?"

"Anything and everything."

"Anything and everything?"

"Yes, anything at all. Sausages, cars, houses, shirts, bridges . . ."

The mayor stepped forward. "Did you say bridges? You sell bridges?"

"But of course. Bridges. All sorts of bridges. Big ones, small ones, medium-sized ones. Made of wood, iron, even concrete."

The mayor scratched his head. "It just so happens that, at this time, we are in need of a bridge. A solid bridge with two or three arches."

"Easy!" said the stranger with a soft little laugh.

"And what is the price of a bridge?" demanded Madame Barbette defiantly.

"Nothing at all."

The four inhabitants of Framboisy jumped for joy, but the teacher said, "that can't be true. If you build us a new bridge, certainly you will ask us for something in exchange."

"Almost nothing," said the stranger.

"What would you ask of us?"

"Your words."

To the astonishment of his audience, the stranger explained, "You give me your words, and I will build you a beautiful bridge in five seconds. Note that I am not asking for all your words; I will leave you a few for your daily needs . . . drink, eat, sleep, bread, butter, coffee . . ."

"I don't understand," murmured the teacher. "What are you going to do with our words?"

"That's my business," said the stranger. "Promise that you will give me your words, and I will build you a bridge—a magnificent concrete and steel bridge, guaranteed for ten centuries!"

"It's a bad joke," muttered the mayor. "And furthermore, if you take our words, we shall find it very difficult to converse."

"No, no, no. I will leave you enough to satisfy you. Do you really have to talk so much? I'll leave you the most important words. And you shall have an extraordinary bridge in five seconds."

"So you're a magician, then?" asked the innkeeper.

"I have a very advanced technique at my disposal," the stranger replied modestly.

"We could at least give it a try," said Monsieur Leopold.

"All right," said Madame Barbette. "Let him have our words, and we shall have our bridge."

"I object!" cried the teacher. "We should never give up our words. At any rate, it's a crazy joke. Do you really think that a bridge can be built in five seconds?"

"Let us try, anyway," said the innkeeper.

"You agree, then?" concluded the stranger with a somewhat malicious swiftness.

"I leave you a few words—as I said before: bread, milk, eat, drink, sleep, house, chair—and I build you an extraordinary bridge?"

"Agreed," said the mayor, the innkeeper, and the grocer.

The teacher shook his head in refusal. Too late. The stranger was already turning toward the dilapidated bridge, pointing his index finger. And all of a sudden there arose a beautiful three-arched bridge, silhouetted against the sky.

The mayor nudged the innkeeper and said, "Bread, butter, eat, drink."

The innkeeper looked at him and replied, "Drink, sleep, house, chair."

## Identifying Major Understandings

Now, read the story a second time, with a pencil in hand, and mark phrases/sentences in the text in which the author provides information about key story elements, such as the condition of the bridge, the town's inability to pay for a new bridge, and the town's desperation.

Our choice of important content follows:

- The bridge that spanned the River Clarinette was about to collapse.
- The citizens of Framboisy would lose touch with the rest of France.
- But Framboisy was poor.
- Business is falling off.
- The council examined various bridge plans.
- "We'll never be able to pay for it."
- "Without a bridge we're ruined."
- "Stranger! Impossible! He wasn't afraid to cross."
- "But what an odd sort of person, all dressed in red and black and hopping from side to side. Look at his strange, uncanny smile, and the glint in his eyes."
- "You give me your words, and I will build you a beautiful bridge in five seconds."
- "I will leave you a few for your daily needs . . . drink, eat, sleep, bread, butter, coffee . . ."
- "So you're a magician, then?" "I have a very advanced technique at my disposal."

With the plot in mind and having identified text sentences that elaborate the plot, a teacher has the grist needed for stating the major understandings. Below is our take on the major understandings for this text:

The people in a small town had a dilapidated bridge. It needed to be replaced because it was their only connection to the rest of the world. But they were too poor to build one. Although there was some disagreement, the people made a deal with a strange character (charlatan, magician, devil?) to trade their words for a new bridge.

## Identifying Potential Obstacles

Given that the major understandings have been established, the next step is to think about places in the text that might pose obstacles for students. Because this text is translated from an original French story, the following two titles may be unfamiliar to students: *Monsieur* and *Madame.*

In addition to the titles, there are some words and phrases that may be unfamiliar or are particularly interesting Tier Two words that could benefit students beyond comprehension of this particular text:

> *inhabitants*
> *lose touch*
> *dilapidated*
> *uncanny*
> *defiantly*
> *malicious*

Beyond consideration of words, it's important to think about any other aspects of text that might interfere with comprehension. Our experience with this story is that the most common obstacle for students is figuring out who the stranger is. Although it's an area that is a potential problem, it also is a topic that leads to rich discussion. Another major understanding that causes confusion is working through the deal—the idea that this stranger is able to give the people of the town a bridge for their words and that the people are willing to forgo their words for the bridge.

## Developing Text Segments and Queries

Having determined major understandings and potential obstacles, the next task is to think about segmenting the text and designing Queries. In segmenting, we want to identify places to stop reading and initiate discussion. The major understandings and places with potential obstacles drive decisions about stopping points, rather than paragraphs or page breaks.

There is a strong connection between identifying stopping points and designing open, text-based Queries that provide students with the opportunity to discuss a portion of text as well as clearing up potential points of confusion. Let's look at how we thought through those decisions and the Queries we designed for each text segment.

Before turning to the text, read the title, author, and translation information to students: "'The Bridge on the River Clarinette' by Pierre Gamarra. Translated from the French by Paulette Henderson." Explain that since the story was originally written in French, the words *Monsieur* and *Madame* may be unfamiliar and that they mean the same as *Mr.* and *Mrs.*

In the following planning chart, the first column explains our decision for the stopping points and what story content we want to target for the segment. Discussion of the target information reflects the responses we anticipate from students, and we have formulated our Queries to elicit that information. Keep in mind, also, that the wording of our Queries is only one way to ask students to address a particular issue.

| FIRST SEGMENT | |
|---|---|
| The inhabitants of the little town of Framboisy-sur-Clarinette were worried. The bridge that spanned the River Clarinette was about to collapse. And if the bridge did collapse, the citizens of Framboisy would lose touch with the rest of France. There would be no more trade, no more traffic, no more tourists.<br><br>    It was therefore necessary to reconstruct the bridge. But Framboisy was poor, and the town council was deeply troubled. | |
| **Decisions and Comments** | **Queries** |
| There are two reasons for this stopping point. First, the opening paragraphs set the stage for the town's problem—the bridge is about to collapse, but the town is too poor to replace it. Second, *inhabitants* might be an unfamiliar word, and the students might not recognize the importance of the phrase "lose touch" to the town's dire problem. | "The story begins with the sentence 'The inhabitants of the little town of Framboisy-sur-Clarinette were worried.' Who are *inhabitants*?"<br><br>(If needed, tell students that inhabitants are people or animals that live in a particular place. In this case, they are the people of Framboisy.)<br><br>**Query:** "Now, what's going on so far in the story?"<br><br>**Follow-up:** "So how does this phrase 'lose touch' connect to what you just told me? What does that phrase mean?" |
| SECOND SEGMENT | |
| Just the other morning—on Framboisy's large central plaza—Monsieur Leopold, the owner of the Green Swan Inn, greeted Madame Barbette, the grocer. "How are things with you this morning, Madame Barbette?"<br><br>    "Very bad, Monsieur Leopold. Business is falling off. I did not sell more than one package of macaroni last week. People just don't have money anymore." Monsieur Leopold sighed. "As for me, I don't have customers either. The tourists don't dare cross the bridge nowadays."<br><br>    "Did it split last night?"<br><br>    "Yes, it did; I heard it. It's a disgrace. It could cave in at any moment." | |

| SECOND SEGMENT (continued) |
|---|

"What's to become of us? What we need is a new bridge."

At that moment Monsieur Leopold and Madame Barbette saw the mayor and the teacher coming out of the town hall.

"Well, well, gentlemen," said Monsieur Leopold, "how are town matters going? Are we going to rebuild the bridge?"

The mayor shook his head with infinite sadness. "The council has examined various bridge plans. But it's an outrageously expensive undertaking. We'll never be able to pay for it."

"Nevertheless, you must make a decision," insisted Madame Barbette, nearly stabbing the mayor with her long, pointed nose. "Without a bridge we're ruined. No one dares to venture across our dilapidated old bridge."

| Decisions and Comments | Queries |
|---|---|
| The second segment provides more detail about the two major problems mentioned in the opening paragraphs: the town needs a new bridge and is too poor to pay for it. Stopping here allows students to deal with the desperation of the inhabitants because the bridge is in such bad shape that something needs to be done immediately.<br><br>This segment also includes a fabulous vocabulary word, *dilapidated*, that will support students' understanding of the poor shape of the bridge, so it is important to highlight it here. | **Query:** "How do things look for the people?"<br><br>**Follow-up:** "Given what you know about the condition of bridge, what do you think *dilapidated* means?"<br><br>(If needed, explain that dilapidated means something that is in such bad shape it is about to fall apart.) |

| THIRD SEGMENT |
|---|

The teacher shaded his eyes and gazed in the direction of the bridge. "Someone is coming!" he called.

"Stranger! Impossible! He wasn't afraid to cross," cried Monsieur Leopold.

"Amazing!" agreed the teacher. "But what an odd sort of person, all dressed in red and black and hopping from side to side. Look at his strange, uncanny smile, and the glint in his eyes."

| Decisions and Comments | Queries |
|---|---|
| The third segment introduces a peculiar stranger. It's important that students pick up on the idea that there is something different about this person.<br><br>There is a great vocabulary word, *uncanny*, in this section. It is a nice | **Query:** "What just happened?"<br><br>**Follow-up:** "What do you think of this new character? The author says that the stranger has an uncanny smile." (If needed, explain that something uncanny |

| THIRD SEGMENT (*continued*) ||
| **Decisions and Comments** | **Queries** |
| example of author's craft, as the word reflects the mysterious, creepy feel of the stranger. | is so strange and unfamiliar that it seems unnatural.) "What does that tell us about him?" |

| FOURTH SEGMENT ||

The stranger approached the group and bowed to each of the citizens with great respect. His eyes glowed like deep red rubies. "I am very honored," he said, "to be visiting the distinguished inhabitants of Framboisy-sur-Clarinette."

"Monsieur is travelling?" the innkeeper asked politely.

"I'm going about the land on business."

"Monsieur is a businessman, then?" queried the teacher.

"Yes, I buy and I sell."

"And what is it that you sell?"

"Anything and everything."

"Anything and everything?"

"Yes, anything at all. Sausages, cars, houses, shirts, bridges . . ."

The mayor stepped forward. "Did you say bridges? You sell bridges?"

"But of course. Bridges. All sorts of bridges. Big ones, small ones, medium-sized ones. Made of wood, iron, even concrete."

The mayor scratched his head. "It just so happens that, at this time, we are in need of a bridge. A solid bridge with two or three arches."

"Easy!" said the stranger with a soft little laugh.

"And what is the price of a bridge?" demanded Madame Barbette defiantly.

"Nothing at all."

The four inhabitants of Framboisy jumped for joy, but the teacher said, "that can't be true. If you build us a new bridge, certainly you will ask us for something in exchange."

"Almost nothing," said the stranger.

"What would you ask of us?"

"Your words."

To the astonishment of his audience, the stranger explained, "You give me your words, and I will build you a beautiful bridge in five seconds. Note that I am not asking for all your words; I will leave you a few for your daily needs . . . drink, eat, sleep, bread, butter, coffee . . ."

| **Decisions and Comments** | **Queries** |
| The fourth segment reveals the stranger's offer. He will give them a new bridge in exchange for most of their words. It's also a good place for students to continue to | **Query:** "What did we learn from this conversation?"<br><br>**Follow-up:** "What do you think of the stranger's offer?" |

| FOURTH SEGMENT (*continued*) | |
| --- | --- |
| **Decisions and Comments** | **Queries** |
| develop their understanding of the stranger's character by connecting his actions to their previous thoughts about him. | **Follow-up:** "The last paragraph begins with 'To the astonishment of his audience . . . ' So, based on that description, how are the people reacting to the stranger and his offer?" |

| FIFTH SEGMENT | |
| --- | --- |

"I don't understand," murmured the teacher. "What are you going to do with our words?"

"That's my business," said the stranger. "Promise that you will give me your words, and I will build you a bridge—a magnificent concrete and steel bridge, guaranteed for ten centuries!"

"It's a bad joke," muttered the mayor. "And furthermore, if you take our words, we shall find it very difficult to converse."

"No, no, no. I will leave you enough to satisfy you. Do you really have to talk so much? I'll leave you the most important words. And you shall have an extraordinary bridge in five seconds."

"So you're a magician, then?" asked the innkeeper.

"I have a very advanced technique at my disposal," the stranger replied modestly.

"We could at least give it a try," said Monsieur Leopold.

"All right," said Madame Barbette. "Let him have our words, and we shall have our bridge."

"I object!" cried the teacher. "We should never give up our words. At any rate, it's a crazy joke. Do you really think that a bridge can be built in five seconds?"

"Let us try, anyway," said the innkeeper.

| **Decisions and Comments** | **Queries** |
| --- | --- |
| In this segment, it's important for students to understand that not all the townspeople are in agreement, and a couple of people, especially the teacher, express their concerns. Again, this is a nice place to pull in some great vocabulary words that reflect authors' craft. The stranger describes the bridge as *magnificent* and *extraordinary*—two great words that are sure to influence the people's decision to agree to the deal.<br><br>We also find out a little more about the stranger that adds to his mysterious character. He tells the people that he has a very advanced technique at his disposal. | **Query:** "Now what's going on with the townspeople?"<br><br>**Follow-up:** "The stranger has used the words *magnificent* and *extraordinary* to describe the bridge he'll build. What effect do you think those words have on the people?"<br><br>**Follow-up:** "The stranger also tells the townspeople that he has 'an advanced technique.' What does all that tell us about this character?" |

| SIXTH SEGMENT | |
|---|---|
| "You agree, then?" concluded the stranger with a somewhat malicious swiftness. "I leave you a few words—as I said before: bread, milk, eat, drink, sleep, house, chair—and I build you an extraordinary bridge?" | |
| "Agreed," said the mayor, the innkeeper, and the grocer. | |
| The teacher shook his head in refusal. Too late. The stranger was already turning toward the dilapidated bridge, pointing his index finger. And all of a sudden there arose a beautiful three-arched bridge, silhouetted against the sky. | |
| The mayor nudged the innkeeper and said, "Bread, butter, eat, drink." | |
| The innkeeper looked at him and replied, "Drink, sleep, house, chair." | |

| Decisions and Comments | Queries |
|---|---|
| The townspeople now have a beautiful bridge but are left with only a handful of words.<br><br>This is another place where a great vocabulary word, *malicious*, is used, and it reinforces what we know about the stranger. | **Query:** "How did things turn out for the town and its people?"<br><br>**Follow-up:** "The author tells us that the stranger concluded the deal with a malicious swiftness." (If needed, explain that malicious means wanting to cause harm.) "What does that tell us about the stranger?" |

| Decisions and Comments | Wrap-up Queries |
|---|---|
| This is an intriguing and quirky story that can prompt great discussion about the point of the story and who, really, the stranger is. | **Query:** "What point is the author trying to make in this story?"<br><br>**Query:** "Who was the stranger in the story?" |

Following the interspersed reading and discussion of a text, a QtA lesson can be wrapped up or can provide for extended work, such as interpretive discussion and writing. These topics will be developed at length in later chapters. Here we've offered a simple possibility for a story wrap-up.

# Planning for an Expository Text

Having illustrated the planning process for a narrative text, we next model how we think through the steps of planning for an expository text. However, there is no particular planning process for any genre. It always comprises identifying major understandings and potential obstacles, segmenting text, and developing Queries. The particulars of any text, be they content or structure, dictate how those considerations play out. Thus, as we did with the narrative text, we will discuss decisions for major understandings and potential obstacles, and then provide segment points and Initiating and Follow-Up Queries. The expository text we've selected is "Polar Bears, the

Giants of the Arctic" by Nancy Curry (2019).[2] This text also ranges broadly from fifth grade through middle school. A copy of the story formatted for ease in making multiple copies for the classroom appears in the Appendix (pp. 175–176) and also on the book's companion website (see the box at the end of the table of contents).

Just as we suggested for the narrative text, it is useful to read the text two times. The first read is to get familiar with the content.

### Polar Bears, the Giants of the Arctic
#### by Nancy Curry

Polar bears, the most powerful carnivores on land, live in the Arctic portions of Norway, Greenland, Russia, the United States (Alaska), and Canada (Manitoba). They can be as tall as 10 feet and weigh over a ton (1,400 pounds). That is equivalent to about ten men. Polar bears are exceedingly dangerous animals as they are predators who are not prey to any other animal. Moreover they have no fear of human beings.

For many thousands of years, polar bears have been important to the indigenous peoples around the Arctic. Most of those people have been called Eskimos, but the term Eskimo includes six groupings of people, each of which has its own culture and language, and they prefer to be known by their own names, such as Inuit and Yupak. Indigenous people still hunt polar bears as they are essential to living at a subsistence level. And, much of a polar bear's remains are used. For example the hide is made into clothing, the meat is eaten, the bones are carved into tools and used to make crafts.

Seals are as important to polar bears as polar bears are to the indigenous people. The bears hunt their favorite food by remaining on sea ice floes for long periods. These huge bears have three characteristics—stealth, patience, and excellent sense of smell—that they put to good use to hunt seals. And seals "help" to the extent that they need to carve out breathing holes in the thick polar ice. A polar bear with its outstanding sense of smell locates a breathing hole and stealthily moves on the ice floe as close to the hole as possible, biding its time until a seal raises its head through the hole for a breath. POW! The bear zooms to the hole and catches his favorite prey. Well, not all the time. Seals are fast and many get away, so the polar bear will have to use its patience and await another opportunity.

When the sea ice melts in the spring, some polar bears go north to find hardened ice, but others go onto land. On land they do not hibernate like other bears, but they do rest and are not very active. During that time, polar bears live off the blubber that their bodies have accumulated from their fat rich diet of seals, and they will scavenge for food. These great animals will eat any vegetation they can find and anything else—including human

---

[2] From Curry (2019). Used by permission of the author.

garbage. They have been seen eating tin cans, broken furniture, batteries and other such debris, as well as left over human garbage.

In late fall before the ice has hardened, in Manitoba, Canada, polar bears begin to congregate near the small town of Churchill, waiting for the sea ice to harden. It has been said that about 1,000 bears may congregate in October and November. It is at that time when visitors go to Churchill to see the bears. Tourist agencies in Churchill, and countries other than Canada that are near the Arctic Ocean, have the expertise and equipment to get tourists close to the bears safely.

The fall is also the time when the hungry bears—whose diet is very reduced during the summer—may wander close to where people live. In the early 2000s Churchill had serious invasions of bears that with their excellent sense of smell found feasts at the town dump. Since people dump garbage close to where they live, the bears wandered near to residential housing. Churchill tried scaring the bears with lights and trucks and noisemakers, but they came back to their feasts.

Eventually officials in Churchill rounded up troublemaker bears and put them in "polar bear jail" until the ice had hardened. To get them back to the ice or far away from town, they tranquilized them and helicoptered them out. But that was only a short-term solution. They tried to secure the dumps by installing fences and light fires to burn the trash, but the bears were stubborn and there are images from videos that show fires burning behind polar bears eating. In 2005, the town opened what became known as the "Alcatraz of garbage," a secure building with concrete floors and bars on windows, where garbage could be securely stored until taken to a place where it could be buried deeply. The following year, there were fewer reports of bears near the town.

On the other side of the Arctic Ocean, some 15 years later, in 2019, several small towns in the Arctic area of Russia declared states of emergency because polar bears had "invaded" their communities. Tass, a Russian news agency, reported that about 50 polar bears, had visited the small town of Belushya Guba. In fact, at any one time there were from six to ten bears partaking of what the dump had to offer. The people in Belushya Guba were on edge, and who wouldn't be. Not only had the bears come near to where people lived, some had actually entered houses and other buildings. There is a photo from a video of a bear walking down a hall in an apartment building and another of a female bear and her two cubs sauntering in the courtyard of a residential area.

Polar bears have come closer to human communities to solve a problem that has arisen because of rapidly melting ice in the Arctic caused by global warming. Melting ice means that there are fewer ice floes near shore where the bears can hunt their food. The bears need to go further out from the shore to find breathing holes or attack seals in the open sea. That can be dangerous for the bears. Although they are mighty swimmers, they are not as fast as their favorite prey. Instead of going out further on the ice floes, some bears have chosen to find food by migrating north where the ice is still hard. That means they have to be on land longer than in the past, but on land they cannot find the prey that are so important for their well-being. This makes for hungry polar bears. So when they encounter the attractive odors from human garbage dumps, they go off to the banquet.

It has been estimated that these magnificent animals have been on this planet from about 400,000 to 600,000 years. Now with global warming, many people are worried that if the ice continues to melt at the present rate, polar bears will become extinct. The hope is that scientists who study global warming and those who study polar bear behavior will provide solutions that the people of the earth will embrace.

## Identifying Major Understandings

Now during the second read, mark the phrases/sentences that represent, support, and connect the big ideas, such as the power of the polar bears, the troubles they face and why, and the ways in which they attempt to overcome those troubles. The text material we identified that reflects those ideas follows:

- Polar bears are the most powerful carnivores on land.
- Polar bears remain on ice floes for long periods hunting their favorite food, seals.
- When the sea ice melts in the spring, some polar bears go north to find hardened ice, but others go onto land.
- . . . hungry bears—whose diet is very reduced during the summer—may wander close to where people live.
- Polar bears have come closer to human communities to solve a problem that has arisen because of rapidly melting ice in the Arctic caused by global warming.
- Melting ice means that there are fewer ice floes near shore where the bears can hunt their food.
- Now with global warming, many people are worried that if the ice continues to melt at the present rate, polar bears will become extinct.

After identifying the important ideas and the sentences and phrases that support those ideas, the content needed for major understandings has been established. Our version of the major understandings follows:

Polar bears are in danger of becoming extinct due to global warming. Because of the melting ice, some polar bears travel north where the ice is still frozen and others find food on land. Neither of these solutions will enable polar bears to survive. In fact the situation endangers both bears and humans since their search for food brings them close to where people live. Unless scientists develop better solutions, the future of the polar bear may be grim.

## Identifying Potential Obstacles

With the major understandings established, the next step is to determine places in the text that might cause problems for students. The following are words, phrases, or ideas that may be unfamiliar to students; some are interesting, high-utility Tier Two words. Also, as you think about potential obstacles to comprehension, remember to keep in mind the continuum of potential obstacles—from unfamiliar words and content to places where inferences and pieces of background knowledge are needed.

> *predator*
> *prey*
> *indigenous*
> *subsistence*
> *ice floes*
> *stealth*
> *Alcatraz*
> *sauntering*
> *congregate*
> *stealth*
> *global warming*

Although students are probably familiar with the term *global warming*, we included it because they may not fully grasp the concept and especially its consequences, as well as holding misunderstandings about the concept.

## Developing Text Segments and Queries

With major understandings and potential obstacles established, the next step is to segment the text and design Initiating and Follow-Up Queries. Again, the major understandings and potential obstacles drive the decisions about stopping points and Queries. Below we provide our thinking about those decisions.

| FIRST SEGMENT |
| --- |
| Polar bears, the most powerful carnivores on land, live in the Arctic portions of Norway, Greenland, Russia, the United States (Alaska), and Canada (Manitoba). They can be as tall as 10 feet and weigh over a ton (1,400 pounds). That is equivalent to about ten men. Polar bears are exceedingly dangerous animals as they are predators who are not prey to any other animal. Moreover they have no fear of human beings. |

| FIRST SEGMENT (*continued*) | |
|---|---|
| **Decisions and Comments** | **Queries** |
| The first paragraph introduces the topic and establishes the polar bears' power and predatory nature.<br>    The terms *predator* and *prey* are found in primary grades curricula, so the follow-up is targeted to checking that students know the terms. | **Query:** "What have we learned in this first section?"<br><br>**Follow-up:** "What does it mean that polar bears are predators, and prey to no other animal?" |

| SECOND SEGMENT |
|---|
| For many thousands of years, polar bears have been important to the indigenous peoples around the Arctic. Most of those people have been called Eskimos, but the term *Eskimo* includes six groupings of people, each of which has its own culture and language, and they prefer to be known by their own names, such as Inuit and Yupak. Indigenous people still hunt polar bears as they are essential to living at a subsistence level. And, much of a polar bear's remains are used. For example the hide is made into clothing, the meat is eaten, the bones are carved into tools and used to make crafts. |

| **Decisions and Comments** | **Queries** |
|---|---|
| This segment uses the term *indigenous* people and deals with the importance of the polar bear to the existence of the Arctic indigenous people. Indigenous is a Tier Three word, and a term that will likely be found in history as well as biology classes (e.g., there are indigenous plants). *Indigenous* comes up in the first sentence, and the rest of the segment is about indigenous people. So it's important to deal with *indigenous* when it comes up.<br>    *Subsistence* may also be unfamiliar, and understanding subsistence living supports understanding how the people use the polar bear. | Read the first sentence and explain that indigenous people are the people who first live on a land. Also mention that in some countries indigenous people are referred to as the First People or as Native People.<br><br>**Query:** "Now what's the author told you about polar bears?"<br><br>**Follow-up:** "A *subsistence level* means that you are only able to get the minimum of things you need to live, like food and shelter. How does that connect to how the people use polar bears?" |

| THIRD SEGMENT |
|---|
| Seals are as important to polar bears as polar bears are to the indigenous people. The bears hunt their favorite food by remaining on sea ice floes for long periods. These huge bears have three characteristics—stealth, patience, and an excellent sense of smell—that they put to good use to hunt seals. And seals "help" to the extent that they carve out breathing holes in the thick polar ice. A polar bear with its |

| THIRD SEGMENT (*continued*) | |
|---|---|

outstanding sense of smell locates a breathing hole and stealthily moves on the ice floe as close to the hole as possible, biding its time until a seal raises its head through the hole for a breath. POW! The bear zooms to the hole and catches his favorite prey. Well, not all the time. Seals are fast and many get away, so the polar bear will have to use its patience and await another opportunity.

| Decisions and Comments | Queries |
|---|---|
| This third section provides information about the polar bears' preferred food and the characteristics that make them successful hunters. Students also might be confused about how the seals "help" the polar bears find their food.<br><br>    This section includes a great Tier Two word (*stealth*) that will be discussed as part of vocabulary instruction in a later chapter. The phrase *ice floes* may be unfamiliar and need a brief explanation. | **Query:** "Now let's talk about what we just read. What is this section all about?"<br>    (If necessary, provide the following explanation for ice floes: ice floes are huge masses of floating ice, many miles in size.)<br><br>**Follow-up:** "It says that seals help polar bears as they hunt seals for food. That's confusing. What do you think that means?"<br><br>**Follow-up:** "The author says the bears use stealth in hunting and that the bears move stealthily. What do you think the word means?" (*Stealth* means doing something quietly and carefully so that it is not noticed.) |

| FOURTH SEGMENT | |
|---|---|

When the sea ice melts in the spring, some bears go north to find hardened ice, but others go onto land. On land they do not hibernate like other bears, but they do rest and are not very active. During that time, polar bears live off the blubber that their bodies have accumulated from their fat-rich diet of seals, and they will scavenge for food. These great animals will eat any vegetation they can find and anything else—including human garbage. They have been seen eating tin cans, broken furniture, batteries and other such debris, as well as left over human garbage.

| Decisions and Comments | Queries |
|---|---|
| This section addresses a problem the polar bears face: when the ice melts they must search for food elsewhere. This means going further into land and scavenging for food. | **Query:** "Now what's going on with the polar bears?"<br><br>**Follow-up:** "The text says the bears scavenge for food; they find and eat anything including garbage. So what do you think it means to *scavenge*?" (To *scavenge* means to search among things that have been thrown away.) |

## FIFTH SEGMENT

In late fall before the ice has hardened, in Manitoba, Canada, polar bears begin to congregate near the small town of Churchill, waiting for the sea ice to harden. It has been said that about 1,000 bears may congregate in October and November. It is at that time when visitors go to Churchill to see the bears. Tourist agencies in Churchill, and countries other than Canada that are near the Arctic Ocean, have the expertise and equipment to get tourists close to the bears safely.

The fall is also the time when the hungry bears—whose diet is very reduced during the summer—may wander close to where people live. In the early 2000s Churchill had serious invasions of bears that with their excellent sense of smell found feasts at the town dump. Since people dump garbage close to where they live, the bears wandered near to residential housing. Churchill tried scaring the bears with lights and trucks and noisemakers, but they came back to their feasts.

Eventually officials in Churchill rounded up troublemaker bears and put them in "polar bear jail," until the ice had hardened. To get them back to the ice or far away from town, they tranquilized them and helicoptered them out. But that was only a short-term solution. They tried to secure the dumps by installing fences and light fires to burn the trash, but the bears were stubborn and there are images from videos that show fires burning behind polar bears eating. In 2005, the town opened what became known as the "Alcatraz of garbage," a secure building with concrete floors and bars on windows, where garbage could be securely stored until taken to a place where it could be buried deeply. The following year, there were fewer reports of bears near the town.

| Decisions and Comments | Queries |
|---|---|
| Although this is a longer chunk of text, both paragraphs build on previous learning by providing more information about how polar bears deal with the issue of melting ice. During the fall, they wander into towns, and the towns have various ways of dealing with the problem. | **Query:** "How does this text segment deal with the bears' problem that the author has been describing?" (If needed, explain that when the text talks about the bears congregating in Churchill it means they come together as a group.) |
| Students may not know that Alcatraz was a very secure and strict prison, and thus will likely not understand the phrase "Alcatraz of garbage." A point of the Follow-Up Query is to encourage students to appreciate the townspeople's choice of words to describe where their garbage is stored. | **Follow-up:** "Imagine what it's like in this town! What do you think of how the town is handling all this?"

**Follow-up:** "The author says that the town opened up an 'Alcatraz of garbage.' Why would the author describe the place that garbage was stored as the 'Alcatraz of garbage?'" (If needed, explain that |
| *Congregate* may be unfamiliar and need a brief explanation. | Alcatraz was a very secure and strict prison.) |

| SIXTH SEGMENT |
|---|

On the other side of the Arctic Circle, some 15 years later, in 2019, several small towns in the Arctic area of Russia declared states of emergency because polar bears had "invaded" their communities. Tass, a Russian news agency, reported that about 50 polar bears had visited the small town of Belushya Guba. In fact, at any one time there were from six to ten bears partaking of what the dump had to offer. The people in Belushya Guba were on edge, and who wouldn't be. Not only had the bears come near to where people lived, some had actually entered houses and other buildings. There is a photo from a video of a bear walking down the hall in an apartment building and another of a female bear and her two cubs sauntering in the courtyard of a residential area.

| Decisions and Comments | Queries |
|---|---|
| This section broadens the idea about polar bears' desperation for food by describing yet another place where bears are going into towns.<br><br>    This also is another segment that includes an interesting Tier Two word (*sauntering*) that we would include in vocabulary instruction after the text discussion. For the text, understanding that word helps create a picture of the bears as rather comfortable around humans. | **Query:** "How does the information in this section add to our understanding of what's happening with the polar bears?"<br><br>**Follow-up:** Reread the first sentence: "On the other side of the Arctic. . . ." "What does this suggest about the polar bears' problem in finding food?"<br><br>**Follow-up:** "The text says that a female and her cubs sauntered in a courtyard. That means that the family was kind of strolling or walking leisurely. So, based on the meaning of that word, what point is the author making about the bears?" |

| SEVENTH SEGMENT |
|---|

Polar bears have come closer to human communities to solve a problem that has arisen because of rapidly melting ice in the Arctic caused by global warming. Melting ice means that there are fewer ice floes near shore where the bears can hunt their food. The bears need to go further out from the shore to find breathing holes or attack seals in the open sea. That can be dangerous for the bears. Although they are mighty swimmers, they are not as fast as their favorite prey. Instead of going out further on the ice floes, some bears have chosen to find food by migrating north where the ice is still hard. That means they have to be on land longer than in the past, but on land they cannot find the prey that are so important for their well-being. This makes for hungry polar bears. So when they encounter the attractive odors from human garbage dumps, they are off to the banquet.

| Decisions and Comments | Queries |
|---|---|
| This section explains that global warming is causing polar bears to face the | **Query:** "What did we find out in this section?" |

| SEVENTH SEGMENT (*continued*) ||
|---|---|
| challenge of finding food and addresses why their solutions aren't really working. | **Follow-up:** "What does the author mean when she says that polar bears come into towns to solve a problem?" |

| EIGHTH SEGMENT ||
|---|---|
| It has been estimated that these magnificent animals have been on this planet from about 400,000 to 600,000 years. Now with global warming, many people are worried that if the ice continues to melt at the present rate, polar bears will become extinct. The hope is that scientists who study global warming and those who study polar bear behavior will provide solutions that the people of the earth will embrace. ||

| Decisions and Comments | Queries |
|---|---|
| This last section reinforces global warming as causing polar bears serious food shortages and explains that without a solution, they are in danger of becoming extinct. | **Query:** "What point is the author making in this last section?" |

We have not provided a Wrap-Up Query here because the Query for this final section seems to adequately play that role. However, the text offers plenty of grist for further follow-up, which could go in many directions depending on what the particular group of students knows about these issues or what they are currently studying about them.

## Some Final Words

We would like to say that we have provided plans for two ideal, foolproof text lessons. But alas, we have not. As with all planning endeavors, the old saw "the best-laid plans of mice and men often go awry" applies here. Given that we are dealing with young humans, this will be true of any set of plans we provide or that you create based on QtA. Your students may disappoint you, distress you, amaze or impress you. But undoubtedly the lessons will not unfold precisely as you envisioned them. Over the years we have faced surprises countless times and have developed, along with the teachers we have worked with, many strategies for dealing with the unexpected and spontaneous. We will delve into those ideas in the subsequent chapters.

### ENDING NOTES

- To begin the QtA planning process, read the text twice, first to get a general sense of the text, and a second time to identify:

○ for a narrative text, information that reflects key story elements.

○ for an informational text, the major ideas.

- Underline the important content in the text, including words, phrases, and sentences, and then create the major understandings from the material you underlined.

- Create a list of potential obstacles, which may include unfamiliar vocabulary or difficult content.

- Using the information you gathered when underlining the important content, the major understandings you created, and your list of potential obstacles, begin to segment the text and design Queries.

- When segmenting, think about why you are stopping at a particular place and what you want to accomplish in the discussion.

- Keep the Queries open and think about anticipated student responses.

- Consider creating some Follow-Up Queries for when students are not able to address the Initiating Query.

- Always remember that there is no such thing as a foolproof plan!

# CHAPTER 5

# Digging into Initiating and Follow-Up Queries

Chapter 4 included Queries we had designed for each text segment of two example texts. Beyond that, we did not go into much depth about Queries in Chapter 4, as we wanted to keep the focus on the lesson sequence and thus keep the lessons as uncluttered as possible. In this chapter we bring forward the concept of Queries and discuss them in some depth. We start, however, by noting our comment in Chapter 1 that Queries are indeed questions, and that we initiated the term *Queries* to emphasize their distinctive features and reduce the chances that they will get confounded with other labels for types of questions in the field (e.g., literal, interpretive).

Questions are a way of life in classrooms. It is hard to imagine how a teacher would teach without using questions. So it follows that questions have been a topic in both instruction and research for many years. Questions used to support reading comprehension are often categorized by levels of comprehension or cognitive activity, or according to specific processes that readers use to deal with text. Levels of comprehension characterize question taxonomies, which were intended to offer a hierarchy of comprehension. For example, Bloom's taxonomy (1956) features knowledge of specific facts; describing in one's own words (labeled comprehension); application of information; analysis; synthesis; and evaluation. Barrett's taxonomy (1967) was developed to help teachers write comprehension questions. Similar to Bloom's, it features literal comprehension, reorganization, inferential comprehension, evaluation, and appreciation.

Questions are also sorted into those that tap lower and higher cognitive activity. Lower cognitive questions tap the recall of information and go by labels such as fact, closed, direct, recall, and knowledge questions. Higher cognitive questions require mental manipulation of information to produce a response and include open-ended, interpretive, evaluative, inquiry, inferential, and synthesis questions.

Questions aligned to readers' processes include those that ask a reader to summarize information or draw inferences. Regardless of the classification, traditional wisdom holds that the questions that recruit higher levels of thinking, beyond recall of factual information, lead to higher-quality answers and increased learning and achievement. So where do Queries fit?

# Backdrop to Queries

We developed Queries against a backdrop of two kinds of instructional approaches to questioning students about text they read that were prominent in classrooms at the time, what we call traditional IRE questions and comprehension strategies.

## Traditional IRE Questions

We refer to these as traditional questions because of their dominance in both reading and content-area classrooms over many decades (see, e.g., Bellack, Kliebard, Hyman, & Smith, 1966; Mehan, 1979; Alvermann, O'Brien, & Dillon, 1990). The IRE pattern is that, after text has been read, a teacher **I**nitiates a question—usually fact or retrieval oriented; a student **R**esponds, most often briefly; and the teacher then **E**valuates, such as "Good," "Right."

## Comprehension Strategies

The comprehension strategies approach centers on the direct teaching of specific procedures in working with text, such as summarizing, making inferences, and generating questions. The approach is intended to engage students with text through execution of such routines. So, for example, as a text is being read in a classroom, the teacher might stop and ask the students to summarize a portion of the text just read. Typically the teacher would follow up a student's summary by asking other students if it was a good summary and why or why not. Thus the focus of questioning is on the strategy itself.

We found both approaches to improving and facilitating comprehension problematic. The wording of IRE questions makes them more suited to assessment than guiding comprehension. At best, they tend to encourage students to recall what they have read. Although a question is directed to the entire class, only one student provides the answer. The classroom dynamic can take on the character of a quiz show, featuring quick question/answer bursts.

Our major issue with comprehension strategies instruction is that students are being asked to do something in addition to making sense of the text. It is the case that all human beings have a limited capacity for active mental engagement. So if some mental resources are devoted to calling up strategies, the mental resources needed for comprehension are reduced. The goal of comprehension strategies instruction and QtA are the same—to encourage active processing. The difference is that strategies do that by adding a layer of strategic actions, while Queries keep the focus on the content.

## How Queries Are Different

The two keys to Queries are that they are content focused and they are directed to keep students striving for meaning. That is, Queries emerge from and focus on the content of what is being read, and comprehension enhancement is achieved by continually seeking understanding as reading of a text moves along. Queries are directed to support students as they dig in to make sense of what they are reading. In contrast to IRE and strategies approaches, the focus is on the quality and depth of the meaning that students are constructing rather than on the accuracy of the response they give or on calling up a strategies routine.

Queries are used in the course of the initial reading of a text. Let's consider the effects. When teachers ask questions after reading, students may get some messages that teachers may not intend. Students may assume that questioning is a different and perhaps unrelated exercise from reading. Is this the message we want to convey to students? Isn't it a more accurate message that readers are always questioning as they read? Questioning and reading are symbiotically related to each other; one enhances the other in mutually beneficial ways.

Queries are designed to change the role of the teacher to facilitator of discussion. A teacher who uses Queries evaluates student responses not as right or wrong, but with the goal of encouraging students to consider an author's ideas and to respond to each other's interpretations of those ideas. As a result, student-to-student interactions tend to increase. We speculated that the increase was the result of the teacher becoming one of the collaborators toward developing understanding. The context for learning in QtA does not resemble an IRE pattern, but rather a classroom of spirited learners grappling with an author's text and working together to understand it.

One of our favorite anecdotes of student grappling came from an incident in a fifth-grade class whose language arts and social studies teachers had implemented QtA. But in this case, the student was in science class, where QtA had not been implemented. In the midst of students silently reading two pages that the teacher had assigned, one of the students blurted out to another sitting near: "I can't get what this dude's [the author] trying to say," and the other replied, "Yeah, we better do Questioning the Author." The first student recognized that he wasn't understanding what he was reading, and the other student used her version of an Initiating QtA Query.

## Types of Queries

We refer to Queries as either Initiating or Follow-Up. The goals of Initiating Queries are to make public what the author has presented and to launch discussion. The goal of Follow-Up Queries is to focus discussion once it is under way by encouraging students to elaborate and integrate ideas.

Note that the Initiating Queries in Table 5.1 are open and minimally directive. They are intended to focus students on the overall situation in a text segment rather

**TABLE 5.1.** Initiating and Follow-Up Queries for the First Five Text Segments for "The Bridge on the River Clarinette"

| Segment | Initiating Queries | Follow-Up Queries |
|---|---|---|
| 1 | "What has the author told us so far?" | "What's the meaning of the phrase 'lose touch' in the context of the story?" |
| 2 | "How do things look for the people?" | "Given what you know about the bridge, what does *dilapidated* mean?" |
| 3 | "What just happened?" | "What do you think of this new character?" |
| | | "The author says that the stranger has an uncanny smile. What does that tell us about him?" |
| 4 | "What did we learn from this conversation?" | "How does the new information add to our understanding of who he might be?" |
| | | "The last paragraph begins with 'To the astonishment of his audience . . .' Based on that description, how are the people reacting to the stranger and his offer?" |
| 5 | "Now what's going on with the townspeople?" | "What else did we learn about the stranger? How does this new information add to our understanding of his character?" |

than a specific event or fact. However, students unaccustomed to such questions might interpret their task more traditionally, and respond in a closed way. For example, a student might simply say, "The guy is gonna build a bridge in 5 seconds" in response to the Query for the fourth segment, "What did we learn from this conversation?" This is where Follow-Up Queries come in. The role of Follow-Up Queries is to prompt students to clarify, explain, reconsider, and the like. That's where the teaching, or maybe the better word is coaching, of comprehension occurs. We consider Follow-Up Queries more closely next.

## Follow-Up Queries

In planning, a teacher develops Queries to ask at stopping points, which include an Initiating Query and can include Follow-Up Queries as well. Follow-Ups do *not* have to be asked if the Initiating Query is sufficient to draw out the content that is targeted for the segment. It is the ongoing discussion that informs the teacher whether a Follow-Up is needed. As a lesson plays itself out, just as the planned Follow-Up Queries may not be required, a teacher may need to spontaneously create additional Follow-Ups to help students develop target understandings.

Being ready to improvise Follow-Ups to draw out student responses is an important part of guiding a successful QtA lesson. The need for improvised Follow-Ups occurs because students' responses may not fully address the issue tapped by a Query. This is a natural outcome of QtA Queries being open, rather than being the kind of questions that provide so much structure and content that they leave space for only a limited student response. We intend to prompt student thinking and have students take responsibility for generating ideas. But sometimes additional assistance is required. Let's take a closer look at each of the Queries in several of the segments shown in Table. 5.1.

In the first segment of the lesson, the first Query is a broad Initiating Query to establish the set-up of the story. The text states that a small town's bridge was about to collapse, which would leave the town's inhabitants disconnected from the rest of the country. So the thinking is that that point is not difficult to understand, with the assumption that the general meaning might not require following up. However, we chose to address the phrase "lose touch"—not simply the meaning of that phrase, but, importantly, how it reinforces the dire consequences of a bridge collapse.

Now to the second segment of the "Bridge" text, which focuses on the dire situation the town would face without a bridge and the fact that they can't afford to build a new one. The planned Initiating Query for the segment is: "How do things look for the people?" and it is meant to prompt a discussion of aspects such as the bridge being in such bad shape that merchants have no customers because people are afraid to cross, but that funds are not available to rebuild the bridge. Yet we have seen instances where a student responds to a Query like "How do things look now?" by simply saying "Bad." Of course that is not what is needed to develop understanding or explore what's going on in the text! So it becomes time for a teacher to think on his or her feet! Example Follow-Ups that might prompt students to extend and elaborate include "What do you mean by bad?" or "What's so bad about their situation?" or "What do you think the author wants us to understand about this bad situation?"

The wording of a Follow-Up Query should signal students to continue along the same line of thinking and not just bring up another fact from the text. You want students to give more information, but be wary of simply asking, "What else?" or "Tell me more?" or "Does anyone have something to add?" Although that kind of wording can sometimes do the job, it may not guide students toward building on ideas, but instead encourage them to contribute random pieces of text information. For example, after the segment that introduces the strange character in the "Bridge" story, the Initiating Query asks, "What just happened?" Our purpose for that Query was that students discuss this odd character. However, we want to be prepared in the event students merely mention that a new character was introduced. Rather than simply saying, "What else?," which might encourage them to talk about other topics, we follow with "What do you think of this new character?" which keeps them focused on the topic being discussed, the stranger.

Let's consider one more example from the "Bridge" story. In the fifth segment the townspeople are reacting to the stranger's offer to build a beautiful new bride in exchange for their words. There appears to be some consternation among the villagers, and people have a variety of reactions. The planned Query is "Now what's going on with the townspeople?" Imagine that a student responds by describing just one of the responses, such as "the mayor thought it was a bad joke."

The task here is to ask a Follow-Up that signals students not to just reiterate what the individual people have said, but to develop the overall idea of people being a bit confused and in disagreement about how to take the stranger's offer. A Follow-Up Query might first invoke the student's response—"OK, that's how the mayor reacted"—and then ask, "How does that fit in to what's going on here?" Such a Query can encourage students to look at the whole picture and how the pieces fit together.

In the previous two examples, the student responses, although incomplete, were on the right track of the major ideas. But what happens if a response does not focus on accurate information? The task then is to use a Follow-Up Query to redirect student thinking. For example, after the fourth segment, the Query asks what was learned from the conversation between the townspeople and the stranger. The stranger has told them that he buys and sells things, but he has offered to build the bridge in exchange for their words. Imagine a student responding that "the stranger wanted to sell them a bridge." A useful Follow-Up Query might be "Does he? What does the author tell us about that?" The move here should be for students to go back into the text and perhaps even read aloud the portion that suggests otherwise. In fact, directing students back to the text to check whether a response and the text are in sync is a very useful move. Going back to the text is especially useful if students are unable to respond to an Initiating Query at all, because going back will likely focus them on the information targeted by the Query.

Follow-Up Queries should keep students mindful of the text and mindful that their task is to focus on key ideas and consider how they connect. Queries not only lay a plan for guiding students through a particular text, they offer a framework for students' approach to text more generally. Thus Queries that are worded to signal linkage among ideas will help students focus their comprehension resources on connecting and integrating text ideas.

## Follow-Up Queries on the Fly

The Follow-Up Queries we discussed above were written in anticipation of what might be needed if students' responses to an Initiating Query were limited, wrong, or confounded. To develop Follow-Up Queries, teachers use their knowledge of the kinds of readers sitting in front of them, their verbal abilities, the students' standards of attention, and of course the nature of the text: Is it challenging? What background knowledge is needed? What's the vocabulary burden? and the like.

A good way to prime the development of Follow-Up Queries is to consider how students might respond to the Initiating Query. This helps to ground the planning process—to focus on real students that you know, rather than on abstract possibilities. Anticipating students' actual responses may also help to uncover additional potential obstacles that you may not have considered initially.

Developing Follow-Up Queries as you plan may seem like an extra step, but at least in the beginning of using QtA, we find it an invaluable one. As teachers get more accustomed to QtA, following up on the fly—creating spontaneous Queries in response to students' contributions—often becomes the norm. Indeed, we have noticed that for teachers who are practiced with QtA, following up in discussions begins to take on distinctly personal features. We recall several teachers who simply made characteristic sounds that would tip off their students that "something was up." This typically caused students to sharpen their attention or go back to check the text and then realize that they had a lot more to say. We saw other teachers use wait time as an effective tool. This can work when no responses seem forthcoming initially. Or it can be used if an initial response is incomplete or problematic. Teachers often find they can rely on their class to spontaneously add to or redirect what a peer has said, just by pausing and allowing students the thinking time. The big point is that Follow-Up Queries are useful, but not always required. More important is the concept of keeping discussion on track. Find ways to keep interactions around text ideas going until a good representation of the text situation has been built.

In order to illustrate a few more points about the use of Follow-Ups as a lesson proceeds, we consider brief excerpts from a transcript of a lesson from a sixth-grade social studies lesson on Egypt. Note in particular the role of Follow-Up Queries.[1]

## "The Life of a Scribe": Discussion Excerpts

### Excerpt 1

The initial text segment under discussion describes how the Egyptian pharaohs depended on written records to keep government organized. These records were developed by writers called scribes, who traveled the country to record information such as how much grain farmers harvested and how much farmers owed to the government. Scribes were also responsible for writing letters and marriage contracts for people. Few people were taught to write, so scribes were highly respected and it was a great honor to be a scribe.

> TEACHER: So what's the big idea; what do you think the author wants you to know?
>
> JAYLA: People who wrote stuff were called scribes, and they kept records.
>
> ETHAN: I want to add on to what Jayla said. Um, scribes also recorded how much grain farmers harvested.
>
> TEACHER: Okay, so you've picked up on the idea that scribes kept records, but how does that information fit in with what else we know about scribes?

---

[1] A version of these lessons appeared in our earlier QtA book. Since then we recorded subsequent lessons with the same teachers, who continued to use these texts. The excerpts presented here have integrated the early and later versions to highlight our points about Queries.

Notice that the first two students addressed only one aspect of the life of a scribe, the idea that scribes were able to keep records. Because the teacher wanted them to move beyond that idea, she asked a Follow-Up Query that challenged them to think about the connection between keeping records and being highly respected by asking how the information might fit with the rest of what had been read. Below, Elia and DiMajio work together to make the connection.

> ELIA: It says that scribes were highly respected, so people thought it was a pretty big deal to be a scribe.

> DiMAJIO: Yeah, cause not everybody knew how to write, so these scribes were like the only people who knew how to write, so they were respected by everyone.

> TEACHER: Okay, I think Elia and DiMajio hit on the big idea, so let's move on.

The teacher recognized that Elia and DiMajio had identified the big idea, and she moved on to the next segment.

## Excerpt 2

The text segment for this excerpt explains that boys who are training to be scribes needed to learn hieroglyphics used for record keeping, and then began to write on papyrus. The text explains that papyrus is a reed plant that ancient Egyptians used to make a kind of paper, also called papyrus, and then draws attention to the similarity between *papyrus* and *paper,* commenting that the word *paper* comes from the word *papyrus*.

The segment continues, describing the reeds that scribes used as pens, and noting that scribes had to have good penmanship and also needed to be good at math because their duties included figuring out the number of workers and the amount of materials needed to complete building projects. The segment ends by emphasizing that scribes had to keep correct records for the pharaoh.

> TEACHER: The author has given us a lot of information in that section, but what do you think is important to know about scribes?

> KA' RAUN: They wrote on papyrus paper.

> NATALIE: And they used reeds.

The first two responses repeated bits of information from the text, but they didn't address the important idea. So the teacher followed up by pushing students to move beyond pulling details from the text: "Okay, so you've mentioned a couple of details from the passage, but how are those details important to our understanding of scribes?"

In the next exchange, students piece together that it was a challenging job, connecting to the previously established idea that scribes were highly respected.

> ROBERTO: It was a really hard job. Like, you had to have good penmanship and be good at math.

> HEAVENLY: Roberto said, like, you have to be good at what you do, and I wanted to add on that you have to be good at what you do because you were working for the pharaohs, so you had to be, like, perfect.

The teacher recognized that Roberto and Heavenly were on the right track, but they still weren't making the connection between the challenging aspects of the job and being well respected, so she asked another Follow-Up Query that provided students with the opportunity to make that connection.

> TEACHER: Okay, so Roberto and Heavenly have explained how hard the job of a scribe is. So how does that connect with what we already said about scribes?

> ETHAN: They were well respected because their job was really important and they were under, like, pressure because they were keeping all these records for the pharaohs.

Let's summarize the specific effects of the Follow-Up Queries in the "Life of a Scribe" transcript. First, we can see that with the teacher's guidance, the students were able to identify the big ideas and make connections between already-established ideas and new information. Second, students worked together to build on each other's ideas and cited specific examples from the text in establishing those ideas. Finally, meanings and explanations emerged from several sources, not from the students alone, not from the teacher alone, not from the text alone, but from a collaboration that involved all three.

## Queries and Text Genres

In considering the differences between two major text genres, expositions (currently often called informational texts) and narratives, we have long been fond of Black's (1985) succinct distinction: "Expository texts are the ones that convey new information and explain new topics to people. In contrast stories and other narrative texts mostly describe new variations of well-known themes." Our first QtA work grew out of our concern with the poor comprehension we observed in the course of doing several studies on students' comprehension of social studies textbooks, which were at the time notorious for being less than coherent. We developed Queries and interspersed discussion to support students in making sense of text material that was poorly presented (Beck et al., 1989). We learned that interrupting reading and asking Queries had a beneficial effect on students' comprehension.

Later, we tried out Queries and interspersed discussion with narratives and learned that the same Queries worked with narrative texts but found that some additional Queries were especially helpful for targeting features of narrative texts. These additional Queries take into account the special characteristics of narrative texts in terms of purpose, structure, and author's craft.

Some of the problems in understanding narrative texts are the same kinds of problems expository texts offer, such as difficult language, unfamiliar content, and density of content. One kind of difficult language is unfamiliar vocabulary, which can be found in both genres, but there is one distinction that is exemplified in the two example texts used in Chapter 4. Our narrative text includes more potentially unfamiliar Tier Two words—for example, *dilapidated, uncanny, malicious*—whereas the expository text includes more potentially unfamiliar Tier Three words—*ice floes, global warming, indigenous*—as well as potentially unfamiliar Tier Two words—*stealth, sauntering, congregated*. Those differences in vocabulary generalize to most texts. Particular to the language of narratives is the authors' deliberate and artful forms of expression that suggest rather than demonstrate, which can make understanding difficult.

Finally, the structures of expository and narrative texts differ. In narrative texts, there are unique elements of structure and author's style that can present challenges for readers. Plot structure, for instance, is influenced by such elements as character motivation, setting, foreshadowing, conflict, and resolution. Techniques of an author's style can include the use of metaphor, analogy, mood, and idioms.

We will consider six Queries that have been particularly useful in addressing the unique aspects of narrative text. These first two Queries, below, help students think about character motivation and consider the "big picture" of where a character is and how he got there.

- "How do things look for this character now?"

- "Given what the author has already told us about this character, what do you think he's up to now?"

Just as the author constructs a character and a set of circumstances in which that character acts in believable and consistent ways, the reader must also understand the character well enough to construct his or her own representation of the character. Note that the above Queries ask students to think about future actions of a character, based on what they have gleaned to this point. Thus we do not consider them prediction questions. This reflects the understanding that good readers do not spend resources on frequent and unfounded predictions but save the formation of predictions for when evidence points to a likely event (Graesser et al., 1994).

Three other Queries can be effective in focusing students' thinking on the author's crafting of the plot and characters:

- "How has the author let you know that something has changed?"

- "How has the author worked that out for us?"

- "How is the author making you feel right now about these characters?"

Those Queries can enhance students' awareness of the author and remind them that plots are created by authors who plan complications and resolutions.

The use of conversation to provide information or move the plot is a common device that authors employ in narrative texts. A useful Query to draw attention to the idea that the author is revealing something beyond the words of the conversation is:

- "What more did we learn from this conversation?"

Let's see how some of the additional narrative Queries play out in an actual lesson by looking at a series of exchanges taken from the transcript of a narrative text lesson. In this lesson, a sixth-grade class is continuing their reading of the book *Tuck Everlasting* (Babbit, 1975). The book is a story of a family that has found eternal life by drinking from a secret spring. A girl, Winnie, has discovered their secret, and thus the family—Mae, Tuck, and their teenage son Jesse—has taken her with them to keep their secret safe. In the portion of text the class is working with, the Tucks have gone to bed and left Winnie to sleep on their couch.

## *Tuck Everlasting*: Discussion Excerpts

### Excerpt 1

In this text segment, Mae has come out to talk to Winnie, explaining that since Winnie had discovered their secret, they did not know what else to do but take her with them. Mae then tells Winnie that because they have been alone so long, it feels good to have her with them. "I wish you was . . . ours," she tells Winnie.

TEACHER: So what have we learned from this conversation between Winnie and Mae?

DRAVON: Mae's apologizing for kidnapping Winnie.

TEACHER: What does that tell us about Mae?

SARA: She's, like, a good person.

MEGAN: Can I ask a question cause I kinda disagree with Sara? Like, if she's a good person then why would she kidnap somebody?

TEACHER: Well, that's a good question. What do the rest of you think about that?

ANGEL: I agree with Sara. I think she is a good person cause it says that Mae said that she wishes Winnie was theirs.

TEACHER: Hmm, Winnie was theirs? What's that about? How does that connect with Mae being or not being a good person?

ROBERT: 'Cause, like, they never see nobody or have no visitors, so if she was theirs, maybe, she'd, like, live with them and always be there.

MARINA: And then they wouldn't be lonely no more.

TEACHER: So how does all of this fit together? Can someone pull together what everyone is saying and answer Megan's question?

JAKE: Yeah, like Mae knows what they did was, like, wrong, and um, that's why she's apologizing for it. And she's telling us, like, why she wants her [Winnie] to live with them. So, yeah, they kidnapped her, but it was, like, for good reasons, so she can still be a good person.

Notice how the teacher begins the discussion by asking what the conversation reveals about the two characters. Dravon begins by sharing that part of the conversation is Mae's apology, and Sara comments that the apology shows that Mae must be a good person. Megan offers a different perspective by pushing students to think about how someone who kidnaps can be a good person. Students work together to justify how the two ideas might not be in conflict, and the teacher wraps up the exchange by asking a student to pull together their ideas.

## Excerpt 2

Mae has gone back to bed, but Tuck now appears. He tells Winnie that he didn't mean to disturb her, but thinks that he ought to be keeping her company out in the living room. Winnie finds herself surprised and touched by Tuck's concern, and tells him that she is all right, assuring him he needn't sit up with her.

TEACHER: Hmm, now what's going on with Winnie?

JESSICA: I think Winnie is kinda changing how she feels about them.

TEACHER: Why do you say that?

JESSICA: Because before she, like, thought like they were bad people or something cause they kidnapped her, but now she's, like, saying she was touched and surprised.

TEACHER: She was touched and surprised. What does that tell us?

TONY: Like, she's changing how she feels about them a little. It's like she felt good that he kinda checked on her, but she was kinda surprised that she felt that way.

The teacher wanted students to notice how Winnie is beginning to change her attitude, but she wanted to begin with a Query that allowed the students to acknowledge that a change is taking place. In asking "What's going on with Winnie?," the teacher is allowing students to recognize the change without pointing it out to them. Her simple follow-up, "Why do you say that?," allows students to elaborate on how Winnie's feelings are changing.

## Excerpt 3

Winnie is now lying awake feeling cared for and confused. She reflects on having initially thought of the Tucks as criminals. The segment concludes as Winnie's thoughts continue to vacillate: "Well, but they *were*. And yet . . . "

> TEACHER: Okay, so we just talked about how Winnie's feelings are changing, but let me ask you how the author is making *you* feel right now about the Tucks?
>
> SHAYLA: I didn't like them at all 'cause I thought what they did to Winnie was wrong. I don't know, but now, I'm kinda feeling like how Winnie feels right now, like maybe they're not too bad.
>
> SIERRA: The author's making me feel like I might kinda like them.
>
> MONTAE: I agree with Sierra. I think I'm starting to like them. Like, the author wants us to change how we feel about the Tucks. Like at first the author made them seem like really bad people, but now it's like, it's like, the author is showing maybe a different side to them.

This exchange speaks to an author's ability to engage a reader with the characters in a book and capture how a reader feels about them. The teacher's Query acknowledges the conversation the class just had about Winnie's feelings and pushes students to think about their own feelings toward the Tucks. Notice how Montae explains that he thinks the author is intentionally trying to change the reader's mind.

## Excerpt 4

Now the Tucks' son Jesse appears and gently suggests to Winnie that she consider staying on with them. After Jesse leaves, Winnie is wide awake, considering what her future might be. She is feeling even more confused, and clearly finds Jesse appealing.

> TEACHER: What's going on with Winnie?
>
> JAKE: She's really confused 'cause now Jesse was talking about wanting to get married.
>
> DEMIAH: And, like, she don't know how she should feel. It's like, should she still be mad at them for kidnapping her, or like them 'cause now they're being nice?
>
> MALIK: Or, like, be in love with Jesse?

The Query "What's going on with Winnie?" allows students to think about how Winnie is reflecting on the ongoing and changing situation. Student responses demonstrate that they are able to consider the range of emotions Winnie is feeling and further build on the idea that this range of emotions is causing Winnie to feel confused and not truly understand how she should feel about the characters.

In Table 5.2 we have pulled together examples of the types of Queries discussed in this chapter—Initiating, Follow-Up, and some worded specifically for narratives. The table is meant to show the typical ways Queries of each type are worded, and in each case their open nature.

## The Bottom Line on Queries

We can boil down the purpose of Queries, whether Initiating or Follow-Up, to two categories: to prompt students to figure out what a text segment is about, and to connect ideas. Initiating Queries prompt the process of considering and connecting information, and Follow-Up Queries help to focus and clarify those considerations, and to further support building text connections.

But as we have demonstrated, there is a large variety of ways that Queries can be worded beyond "What's that all about?" and "How does that connect?" That is because the Queries are often worded to help draw students' attention to specific text elements. For example, a teacher might want to focus attention on a character with a Query such as "What have we learned now about the old man?" Or a teacher might want to prompt information about a situation that needs to be inferred, so a Query might ask, "What did we learn from this conversation?" or "What does the author mean that polar bears come into towns to solve a problem?" Such Queries are,

**TABLE 5.2.** Examples of Queries: Initiating, Follow-Up, and Narrative

| Initiating | Follow-Up | Narrative |
| --- | --- | --- |
| "What is the author saying here?" | "That's what the author said, but what did the author mean?" | "How do things look for this character now?" |
| "What's the big idea?" | | "How does what we just read add to our understanding of this character?" |
| "What's going on here?" | "Does that make sense with what happened before?" | |
| "What do you think the author wants us to know?" | "How does that fit in with what the author has told us?" | "How has the author worked that out for us?" |
| "What is the author talking about?" | | "Given what we already know about this character, what do you think he's up to?" |
| "What's this all about?" | "But does the author tell us why?" | |
| | "How does that connect with what we just read?" | "What have we learned from this conversation?" |

at their core, asking students to figure out the important ideas in a segment of text. But by varying the wording and directing students' attention to certain elements or situations, we are helping to shape the comprehension process, specifically, that comprehension requires decision making.

A reader's goal is not just to recite major text information, but to decide on which information is most important to carry forward as reading proceeds. As additional segments of text are read, a primary goal of the reader is to connect ideas from segment to segment to build a meaningful representation of the text. Queries that prompt connections are often quite straightforward, such as "How does that connect to what we already knew?" or "How does this fit in with what is going on?" The bottom line is that the point of any Query is to prompt students to develop the understandings that the teacher has identified as key.

## ENDING NOTES

- Queries differ from some traditional questions in that Queries are more process oriented—intended to assist students in the process of comprehending.

- In contrast, some questions are more product oriented because they assess understandings that are the products of comprehension.

- Initiating Queries function as the mechanisms for making text information public and launching discussion.

- Follow-Up Queries encourage students to keep the discussion focused and integrate ideas.

- Narrative texts require additional Queries because authors of narrative texts use literary techniques that can pose special challenges to readers.

- A general way to think about Queries is that, whether Initiating or Follow-Up, their purpose comes down to one of two categories: to prompt students to figure out what a text segment is about, or to connect ideas.

# CHAPTER 6

# Specific Plans for a Narrative and an Expository Read–Aloud Text

QtA was developed for middle elementary students and above, that is, students already reading on their own. Prompted by our own observations and questions from primary grades teachers, we began to think that a similar process could work for very young students. We subsequently developed an approach called Text Talk (Beck & McKeown, 2001), targeted to developing young learners' language and comprehension abilities through in-depth experiences listening to stories read aloud. In particular, we wanted to give students experiences responding to ideas communicated through printed language.

The language of texts is referred to as decontextualized language because it is beyond the here and now of everyday conversational contexts. Helping children respond to text language forms the basis of comprehension ability. Developing young learners' comprehension ability means helping them to understand that interacting with text is about building and connecting ideas. This was the goal of Text Talk, and of course an important aspect was having students interact with those ideas through interspersed reading and talk.

In Text Talk, we particularly targeted some tendencies that young students have when first asked to respond to text ideas:

• *Responding with what is in the pictures.* Of course charming pictures are a hallmark of good read-aloud texts and add delight to experiences with books. However, if children rely on getting information from pictures, it diminishes their attention to the language of the book. If interactive experiences with books are to lead to comprehension, attention needs to be on the language. This of course does not mean ignoring pictures, but rather recognizing the role of pictures versus language in interactions with text.

• *Responding with background knowledge rather than story information.* Integrating background knowledge with text information is a vital part of successful comprehension. But an important part of using prior knowledge is understanding what knowledge is and is not relevant to the text. Children often form quick associations to pictures or words in a text that can lead them astray. For example, in one of our kindergarten observations, one of the *Curious George* (Rey, 1941) stories was being read. The text introduced the character as a little monkey who sometimes got into trouble. Asked what the story was telling us about George, a girl answered, "He likes bananas." She was recalling a fact about monkeys, but it was not related to the text. We do want children to be active readers who connect what they know to what they read. But we want them to develop the habit of attending to text language first, and then activating knowledge that is in keeping with that.

Read-alouds are excellent vehicles for getting young students accustomed to getting information from text. They allow students to develop their thinking and comprehension abilities by offering much more sophisticated material than is possible in texts that young students read on their own. So whether we call it Questioning the Author or Text Talk, experiences built around discussion of text as it is read can benefit literacy development.

In developing lessons for primary grades students, we point to some differences to keep in mind. There may be even greater need to follow up the Initiating Queries with more particular probes, because the notion of dealing with text ideas is still so new. We do, however, still want to begin with open Queries, but just be even more prepared with Follow-Ups than might be needed with older students. Following up may be of greater need because of another tendency of young students in responding to text questions. That is, we noted in our observations that students very often responded by simply repeating lines from text, even when the question was asking something beyond that. Follow-Ups can encourage students to talk about what's happening in a text using their own words, rather than retrieving language of the text.

Follow-Ups also encourage students to produce more language. This concerns another issue we observed. Students often produced single-word answers in response to questions about a text. Sometimes they were actually set up to do so, as when a teacher said, "After she ate all those raspberry tarts, she felt how?" Of course this draws students to say "sick." We found this kind of fill-in-the-blank questioning quite prevalent. So naturally students develop the habit of not saying much. We aim to change that!

Lessons with young students often tend to have more stops, some of which are intended to be quick stops to draw attention to features of text content and make sure that students are focusing on important ideas. The point of such stops is not to invite discussion, but to kind of put some markers down to guide students' thinking. For example, if something happens that students had anticipated, a teacher might make a comment such as "Oh, it was exactly as we thought!" Or if a character from earlier suddenly reappears, the teacher might say, "Oh, we remember this guy from before, right?"

Stops that are intended to prompt talk about the text often include more rereading of portions of the text. In read-alouds students do not, of course, have the text in front of them, so it is especially important to reestablish attention to the text through rereading key sentences. This helps provide the grist students need for responding.

In this chapter we offer two plans for texts meant to be read aloud to young learners, targeting first graders, although they could work for kindergarten or second grade depending on the group. As in Chapter 4, we go through the planning process for a narrative and then for an expository text. In each case we discuss the thinking for every decision we made within each of the three planning categories: (1) determining major understandings and identifying potential obstacles, (2) segmenting the text, and (3) developing Initiating and Follow-Up Queries.

## Planning for a Narrative Read-Aloud

The narrative text that we use for planning is "A Donkey for Fifty Cents," a Puerto Rican folktale adapted by Jean Acosta (2019).[1] A copy of the text formatted for ease in making multiple copies for the classroom appears in the Appendix (pp. 177–178) and also on the book's companion website (see the box at the end of the table of contents).

### *A Donkey for Fifty Cents*
#### Puerto Rican folktale adapted by Jean Acosta

This is the story of a boy named Pablo who lived in a small village in Puerto Rico. Is it a true story? Who knows! But the people in Puerto Rico have told this tale for many years. Pablo wanted a donkey. He told his parents that if he had a donkey of his own, he could help them out by carrying things from the store and back and forth from his family's fields. They told him he could get a donkey if he paid for it himself.

Since he was just a boy, Pablo did not have much money. He scraped together the few coins he had and went out to look for a donkey. After walking a little ways, Pablo ran into an old man who was leading three donkeys. He called to him, "Kind sir, are you interested in selling one of your donkeys?" The man looked at Pablo and smiled, for he was quite surprised to have a young boy wanting to buy a donkey.

"Now, what are you going to do with a donkey, son?" the man said, with kindness in his eyes.

"I want to have something of my own to take care of," replied Pablo. "And if I have a donkey then I can be of more help to my parents. With a donkey I can carry things so my mother and father don't need to make so many trips to the store and in and out from their fields."

The man was very pleased with Pablo's answer. He liked the idea that

---

[1] From Acosta (2019). Used by permission of the author.

a young boy wanted to take care of another creature. And he was very impressed that Pablo wanted to help his parents. So he said to the boy, "Yes, I will sell you a donkey."

Pablo smiled broadly. Then his face changed and he said, "Sir, I have only fifty cents."

The man said, "Well, what luck! That is exactly the price of this donkey," as he pointed to the smallest animal.

Pablo was so excited! He dug the fifty cents out of his pocket, handed it to the man, and took the reins of the donkey. As he walked back home with his donkey, a man called to him from the side of the road, "How much did you pay for that donkey?"

"Fifty cents," he called.

Before he got home, three more people stopped him to ask about the cost of the donkey. "Fifty cents," he said each time.

The next day Pablo was so excited to go out with his new donkey. He asked his mother if he could get anything from the store, and she gave him a list. He set out, proudly leading his donkey. And it began to happen again. Everyone kept asking him how much he paid for the donkey. "Fifty cents," he would say, again and again.

Day after day as he walked about with his donkey, people kept asking him how much he paid for it. "Fifty cents," he would say, again and again. But he got very tired of this. Then one night an idea crept into his mind.

The next day Pablo ran into the old Town Hall. In the back of the hall stood a marble statue of the town's first mayor, Mateo Bonilla, who everyone in town said had magical powers. Pablo went behind the statue and called out, "Go and tell all the people of the town to gather here." The town clerk came out of his office when he heard the voice. He thought that it was the voice of the magical Mayor Bonilla with an important message for the town!

The town clerk did what he was told. He ran and got everyone to come to the town hall and stand in front of the statue. The clerk said to the statue, "I have done what you have asked. All are gathered here now." Then the boy came out from behind the statue. He said, "I'm glad that you are all here. Now let me tell you all—the donkey cost fifty cents. Please do not ask me again."

## Identifying Major Understandings

Now, read the story a second time, with a pencil in hand, and mark phrases/sentences in the text in which the author provides information about key story elements. Our choice of important content follows:

- Pablo was a boy who wanted a donkey.

- [His parents] told him he could get a donkey if he paid for it himself.

- He scraped together the few coins he had, and found a man willing to sell him a donkey.
- The man looked at Pablo and smiled. . . . He was very impressed that Pablo wanted to help his parents.
- "That is exactly the price of this donkey."
- Before he got home, three more people stopped him to ask about the cost of the donkey.
- Everyone kept asking him how much he paid for the donkey. He got very tired of this.
- . . . the town's first mayor, Mateo Bonilla, who everyone in town said had magical powers.
- "Go and tell all the people of the town to gather here." . . . He thought that it was the voice of the magical Mayor Bonilla.
- He said, "I'm glad that you are all here. Now let me tell you all—the donkey cost fifty cents."

Below is our take on the major understandings for this text:

Pablo, a young boy, wanted a donkey and was glad to pay for it himself. He met a man with three donkeys and asked to buy one. Because the man was kind and impressed by Pablo's spunk, he was willing to sell Pablo a donkey for a very low price. Pablo was very happy with his donkey until people kept asking him how much he paid for it. Pablo comes up with a quirky plan to make them stop asking. Using a bit of trickery, he gets the town clerk to gather all the townspeople together. Then he announces to everyone the cost of the donkey and tells them to stop asking him.

## Identifying Potential Obstacles

This is a playful story that begins with a boy's buying a donkey. Early in the story students may not readily understand that the old man is selling his donkey mainly as a kindness to the boy.

But the story ends up being a kind of extended joke, focusing on Pablo's effort to have everyone in town stop asking him about how much the donkey cost. The scene of Pablo entering the Town Hall and hiding behind the statue may cause confusion, since that is a sudden switch in the story. Students may not readily understand that Pablo is trying to make the town clerk believe the statue is speaking, and that such a misbelief is possible because of the mayor's supposed magical powers.

We noticed only two words that may be unfamiliar to students and judged them unlikely to interfere with comprehension, but they may be useful Tier Two words to work with later:

*impressed*
*creature*

## Developing Text Segments and Queries

With major understandings and potential obstacles established, the next step is to segment the text and design Initiating and Follow-Up Queries. You will notice that in these lessons for early students we sometimes mark a Follow-Up Query to be used "as needed." These Follow-Ups are suggested when we anticipate students might not fully respond to the Initiating Query, and they provide a somewhat more directed wording to explore a key point.

In other cases, Follow-Ups are intended to explore a different, secondary point. These are not marked "as needed" and are to be asked even if students are able to address the Initiating Query (e.g., in the Sixth Segment).

As in Chapter 4, the major understandings and potential obstacles drive the decisions about stopping points and Queries. Below we provide our thinking about those decisions.

| FIRST SEGMENT | |
|---|---|
| This is the story of a boy named Pablo who lived in a small village in Puerto Rico. Is it a true story? Who knows! But the people in Puerto Rico have told this tale for many years. | |
| **Decisions and Comments** | **Queries** |
| A brief stop here is called for. First to familiarize students with Puerto Rico and second to encourage students to notice the author's setup of the story as a tale told again and again. | "Puerto Rico is an island that is part of the United States [show on a map]. People who live there speak Spanish."<br><br>**Query:** "What does the author want you to know about this story?" |
| **SECOND SEGMENT** | |
| Pablo wanted a donkey. He told his parents that if he had a donkey of his own, he could help them out by carrying things from the store and back and forth from his family's fields. They told him he could get a donkey if he paid for it himself.<br>    Since he was just a boy, Pablo did not have much money. | |
| **Decisions and Comments** | **Queries** |
| This segment describes Pablo's desire for a donkey and the problem of paying for it. Both of those situations can be dealt with together here. | **Query:** "What do we know about Pablo?"<br><br>**Follow-up:** If needed to draw out that Pablo has little money to buy a donkey, ask, "What problem is Pablo having?" |

## THIRD SEGMENT

He scraped together the few coins he had and went out to look for a donkey. After walking a little ways, Pablo ran into an old man who was leading three donkeys. He called to him, "Kind sir, are you interested in selling one of your donkeys?" The man looked at Pablo and smiled, for he was quite surprised to have a young boy wanting to buy a donkey.

"Now, what are you going to do with a donkey, son?" the man said, with kindness in his eyes.

| Decisions and Comments | Queries |
|---|---|
| The stop here is to establish that Pablo has, perhaps, found a source for a donkey and to consider what the old man's smile might mean. | **Query:** "How do you think things look for Pablo now?" <br><br> **Follow-up** if needed to establish what's going on: "What has happened to Pablo here?" <br><br> **Query:** "What is the author telling us about the old man?" If needed, reread final sentence that ends "with kindness in his eyes." |

## FOURTH SEGMENT

"I want to have something of my own to take care of," replied Pablo. "And if I have a donkey then I can be of more help to my parents. With a donkey I can carry things so my mother and father don't need to make so many trips to the store and in and out from their fields."

The man was very pleased with Pablo's answer. He liked the idea that a young boy wanted to take care of another creature. And he was very impressed that Pablo wanted to help his parents. So he said to the boy, "Yes, I will sell you a donkey."

| Decisions and Comments | Queries |
|---|---|
| Here we stop to give thought to what the old man's reaction might mean for Pablo's donkey buying. These situations help young comprehenders tune in to character motives. <br><br> A good Tier Two word, *impressed*, appears here but it is not needed to understand the context and dealing with it might be too time-consuming. But it would be excellent to come back to its use. | **Query:** Reread "The man was very pleased with Pablo's answer." "What does that tell you?" <br><br> **Follow-up** as needed: If students just talk about what the man said, ask, "Thinking about what the man said, what do you think might happen?" <br><br> If students immediately predict that the man will sell him the donkey: "What makes you think that?" |

## FIFTH SEGMENT

Pablo smiled broadly. Then his face changed and he said, "Sir, I have only 50 cents."

| Decisions and Comments | Queries |
| --- | --- |
| A quick stop here to guide students to pick up on the idea that Pablo worries 50 cents will not be enough to buy a donkey. | **Query:** What does it mean that "his face changed"? <br><br> **Follow-up:** "When he tells the man he has only 50 cents, what do you think Pablo is thinking?" |

## SIXTH SEGMENT

The man said, "Well, what luck! That is exactly the price of this donkey" as he pointed to the smallest animal. Pablo was so excited! He dug the 50 cents out of his pocket, handed it to the man, and took the reins of the donkey.

| Decisions and Comments | Queries |
| --- | --- |
| Stop here to wrap up this sequence of the story, understanding that Pablo has achieved his goal of owning a donkey. <br>    Help students understand that the man might have offered a very cheap price because he likes Pablo and is happy to provide him with a donkey. | **Query:** "What has happened now?" <br><br> **Follow-up:** "The donkey is only 50 cents? What do you think of that?" <br><br> **Follow-up:** "What did the author tell us earlier in the story that might explain why the man is selling the donkey for just 50 cents?" |

## SEVENTH SEGMENT

As he walked back home with his donkey, a man called to him from the side of the road. "How much did you pay for that donkey?"
    "Fifty cents," he called.
    Before he got home, three more people stopped him to ask about the cost of the donkey. "Fifty cents," he said each time.
    The next day Pablo was so excited to go out with his new donkey. He asked his mother if he could get anything from the store and she gave him a list. He set out, proudly leading his donkey.

| Decisions and Comments | Queries |
| --- | --- |
| For this section the goal is to tune attention to Pablo's happiness with his donkey to prepare students for the switch that then occurs. | **Query:** "How is Pablo's day going so far?" <br><br> **Follow-up:** "So what do the people of the town think of Pablo and his donkey?" |

## EIGHTH SEGMENT

And it began to happen again. Everyone kept asking him how much he paid for the donkey. "Fifty cents," he would say, again and again.

| EIGHTH SEGMENT (*continued*) |
|---|

Day after day as he walked about with his donkey people kept asking him how much he paid for it. "Fifty cents," he would say, again and again. But he got very tired of this.

| Decisions and Comments | Queries |
|---|---|
| Here the focus turns to the townspeople asking over and over about the price of the donkey and Pablo's annoyance with it. | **Query:** "What's going on now with Pablo?"<br><br>**Follow-up:** "How does what happened in this section connect to what we just said about the townspeople?" |

| NINE SEGMENT |
|---|

Then one night an idea crept into his mind.

    The next day Pablo ran into the old Town Hall. In the back of the hall stood a marble statue of the town's first mayor, Mateo Bonilla, who everyone in town said had magical powers. Pablo went behind the statue and called out, "Go and tell all the people of the town to gather here."

| Decisions and Comments | Queries |
|---|---|
| Help students realize that Pablo is trying to make it seem like the mayor's statue is speaking. Students may need some help here to put together that the former mayor has been said to be magical, and thus someone might believe his statue was speaking. | **Query:** "What is Pablo up to?"<br><br>**Follow-up:** "What's this about his going behind the statue? What do we know about the statue?" |

| TENTH SEGMENT |
|---|

The town clerk came out of his office when he heard the voice. He thought that it was the voice of the magical Mayor Bonilla with an important message for the town!

| Decisions and Comments | Queries |
|---|---|
| If students did realize Pablo's intent, it is an opportunity to provide feedback on a successful inference. | "Oh, we figured that out! Pablo tricked him into thinking it was the mayor." |

| ELEVENTH SEGMENT |
|---|

The town clerk did what he was told. He ran and got everyone to come to the town hall and stand in front of the statue. The clerk said to the statue, "I have done what you have asked. All are gathered here now."

| ELEVENTH SEGMENT (continued) | |
|---|---|
| **Decisions and Comments** | **Queries** |
| Check that students understand the scene. The townspeople have been called in front of the magical mayor's statue and probably believe they are to hear a message from him. | **Query:** "So why are all those people there?" <br><br> **Follow-up** if needed: Reread the sentence "He thought that it was the voice of the magical Mayor Bonilla with an important message for the town!" from the previous segment and ask, "What do the people probably think is going to happen?" |

| TWELFTH SEGMENT | |
|---|---|
| Then the boy came out from behind the statue. He said, "I'm glad that you are all here. Now let me tell you all—the donkey cost fifty cents. Please do not ask me again." | |
| **Decisions and Comments** | **Queries** |
| Pablo reveals himself and delivers his message. The story ends without reaction from the townspeople, but that may be an interesting point to ponder. | **Query:** "Do you think this will solve Pablo's problem of being asked about the donkey's price?" |
| **Decisions and Comments** | **Wrap-Up Queries** |
| Wrapping up the story could emphasize the humor of the story and that Pablo's solution was quite unusual. | **Query:** "What do you think of what Pablo did?" <br><br> **Query:** "How else could he have solved his problem?" |

# Some Considerations on Expository Text for Young Learners

About two decades ago reading scholars began to discuss the lack of expository text experiences in elementary school and to recommend that young students be exposed to greater amounts of expository text (see, e.g., Duke, 2000). There were generally two reasons that more expository text was seen as beneficial; one was to develop students' content knowledge and the other was to develop understanding of genres beyond narrative. These both are certainly reasonable goals.

There are myriad attractive and delightful expository books for young readers now on the market. But an issue of some concern to our purposes here is that many expository texts for young readers provide a loose collection of ideas around a topic rather than statements that fit together to build main points. That is, they lack coherence, by which we mean a sequence of ideas that makes sense and language that discusses those ideas in a way that makes their nature and their relationships apparent. To a great extent this lack of coherence exists because the explanatory material that would tie together topics and ideas is not conceptually accessible for young readers.

The upshot is that such loosely connected texts can be a fine vehicle for enhancing students' content knowledge. A caveat, however, is that "understanding" these texts consists mainly of recalling literal information; they do not afford opportunities for developing and organizing ideas. Thus their role in helping students to develop comprehension capabilities is limited.

Regarding decisions about when, how, and how much to include expository texts in the curriculum for primary grades learners, teachers need to be aware of the affordances of the text, for example whether a text invites connecting and consolidating ideas or mainly provides familiarization with specific content knowledge. Either has value, and a few texts do manage to provide both. But it is important to take care to balance the goals of building content knowledge and building comprehension.

## Planning for an Expository Read-Aloud

The expository text that we have chosen to use for exemplifying QtA planning for young students, "Let's Explore Caves" by Chloe Davis (2019),[2] is one that we believe does afford building ideas. The topic of the text is caves—what they are, how they form, and examples of caves around the world. Of course, such a text would not be shared with young readers without pictures. In this case, as is true with many expository texts, pictures can aid, and are sometimes required for, explaining ideas in a text. Although we are unable to provide pictures, should you choose to use this text, you can find many pictures of the caves described easily accessible on the Internet. A copy of the story formatted for ease in making multiple copies for the classroom appears in the Appendix (pp. 179–180) and also on the book's companion website (see the box at the end of the table of contents).

### *Let's Explore Caves*
#### by Chloe Davis

On days when it was rainy or too cold to go outside, my mother let my sister and me build a little hiding place under the kitchen table. We would put a long tablecloth over the table and pull in the chairs. It felt like a secret place where we could play and hide. We used to call it our home cave. It probably felt like a cave to us because we felt cozy and protected where no one could see us. But what is a cave?

---

[2]From Davis (2019). Used by permission of the author.

Real caves are big openings in the ground. They can extend deep underground, even for miles. Or they can look like big hollow places on the side of a rocky cliff.

Caves are created when water begins to drip onto rock. Natural chemicals that are in the water dissolve, or wear away, the rock. Over time so much rock dissolves that only large hollow places are left. These large hollow places are caves.

Caves have been useful to people for a very long time. People who lived long, long ago used them for shelter from bad weather or to store food. Sometimes people even used caves as their homes or as a special place for ceremonies.

Caves have always seemed kind of mysterious. Maybe that is because caves are dark inside and when you go into one, you don't know how deep it is. And you never know what you are going to find inside.

There are many, many caves of all different types around the world. And because humans are curious, they like to explore caves. There is a special name for that activity—exploring caves is called spelunking. Would you want to be a spelunker?

We can do some pretend spelunking and find out about interesting caves all over the world!

The largest cave in the world is five and a half miles long! It would take a normal adult nearly 2 hours to walk that distance. This cave is underneath a forest in the country of Vietnam. The cave is called Son Doong Cave, which means "cave of the mountain river" in the Vietnamese language. It is so big that it has a jungle and a river inside it! It is so big that it could hold a 40-story skyscraper inside it!

But this cave was a secret of Nature until 6 years ago. A man who lives near the cave discovered it. Maybe the most surprising thing about Son Doong Cave is that scientists say that it is still growing!

Another amazing cave is Waitomo Glowworm Cave in New Zealand. New Zealand is a country all the way on the other side of the world, near Australia. Tiny glowworms, just a quarter-inch long, hang from the cave ceiling. Glowworms are bioluminescent, which means they are a type of living thing that gives off its own light. The glowworms in Waitomo Cave give off a blue light. There are so many of them along the ceiling that the whole cave looks blue!

Let's talk about one more cave. This one is called Spruce Tree House. It is in the state of Colorado in a park called Mesa Verde. What is special about this cave is that there are ruins of a village where ancient people lived, centuries ago. It has 130 rooms that were built into a cliff in the hillside, and the remains of them are still there for everyone to see. Scientists have figured out that groups of 60 to 80 people lived in the cave and farmed corn, beans, and squash. The cave got its name because it was discovered behind a giant spruce tree. Two ranchers discovered the cave when they were looking for stray cattle.

So we have a cave that has a jungle and a river in it, a cave that has glow-worms hanging from the ceiling, and a cave that has ruins of long-ago cliff dwellers. Which cave would you want to go spelunking in?

## Identifying Major Understandings

We hope that you will continue to follow along with our planning process and now read the text a second time, marking phrases/sentences in which the author provides information about key elements. Our choice of important content follows:

- Real caves are big openings in the ground.
- Caves are formed by water dripping into rock. Chemicals in the water dissolve the rock in a way that creates large hollow places.
- Caves have been useful to people as shelter from bad weather, to store food, as homes or as a place for ceremonies.
- Caves have always seemed kind of mysterious.
- Because humans are curious, they like to explore caves.
- We can find out about interesting caves all over the world.
- Son Doong Cave in Vietnam is so big that it has a jungle and a river inside it.
- Scientists say that Son Doong Cave it is still growing.
- Waitomo Glowworm Cave in New Zealand has glowworms hanging from the cave ceiling.
- Spruce Tree House in Colorado has ruins of a village where ancient people lived.

Below is our take on the major understandings for this text:

Caves are a natural phenomenon formed in rock by the forces of chemical processes (mineralized water). Caves have intrigued people for centuries and have been used for many purposes including as homes. There are many caves that have been discovered across the world, and they offer a variety of amazing natural wonders, such as forests and glowworms. They also offered ancient people a protected place to live.

## Identifying Potential Obstacles

The obstacles in this text are not so much that there is content that may be difficult to grasp. Rather it is the issue that we foreshadowed in the opening section, that it might be difficult to connect ideas and form an overall representation of the text, given that the content consists mostly of a survey of interesting features of a variety of caves.

The obstacle is the challenge of both having students enjoy and learn about various caves yet helping them move toward an overall understanding of caves as a natural, varied, useful phenomenon.

As far as unfamiliar words in this text, there are several Tier Two words that may impact comprehension and that we deal with during reading:

*hollow*
*dissolve*
*ceremonies*
*ruins*

There are also two Tier Three words of note that students should understand for this text. Both are explained in the text and require no further attention—although, as we note, *spelunking* is fun to say!:

*spelunking*
*bioluminescent*

## Developing Text Segments and Queries

We next turn to the text segments and Initiating and Follow-Up Queries we designed for this text. Again, the major understandings and potential obstacles drive the decisions about stopping points and Queries. Below we provide our thinking about those decisions.

| FIRST SEGMENT | |
|---|---|
| On days when it was rainy or too cold to go outside, my mother let my sister and me build a little hiding place under the kitchen table. We would put a long tablecloth over the table and pull in the chairs. It felt like a secret place where we could play and hide. We used to call it our home cave. It probably felt like a cave to us because we felt cozy and protected where no one could see us. But what is a cave? | |
| **Decisions and Comments** | **Queries** |
| A brief stop here is called for to set the topic. The segment prepares students for the text by mentioning some characteristics of caves and indicating that what the author created "probably felt like a cave" but was not a cave. | **Query:** "How has the author started us off?" <br><br> **Follow-up:** "How does the author let you know that what she and her sister created was not a real cave?" |
| SECOND SEGMENT | |
| Real caves are big openings in the ground. They can extend deep underground, even for miles. Or they can look like big hollow places on the side of a rocky cliff. | |

| SECOND SEGMENT (*continued*) | |
|---|---|
| Caves are created when water begins to drip onto rock. Natural chemicals that are in the water dissolve, or wear away, the rock. Over time so much rock dissolves that only large hollow places are left. These large hollow places are caves. | |
| **Decisions and Comments** | **Queries** |
| First we want to clarify *hollow* because it anchors the concept of what caves are and how they are formed.<br><br>Second, the main issue is to have students have some concept of what a cave is and how it develops. | "The author tells us caves are hollow. That means they have a hole or empty space inside them."<br><br>**Query:** "What does the author tell us about how caves become big hollow spaces?"<br><br>**Follow-up:** "The author says that water dissolves rock. If something dissolves, it breaks down into much smaller pieces and then disappears. So what breaks down to make a cave?"<br><br>**Follow-up:** If needed, reread: "Over time so much rock dissolves that only large hollow places are left." And ask the first follow-up again to help students understand that caves are actually big holes in rock. |

| THIRD SEGMENT | |
|---|---|
| Caves have been very useful to people for a very long time. People who lived long, long ago used them for shelter from bad weather or to store food. Sometimes people even used caves as their homes or as a special place for ceremonies. | |
| **Decisions and Comments** | **Queries** |
| This segment presents the word *ceremonies*, which we briefly introduce.<br><br>The point here is to make students aware of the utility of caves. | "The author tells us that caves have been used for ceremonies. Ceremonies are special kinds of celebrations, such as a wedding or a graduation."<br><br>**Query:** "What does the author want us to know about caves?" |

| FOURTH SEGMENT |
|---|
| Caves have always seemed kind of mysterious. Maybe that is because caves are dark inside and when you go into one, you don't know how deep it is. And you never know what you are going to find inside. |

| FOURTH SEGMENT (continued) | |
| --- | --- |
| **Decisions and Comments** | **Queries** |
| The stop here is to prompt students to consider what caves are like inside. | **Query:** "What does the author want us to know about caves?" <br><br> **Follow-up:** "Why does the author want us to think about caves as mysterious?" |

### FIFTH SEGMENT

There are many, many caves of all different types around the world. And because humans are curious, they like to explore caves. There is a special name for that activity—exploring caves is called spelunking. Would you want to be a spelunker?

| **Decisions and Comments** | **Queries** |
| --- | --- |
| We stop here, first, to simply give students an opportunity to enjoy a new word that is fun to say: *spelunking.* <br>     Second we want students to consider curiosity as a motivation to explore, and to connect that to the idea that caves are mysterious and thus invite curiosity. | "The author tells us that the word for exploring caves is *spelunking*! Let's say that word together—spelunking." <br><br> **Query:** "What does the author mean that humans are curious?" <br><br> **Follow-up:** "So how does humans being curious connect to what we learned about caves being mysterious?" |

### SIXTH SEGMENT

We can do some pretend spelunking and find out about interesting caves all over the world!

    The largest cave in the world is five and a half miles long! It would take a normal adult nearly 2 hours to walk that distance. This cave is underneath a forest in the country of Vietnam. The cave is called Son Doong Cave, which means "cave of the mountain river" in the Vietnamese language. It is so big that it has a jungle and a river inside it! It is so big that it could hold a 40-story skyscraper inside it!

| **Decisions and Comments** | **Queries** |
| --- | --- |
| The point here is to have students understand and appreciate the extent of what a cave can be. And it would be our tendency to kick off the Query with an expression of wonder! | **Query:** "Wow! What did we learn about this 'cave of the mountain river'?" <br><br> **Follow-up:** "What helps us understand how huge this cave is?" |

### SEVENTH SEGMENT

But this cave was a secret of Nature until 6 years ago. A man who lives near the cave discovered it. Maybe the most surprising thing about Son Doong Cave is that scientists say that it is still growing!

| SEVENTH SEGMENT (*continued*) | |
|---|---|
| **Decisions and Comments** | **Queries** |
| This segment presents the opportunity to build two concepts. The first is that no one knew of this cave until recently.<br><br>The second, which requires a connection to earlier text, is that caves can grow as water continues to dissolve and further hollow out the rock around a cave. | **Query:** "What does it mean that the cave was a 'secret of Nature'?"<br><br>**Query:** "How could a cave be still growing?"<br><br>**Follow-up:** If needed to understand how caves can grow: "What did the author tell us about how caves are formed? Does that help you figure out why they could still grow?" |

## EIGHTH SEGMENT

Another amazing cave is Waitomo Glowworm Cave in New Zealand. New Zealand is a country all the way on the other side of the world, near Australia. Tiny glowworms, just a quarter-inch long, hang from the cave ceiling. Glowworms are bioluminescent, which means they are a type of living thing that gives off its own light. The glowworms in Waitomo Cave give off a blue light. There are so many of them along the ceiling that the whole cave looks blue!

| **Decisions and Comments** | **Queries** |
|---|---|
| For this section the goal is to have students grasp an image of a blue cave lit by glowworms and enjoy the wonder of it. | **Query:** "What does the author want us to know about the cave in New Zealand?"<br><br>**Follow-up:** "What do you think you would say if you walked inside this cave? What is it about the cave that would make you say that?" |

## NINTH SEGMENT

Let's talk about one more cave. This one is called Spruce Tree House. It is in the state of Colorado in a park called Mesa Verde. What is special about this cave is that there are ruins of a village where ancient people lived, centuries ago. It has 130 rooms that were built into a cliff in the hillside, and the remains of them are still there for everyone to see. Scientists have figured out that groups of 60 to 80 people lived in the cave and farmed corn, beans, and squash. The cave got its name because it was discovered behind a giant spruce tree. Two ranchers discovered the cave when they were looking for stray cattle.

| **Decisions and Comments** | **Queries** |
|---|---|
| The first activity at this stop is to introduce the word *ruins*.<br>    The main goal here is to have | "You might know that if something is ruined, it is so messed up so that it can't be used anymore. Well, ruins of a village |

| NINTH SEGMENT (*continued*) | |
|---|---|
| **Decisions and Comments** | **Queries** |
| students understand that caves served as homes and to consider why caves would be a good place for a home. This latter elicits a connection to earlier text about caves offering protection and shelter. | are what is left over after the buildings of a village have crumbled and the village is gone. That happens after a long, long time if people no longer live there." **Query:** "How is this cave different from the others we've learned about?" **Follow-up:** "Based on what we've learned about caves, why do you think a cave would be a good place to build a place to live?" |

| TENTH SEGMENT | |
|---|---|
| So we have a cave that has a jungle and a river in it, a cave that has glowworms hanging from the ceiling, and a cave that has ruins of long-ago cliff dwellers. Which cave would you want to go spelunking in? | |
| **Decisions and Comments** | **Queries** |
| This segment simply serves to wrap up the text. Also the question at the end serves as a Wrap-Up Query, inviting students to share what they remember and enjoyed about the various caves. | **Query:** "The author asks, 'Which cave would you want to go spelunking in?' Which one would you choose?" **Follow-up:** Encourage students to talk—as a whole class, in small groups, or in pairs—about why they have chosen a particular cave. |

## Some Final Words

Here, as in Chapter 4, we have provided two well-thought-out lesson plans that may lead to highly imperfect lessons! This is true because we assume that you are human and that your classroom is full of small, lively human beings. But if student responses throw you off your game, it is important to remember that this is a learning process—for teacher and students. You may not be able to see exactly what students are taking away from each lesson about reading and about what it means to comprehend text. But those kinds of understandings are the ultimate goal of conducting reading lessons in the QtA way. Progress will grow more and more visible as the process continues.

# ENDING NOTES

- Although QtA was developed for middle elementary students and above, it can also work for very young students.

- We developed an approach, Text Talk, to target young learners' language and comprehension development using stories read aloud.

- Interactive talk around read-alouds gives students experiences responding to ideas communicated through printed language—referred to as "decontextualized language" because it is beyond the here and now of everyday conversational contexts.

- As with QtA lessons for older students, planning includes (1) determining major understandings and identifying potential obstacles, (2) segmenting the text, and (3) developing Initiating and Follow-Up Queries.

- Helping children respond to text language forms the basis of comprehension ability. Developing young learners' comprehension ability means helping them to understand that interacting with text is about building and connecting ideas.

- Interactive talk around read-alouds highlights responding to the *language* of texts, rather than responding based on pictures or on background knowledge alone.

- Read-alouds allow young students opportunities to interact with much more sophisticated material than is possible in texts that they can read on their own.

- In lessons for primary grades students, there may be even greater need to follow up the Initiating Queries with more particular probes, because the notion of dealing with text ideas is still so new.

- Follow-ups can encourage students to talk about what's happening in a text using their own words, rather than retrieving language of the text.

- Lessons with young students often have more stops, some of which are intended to briefly draw attention to features of text content and make sure that students are focusing on important ideas rather than inviting talk.

- Stopping points that are intended to prompt talk often include more rereading of portions of the text, since in read-alouds students do not have the text in front of them.

- It is important to keep in mind that attending to text information and connecting ideas is a learning process that may move gradually, especially for younger learners. But young students can develop the ability to dig into text, which has benefits for their future literacy.

# Special Topics

...................................................................................................................

# CHAPTER 7

# What Comes after Reading
# and Interspersed Discussion?

After a text has been read is typically the time when discussion about it takes place. In QtA there has been much interaction and discussion along the way. But after-text activities provide opportunities to take a step back and consider the text as a whole, to reconsider particularly challenging or important portions of text, and to prompt students to engage in rich analytic and interpretive work. Engaging students in QtA interspersed discussion provides the foundation for students to be successful with such work after reading.

With the current emphasis on preparing students to be college and career ready, there is recognition of the importance of moving students beyond simple comprehension tasks. Today, expectations are much higher than simply understanding a text. However, moving to more cognitively demanding tasks before students have developed an understanding of the text may not elicit the kinds of critical responses that teachers aim for. Students may have limited grist for richer work or their responses may reveal misunderstandings that could not be addressed during reading. For example, a task we see often is to have students analyze the language the author uses and how it gives the reader a better understanding of the characters and events in the text. Although this is a worthy task, if students haven't developed an understanding of the characters and what happens in this story, or have developed misunderstandings along the way, they will have little success engaging with this task.

Engaging students in QtA interspersed reading and discussion on the first read reduces the likelihood of developing misunderstandings and scaffolds students to more challenging tasks such as analyzing, interpreting, synthesizing, and drawing connections across texts. Evidence that QtA prepares students for more challenging work comes from a study that we conducted with middle school students. In the study, we compared students' recalls and responses to analytic and interpretive questions following either a QtA discussion or discussion after a text was read. The QtA students provided longer recalls, which contained a greater number of complex story elements, and higher-rated responses to analytic and interpretive questions (Sandora, Beck, & McKeown, 1999).

The major aim of this chapter is to show how QtA interspersed discussion lays the foundation for more meaningful after-text activities and to offer examples of such activities. After-reading activities can take on greater depth given the discussion that has preceded them. Additionally, the QtA interspersed discussion enables teachers to "see" how students responded to and understood the text. Such insight helps them create a focus for after-text activities that is specifically relevant to students' understandings, misunderstandings, and genuine reactions to the text. For example, in discussions of "Polar Bears, the Giants of the Arctic," students often are upset with what they interpret as cruel treatment of the bears, particularly the segments that talk about tranquilizing the bears and sending them to polar bear jail. An after-reading activity that would allow students to explore their thinking in that space would be to have them look more closely at the actions of the people involved in these instances and respond to the following prompt: "When reading the text, many of you described the treatment of the bears as being cruel. Think about where you stand on this issue. Do you see their actions as being cruel? Support your thinking with specific evidence from the text." The prompt provides students with the opportunity to elaborate on their original thoughts without requiring them to reach consensus.

Similarly, after a text is read can be a time to consider things that did not get done during a QtA text lesson. For example, some nuanced point in the text may have eluded students. Rather than the teacher providing the information for students during reading, or spending excessive time on one text portion trying to elicit the understanding, the teacher might use after-text time to have students revisit the text and reconsider it. For example, in "The Bridge on the River Clarinette," the person who most opposes the stranger's deal is the teacher, but in the Query posed during the discussion ("The last paragraph begins with 'To the astonishment of his audience . . . ' So, based on that description, how are the people reacting to the stranger and his offer?") only addresses the inhabitants' collective reaction to the deal. Considering the role teachers play in our lives, it might be interesting to draw attention to the teacher's reaction by asking students to engage in a quick-write where they respond to the following prompt, "The inhabitants of the town reacted in different ways to the stranger's deal. What can you say about how the teacher reacted? Based on what you know about teachers, why would the teacher have reacted in such a way?" Such a prompt provides students with an opportunity to examine more closely a specific aspect of the text, especially one in which their prior knowledge can support their thinking.

## The Role of After-Reading Activities in QtA

The examples of after-reading activities we present below are not so different from what would occur in a non-QtA class, so they are tasks you may have already used in your classroom. What we offer are ideas for how to use QtA interspersed discussions to lay the foundation for that work, which is more interpretive and analytic than initial comprehension, the primary QtA goal. Comprehension is primary because one needs to comprehend a text before he or she can engage in higher order tasks.

As you plan your Queries for interspersed discussion, think about which Queries will spark student exchanges that might be an entrée to after-text activities. Also, thinking through a lesson this way alleviates the issue of being tempted to stop for extended discussion along the way. Although spontaneous extended stops work at times, too many such stops interrupt the lesson and slow down the discussion. Remember, too, that discussion during the lesson can prompt you to an issue to focus on later.

In the following sections we begin by suggesting activities for the texts for which we presented lessons in Chapters 4 and 6 and tying those to the planned activities during the lessons. We then move to offering after-reading activities for additional texts. In particular we point out how after-reading topics might be seeded within the during-reading interspersed discussion of a QtA lesson.

## Opinion or Argument Writing

One area that receives quite a bit of attention in schools is opinion or argument writing. From primary through secondary grades, students are expected to present their opinion on a subject and provide support for their ideas. One way to develop their ability to be successful with such tasks is to design interpretive prompts that provide students with the opportunity to present their opinions and the evidence to support their ideas. For example, one of the most fascinating characters in "The Bridge on the River Clarinette" is the stranger who makes the deal with the townspeople. Although he is a major character, the author never makes it clear who the stranger is or how he was able to create a bridge. Because of the ambiguity of this character, you may develop a writing prompt that asks students to analyze the character to determine who they think he is and ask for evidence to support their opinions.

Since the question of the stranger's identity is open to multiple interpretations that can be supported by evidence from the text, this task falls nicely into the interpretive category. Note the Queries asked during the QtA lesson that allowed students to talk about this particular character: "What do you think of this new character?"; "So we learn more about the stranger in this section. What's going on?"; "What else did we learn about the stranger?"; "How does this new information add to our understanding of his character?"; and "The author tells us that the stranger concluded the deal with a malicious swiftness. What does that tell us about the stranger?" These Queries allow students to share their ideas about this stranger and provide a scaffold for the independent writing task.

## Genre Study

Another topic we see addressed in classrooms is genre study, and in the early grades fairy tales, tall tales, and folktales receive a lot of attention. Since our story "A Donkey for Fifty Cents" is a Puerto Rican folktale, let's consider the genre study work that can come from the tale.

As mentioned previously, teachers frequently label elements or characteristics for students rather than working with the elements as they are encountered in the text. Often, teachers will introduce a unit on folk or tall tales by telling students the characteristics of a particular genre prior to reading the story. Unfortunately, this may interfere with students' ability to build meaning, as they are now searching for the genre characteristics rather than focusing on the ideas in the story. For example, with folktales, teachers may begin by telling students that a folktale is typically a story that has existed because it is told by word of mouth from one generation to the next, and that other characteristics include having a young main character, and a trickster element.

Rather than *tell* students these genre characteristics, we would rather students discover them during the interspersed discussion. Note that the purpose of our first Query, "What does the author want you to know about this story?," is for students to recognize that it is a "tale told again and again" and to introduce our character, a young boy. Notice, also, that our Queries in the final segments of the story allow students to discuss that Pablo is playing a trick on the townspeople. "What is Pablo up to?"; "What's this about his going behind the statue?"; and "What do you think of what Pablo did?" Providing students the opportunities to work with these ideas through the initial interspersed discussion sets them up to study the characteristics of folktales and revisit the text through this new lens during the after-reading discussion.

For our expository text, "Let's Explore Caves," one of our major understandings is for students to recognize that caves offer a variety of amazing natural wonders and have intrigued people for years. We support students in developing that understanding through Queries such as "Wow, what did we learn about this 'cave of the mountain river'?"; "What does it mean that the cave was a 'secret of Nature'?"; "What does the author want us to know about this cave in New Zealand?"; and "How is this cave different from the others we've learned about?" Because we want students to appreciate the art of spelunking and the interesting features of each of the caves, we included these Queries to specifically target those ideas.

When engaging students in a discussion of the text, it is likely that not all students will agree on which caves are the most interesting. Because of these differences, we designed a follow-up activity that allows students to share their opinions on what they learned about these caves while expressing their creativity. Specifically, the task asks students to choose which cave from the text they think would be the most interesting to explore and then write a letter to the spelunking society convincing them that this is the best choice. They must include in their letter specific evidence from the text to support their thinking.

## Language Analysis

Another area of focus in many classrooms is language analysis and the way in which an author creates a clear picture of what is being discussed in a text. Language analysis works with both literary and informational texts, and is represented in an after-reading activity we suggest for "Polar Bears, the Giants of the Arctic." One of our major understandings for the text was for students to appreciate the power and intimidating size of polar bears. Our Initiating Query, "What have we learned in this first section?," and the follow-up, "What does it mean that polar bears are predators, and prey to no other animal?," target that understanding. Throughout the text, the author uses specific words and phrases to support the idea that polar bears are powerful, magnificent creatures. The title describes them as the giants of the Arctic, the author includes details of their size, shares that they eat furniture, and refers to them as huge bears. An after-reading activity could begin by having students revisit the initial talking point that referenced the size and power of polar bears and then ask them to identify additional words and phrases that the author uses to help the reader see the power and size of the bears. Students can then discuss how these descriptions reflected what the author wanted the reader to "see," especially when sharing the stories of polar bears and the reactions of the people in the towns they visited.

Another area of language analysis we often see teachers focusing on is figurative language and the role it plays in a text. Too often, we see teachers pointing out instances of simile or personification prior to the reading or stopping when reading, pointing out examples, and explaining what they are. We suggest that this kind of structural focus takes away from true conversation around a text and puts the interaction more in the traditional school-task arena.

We suggest embedding discussions of these elements in the context of the story, allowing students to truly understand their purpose and the role they play in the particular story being read. For example, in the children's book *Last Stop on Market Street* by Matt de la Peña (2015), the author provides the following description of a bus: "The bus creaked to a stop in front of them. It sighed and sagged as the doors swung open." A Query such as "So what picture are we getting of this bus?" opens the door for a discussion about how the author is painting a picture of an older and tired bus. Once students have established those ideas, the Follow-up Query "Wait, *sighed* and *sagged*, are they words we use to describe objects? What's the author doing here?" begins the conversation about personification. Notice that the conversation began with an authentic discussion of the ideas in the text and not a definition of personification.

An after-reading activity could have students revisit the text to identify additional examples and discuss how the author used personification to give the reader a better picture of characters or events. Providing students with opportunities to discuss these elements as they are connected to the text, rather than as separate elements, deepens their understanding of how authors use them and increases the likelihood that students will apply them to their own writing.

## Author Study

Engaging students in an author study is work we see in classrooms from PreK to grade 12. Consider a teacher who wants to do an author study on Patricia Polacco, an author popular with many elementary teachers. Her books typically include children who don't always fit in with their peers and who have to overcome challenges.

## Author's Craft

The teacher might begin by planning Queries that set up an analysis of author's craft in terms of style and literary elements as well as content analysis of similar themes or character types. Students can analyze Polacco's books for the great language and dialogue that bring her characters and events to life. For example, in the book *Picnic at Mudsock Meadow* (Polacco, 1992), one of the characters, William, is comparing his costume to a far more impressive one. "And on the end was Hester. Even William had to admit she looked great as a snake charmer. Jewelry rattled on her neck and ankles, and her vacuum-hose snakes shook their tails. William knew his dumb old sheet didn't stand a chance." A simple Query such as "So what picture is the author creating of this scene with Hester and William?" allows students to examine the language the author uses to give the reader a better understanding of both Hester's impressive costume and William's reaction to it.

A Follow-Up Query such as "How does the author let us know that the character William is feeling that way?" again allows them to further examine author's craft. After reading several books by Polacco, an analysis of craft follow-up task could be "Write an essay in which you analyze Polacco's style of writing and the literary elements she uses to bring her characters to life. Cite specific evidence from each text to support your ideas." Because of the teacher's careful planning, students are able to work across texts and engage in the deeper analysis required of this task.

## Themes across Texts

In addition to the analysis of craft work, students can engage in both analysis and interpretive work by examining themes as they look across texts in an author study. While reading each text, Queries such as "So what do you think this story was about?" or "What is the big idea that is important to this story?" support students in responding to a final task that asks them to identify common themes: "We've talked about the various themes that work across all of Polacco's texts. Identify at least two themes evident in the texts we read and then explain which theme you think is most important to the texts. Cite specific evidence from all of the texts to support your ideas." For example, common themes across Polacco's texts are her nod to teachers who are able to reach students who struggle and instill in them the confidence and ability to be successful, and the idea of overcoming challenges. A teacher might begin with *The Junkyard Wonders* (Polacco, 2010) and *Thank You, Mr. Falker* (Polacco, 1998) to allow students to examine these particular themes. Again, the teacher's preplanning for the QtA discussions provides the support for students to be successful in identifying these themes, rather than having the teacher state them.

## Influence of the Author's Life on Writing

Another after-reading activity that works well with an author study is to examine to what extent an author's personal life has influence on his or her writing. Again using the Polacco author study as an example, students could read articles about her life and respond to prompts such as "So what are we learning about Polacco's life?" "How does what happens to Polacco as an adult connect to what we know about her childhood?" They then can apply what they've learned about her life to the texts she's written. For example, as mentioned above, one common theme across Polacco's texts is the idea of overcoming challenges. The challenges often involve students who are bullied at school because they struggle with various issues. After reading about Polacco's personal life, students will learn that Polacco was dyslexic and often dealt with bullying from other students. By responding to a prompt such as "How is what we've learned about Patricia Polacco's life reflected in the books she's written?" students are able to dig deeper into the books she's written and the effect her life had on the characters and events in those books.

# Various Activity Structures

In Chapter 12, we talk about the process of having students transfer what they learned about building meaning when engaging with text during a whole-class Questioning the Author lesson to their independent reading. One of the ways we move students in that direction is through small-group work. Although we acknowledge the important facilitator role the teacher plays in a QtA discussion, we also recognize the importance of students being able to continue the kinds of dialogue demonstrated during a whole-class lesson to partner and small-group work. After-reading questions and activities provide opportunities for students to do just that. For the after-reading activities you design, we suggest that you establish a variety of activity structures, making sure to be consistent with those instructional routines.

In that later chapter we offer some examples of these various structures for the kinds of activities and questions described in this chapter. Keep in mind that some activities may be more suited for small-group work. For example, the activity that has students decide whether they feel that the treatment of the polar bears could be described as cruel and the activity that asks students to take a closer look at the stranger in "The Bridge on the River Clarinette" both lend themselves to a small-group debate setting. Students have to take a stance on an issue and then provide specific evidence to support their ideas. Because these questions are open to more than one perspective or interpretation, students can engage in a debate where they must convince the other group that their interpretation is more logical based on the evidence in the text.

The task that asks students to write a letter to a spelunking society would work well in a partner setting, as each partner would have to make a convincing argument for why his or her chosen cave is the best. When thinking about which format to use, the point is to think about which setting would be most useful in supporting all students to be successful on these after-reading activities.

## ENDING NOTES

- In order for students to engage in analytical and interpretive work, they must have developed a solid understanding of the text.

- QtA discussions lay the foundation for students to engage in cognitively demanding activities that follow the initial reading and discussion of the text.

- After-reading activities can be preplanned, or come from students' genuine interactions with and reactions to the text.

- After-reading activities can include a closer look at authors' craft, including the language used and an author's particular style.

- Interpretive and opinion writing activities provide students with opportunities to dig into a text by expressing an opinion or interpretation, and providing text-based evidence and an explanation to support their ideas.

- When engaging students in after-reading activities, provide them with various activity structures, such as working in small groups or pairs.

- Keep in mind, some structures are better suited for certain activities, so when planning after-reading work, think about which structures would best support a particular activity.

# CHAPTER 8

# Vocabulary in the Context
## of Comprehension

We start this chapter by explaining why a book whose title clearly states that it is about comprehension includes a chapter on vocabulary. There are two reasons. One is that vocabulary knowledge and comprehension are symbiotic. Those who know a lot of words usually comprehend what they read well, and those who comprehend well know a lot of words. Moreover, those who comprehend well learn new words in the course of reading. Unfortunately, those descriptions are far from accurate for the many students who do not know a lot of words. The second reason is that attending to vocabulary around texts read in the classroom is an effective and efficient way to address vocabulary learning because there may be many words in texts that students do not know, and the context of text in which words occur offers a great start for word learning.

Just as we told you a bit of what we did in our research that led to our development of QtA, we will do the same for our vocabulary work by briefly mentioning some of the topics we studied and the resulting instructional development work on vocabulary, in which we were involved for more than three decades. We started our vocabulary work, as we did with our comprehension work, by reviewing the status of vocabulary instruction in the basal readers (Beck et al., 1979) and textbooks used in preservice education courses. What we found was unsatisfactory in terms of which words were called out for instruction, when they were taught, how they were taught, the extent to which there was maintenance of words, and the inadequacy of the dictionary definitions, as well as the quality of the instruction in terms of liveliness and potential student interest.[1] These issues motivated us to investigate how useful those kinds of

---

[1]After our original analyses of 1979 basals, we reviewed the vocabulary instructional materials in 1990 basals and found that the issues we had raised about the previous decade of basals were still present. We can report that there is improvement in the basals in the second decade of the 2000s, though not everything shown to be important has been incorporated.

choices and activities were and to develop and study the kind of vocabulary instruction that might be more effective.

Over the years, we have discussed the features of vocabulary instruction that are effective in various articles and other books. And we will talk about them here, too. What is different here is that all those issues will be discussed in the context of text lessons presented in detail in earlier chapters of this book whose primary goal was comprehension. In this chapter we will go back to those text lessons, identify words that we would target for attention for those texts, and develop lesson plans that provide examples of the features of vocabulary instruction that we discuss in this chapter.

## Which Words to Teach

As we began our work with teachers, we found that they had difficulty selecting words in a text that were beneficial to call out for attention. So we will begin by addressing that issue. In Chapter 3 we discussed briefly our three-tier framework (McKeown & Beck, 1988) of words in our language, which was developed as a way to narrow the choice of which words to teach in reading and language arts. Tier One words are those that are found with high frequency in everyday speech and as such do not need instruction in meaning. We also eliminated Tier Three words by noting that they were the words of content area classes and should be taught in connection to topics in history, biology, civics, and the like. That leaves Tier Two words, the words that characterize written materials. And the sources for those words are the materials students read. Our preference for written materials is that the words are in context, as we are not fans of word lists.

## When to Teach

Since our main source for words to teach is the materials that students read, there are three places words might be called out for some kind of attention: before, during, or after the text is read. In the older basal programs and textbooks used in preservice reading education classes, preteaching words was the norm. In the basals the words that were considered unfamiliar and potentially important to an upcoming text were listed with ways to present their meanings before a text was read. From both our teaching experiences and observations of reading classes we found fault with preteaching. We especially noticed that when some pretaught words were encountered during reading it appeared that several students we followed closely did not recall their meanings. In the instruction we are describing, there were about five to 10 words for each text designated to be pretaught. The instruction provided was typically a brief definition and an example sentence, with no opportunities for students to interact with the words in meaningful ways. Thus it was not surprising that some words were not recalled when needed.

Then there came a time when providing too much information became the norm for preteaching words. Perhaps this was because of the inadequacies of too little attention to words likely to be unfamiliar, so there was a change to providing too much information, which absorbed too much instructional time—time that was taken away from reading and comprehending.

As to when to teach, with a few exceptions, we find it appropriate to clarify words during reading and engage in robust instruction after the text has been read. We will bring back the question of when to teach later.

# What's Better Instruction?

The goal for "better" instruction is that students develop flexible and multifaceted representations of target words. Over the years we have come to call this kind of instruction robust instruction because it is strong and energetic. Below we present a shortened version of the range of components of robust instruction.

## Introduce Words through Explanations in Everyday Language

Our dissatisfaction with dictionary definitions for introducing word meanings resulted in developing our own ways to explain word meanings that we thought would be clearer and more helpful to students. This was the seed of our notion of student-friendly explanations. Since then, we have done research developing our notions of explanatory definitions more systematically, which showed that student-friendly definitions more effectively communicated word meanings to students (McKeown, 1993). As a quick example, consider that a dictionary defined *transitory* as "passing soon or quickly," which made some students think of a passing train, in contrast to our friendly definition, "describes a mood or feeling that only lasts a short time," which helped students understand the sense in which *transitory* is most often used.

## Provide Several Contexts in Which the Word Can Be Used

Several sources of evidence demonstrated to us the need to build into the instruction multiple and varied contexts for each word. An important source was Werner and Kaplan's (1950) classic study showing that learners often imported features of the context into their developing understanding of an unfamiliar word. As former teachers, such findings struck a chord with us, as we could remember students tending to stick to the context in which a word had been initially introduced. For example, when learning the word *implored* from a scene in a story in which one character implored another not to tell a secret, a student might incorporate the notion that a secret was part of the meaning of *implored*. Thus, in the instruction we developed, multiple contexts were an important feature.

## Get Students to Interact with Word Meanings Right Away and Design Activities That Require Students to Process the Meanings of Words

A good explanation of word meaning and several example contexts can provide a strong idea of a word's meaning, but it is still static information. Students need to interact with word information in some way. So we developed quick activities with the words after their meanings were introduced. For example, after being introduced to *nuisance,* kindergarten children were asked, "Where would loud talking be more of a nuisance: on a playground or in the library?" That task requires only lower levels of mental effort and as such may only bring about minimal learning results. But since our goal was that words be known deeply and flexibly enough to enhance higher level verbal tasks, we needed to develop instruction that required deep processing. All this led us to arrange instruction that required students to think about words and their meanings, identify and explain appropriate uses, create appropriate contexts, and engage in various other reflective and analytical activities.

### Provide Examples, Situations, and Questions That Are Interesting

In the course of looking at commercial vocabulary instructional materials, we noted that most examples were obvious and ordinary. It is of some irony that in trying to provide students with the building blocks of language, there wasn't much of an attempt to use engaging examples or to present novel contexts. Doing so was a prime goal for us.

### Gimmicks to Encounter Words

We considered that if students' learning of their new vocabulary was simply a classroom activity, their understanding and use of the words could be limited, and the words would be less likely to become a permanent part of their vocabulary repertoires. So another goal of instruction was to move students' learning beyond the classroom to increase their encounters with words and to enhance the contextualization of the words. To encourage outside learning, we developed gimmicks called *Word Wizard* (Beck & McKeown, 2004b) and *In the Media* (McKeown, Crosson, Artz, Sandora, & Beck, 2013) in which students could earn points by reporting having seen, heard, or used target words outside of class.

## What Evidence Is There That Robust Vocabulary Instruction Works?

On the basis of the issues we raised about vocabulary instruction, we undertook a series of classroom studies in which we attempted to provide better instruction toward improving comprehension and evaluated the instruction by comparing experimental and control students as well as experimental and control words (Apthorp et al., 2012; Beck & McKeown, 2007b; Beck et al., 1982; McKeown, Beck, Omanson, & Pople, 1985). The general outcome of these studies showed that robust instruction improved students' understanding of word meanings and their ability to access the words quickly and flexibly, and to comprehend text that included the taught words. These results were in comparison to students who had not gotten the instruction and to words not taught. Since those studies, there has been an abundance of research by other researchers as well as our team to show the effectiveness of robust instruction for students at all levels. (See, e.g., Carlo et al., 2004; Coyne, Capozzoli, Ware, & Loftus, 2010; Kieffer & Lesaux, 2012; McKeown & Beck, 2014.)

## Words Targeted for Attention from "The Bridge on the River Clarinette"

As discussed in Chapter 3, the teacher identifies words he or she thinks need to be called out for attention while reading the text. The obvious time is during the second read, when the purpose is to identify potential obstacles to comprehension. But sometimes during a first read a word pops out as likely being unknown to your students. Moreover, in the course of segmenting and developing Queries one may notice an additional word, or take a word out. Words tend to be removed because they are not as necessary as initially thought. But it is also the case that all words you identify as likely unfamiliar do not need to be called out. In the course of reading, most of us have come to an unfamiliar word and just ignored it.

With an initial list that you think will likely be unfamiliar to students, ask yourself:

- Is the word important or useful to comprehension of the upcoming text?
- If the word is not necessarily important to comprehension, is it a quality Tier Two word?

The first column in Table 8.1 shows the words from "The Bridge on the River Clarinette" targeted for attention. In Chapter 4, the Discussion and Comments columns in the lesson plan for the story provided the reasons each word was called out for attention, which was either for comprehension purposes and/or as a quality Tier Two word. In the table, every word has been placed under one or both reasons; the second column indicates that a word was targeted for comprehension purposes. The third column lists quality Tier Two words from the story.

Of the six words selected, five were judged to have some effect on comprehension. But keep in mind that comprehension as a concept or as a goal is not an all-or-nothing proposition; a specific reader may comprehend a specific text well, but not really understand a protagonist's goal in another text. Similarly, often a given word has variable influence on comprehension. We tried to indicate the less than singular

**TABLE 8.1.** Words Selected for Attention in a Narrative Text: Why Selected and When Instruction Is Provided

| Words selected | Needed/ helpful for comprehension | Quality Tier Two word | Before reading | During reading | After reading |
|---|---|---|---|---|---|
| *inhabitants* | × | × | × | | × |
| *lose touch* | × | | | × | |
| *dilapidated* | × | × | | × | × |
| *uncanny* | × | × | | × | × |
| *malicious* | × | × | | × | × |
| *infinite* | | × | | | × |

*Note.* × = yes.

effect a given word may have on comprehension by labeling the second column as "Needed/helpful for comprehension," rather than just "Needed." We placed all the Tier Two words from the text that were likely not known in the third column. All Tier Two words are not created equal—some are more potentially useful across a number of topics. We consider some of our decisions below.

## Considerations for Which Words to Teach

The reasons for our choices to place words in either column are not always the same for the words down each column. To explain, we will compare the differences between our reasons for including the phrase *lose touch* and the word *uncanny* as useful for comprehension. In the case of *lose touch,* one concern was that students' experiences with the phrase are likely associated with not losing touch with someone, such as a friend who is moving away. But here the use of *lose touch* indicates a graver consequence for the town. A second concern is that phrases can be notoriously difficult for English learners and students with less vocabulary competence.

In comparing *lose touch* with *uncanny,* we consider the usefulness of knowing the meaning of *uncanny* to comprehension. In the text the stranger is said to have an uncanny smile, which might be another clue to understanding him. The explanation that we provided for uncanny, "something uncanny is so strange and unfamiliar that it seems unnatural," might increase students' appreciation of the stranger's weirdness. One could well think that uncanny is, perhaps, of limited importance to comprehension of the story. Beyond the role of *uncanny* in the story, the word is a useful addition to the repertoire of a mature language user.

One reason for the comparison is to make the point that there are not rigid rules for determining which words to give attention to. Personal judgments may not be perfect, but neither is reliance on word lists, which are disconnected from classroom lessons and students. Our bias is that teacher judgments of words to be taught, made in consideration of lesson goal, the word-learning goal, and the characteristics of the students, lead to the best results. Even if in hindsight a word selection seems less than ideal, understanding that conclusion and the reason behind it is valuable to a teacher.

Before we leave our discussion of selecting words for attention, let us explain why *infinite,* the last entry in the first column, was not selected as important to comprehension. The word appeared in the sentence "The mayor shook his head with infinite sadness." For comprehension purposes it is not essential that a reader know the intensity of the sadness, so we didn't need to bring it up during reading. But we choose to bring it up during after-reading instruction because it is a quality word. Thus the general point is that Tier Two words other than those thought important to comprehension are fair candidates for later instruction.

## When and How Should Words be Taught?

- *When*: before, during, and after reading
- *How*: meaning provided, elicit meaning from students, elicit meaning through use of context clues

Let us state at the outset that our approach generally includes some instruction during and more instruction after reading, mostly providing meaning by eliciting use of context, and rarely asking for meaning. We explain and demonstrate these choices in this section.

The last three columns in Table 8.1 indicate where in the lesson attention will be given to the word in relation to reading and discussing the text. We targeted *inhabitants* as potentially unfamiliar to readers at the lower ages of this story's range. And despite our negative opinion of preteaching, we designated *inhabitants* for before-reading attention.

Our reasoning that we should clarify *inhabitants* before reading went something like the following: We noted that *inhabitants* was the second word in the first sentence of the story. Then we noted that in the third sentence the people referred to as inhabitants were now called citizens. Hmm . . . the subject of these sentences might be questionable. Perhaps that was overthinking *inhabitants*. Nevertheless, we included it because why not? As indicated in the lesson plan, the expenditure of instructional time is minimal. During reading, when a word needs to be clarified we use a short routine.

- The text context for the word is read: "The inhabitants of the little town of Framboisy-sur-Clarinette were worried."
- If the context seems likely strong enough for students to understand the word

meaning, the meaning of the word is solicited from a student: "What are inhabitants?"

- If there is no response or inadequate response, the meaning is provided: "Inhabitants are people or animals that live in a particular place."

Three points about our routine: The first is that we only sparingly ask students for the meaning. This is because that practice so often results in guessing, and then some students have a hard time separating incorrect guesses from accurate word meaning information the next time the word is met. Second, notice how direct the question under the second bullet is. The directness replaces the common "Who knows what *inhabitants* means?" because that encourages students to want to reply, resulting in some students offering left-field guesses.

A related but slightly different point is that the question "Who knows?" seems to indicate that some student needs to know. We have long been amused when a conscientious friend told us that as a young student, when she heard "Who knows . . . " her inference was that the teacher thought she should know, and when she didn't know, she held her breath until someone who knew responded. The bottom line is that when an unknown word that is of value to comprehension comes up during reading interactions, we immediately provide its meaning, because such clarification is usually useful to the primary goal during reading—comprehension.

And the third point has to do with context clues. For decades and continuing recently (e.g., the Common Core State Standards: National Governors Association Center for Best Practices and Council of Chief State School Officers, 2010) the mantra for what to do when one doesn't know the meaning of a word encountered in text is to use context clues. One might think that that pronouncement needs to be followed by helping students learn how to do that. To the best of our knowledge, we know of only one kind of instruction that is supposed to do this—being taught classifications of types of context clues and practice labeling example sentences with the specific context clue. For example, one clue, labeled definition/example clue, explains that sometimes what a word means is provided in the sentence, such as: "The sales associate, the person who showed us several types of popular boots. . . . " Another clue, called contrast/antonym, points out that sometimes a word's meaning can be figured out by contrasting it with a known word, for example, "Harry wanted to go to a fancy restaurant, but George wanted to go to an unpretentious place." Current classification systems seem to include five to seven types of clues.

The problem with these examples is that they are instructional contexts. That is, they were intentionally developed to provide specific context clues. The little evidence that we have ever found about the value to students of learning to identify various types of contexts clues is that students do indeed learn to identify which context clue is represented in instructional contexts. But to the best of our knowledge there has never been a hint of evidence that classifying and identifying word meanings from instructional contexts transfers to identifying word meanings in naturally occurring text. And the reason, of course, is that professional authors do not intentionally provide readers information about the meaning of the words they use because their purpose is to tell a story or explain a phenomenon, not to convey the meaning of some words. Very recently, however, researchers have been working with naturally occurring contexts in children's texts using a 15-type context clue classification system to identify context clues (Dowds, Haverback, & Parkinson, 2016). This new work may eventually lead to work that is useful for education purposes.

Our position on context clues is that if context is present, we can think of little better than in the course of reading for a teacher to help students notice that something in the text's context is a clue to the meaning of an unfamiliar word. So that's where we go now.

*Inhabitants* is the one word of the set we identified for attention that could have been supported by the teacher pointing to a within-sentence clue. We didn't do that because as mentioned above, it was in the first sentence and we thought it a better start to move on to the story. But had the sentence "The inhabitants of the little town of Framboisy-sur-Clarinette were worried" appeared later in the text and had students not been able to indicate what *inhabitants* meant, we could have told them that there was a clue in the sentence, the word *worried,* and ask who was worried.

The availability of context that provides some information on word meaning often doesn't come from within-sentence information. The word *dilapidated* in the story is a good example of sufficient clues to the word's meaning, but those clues are not from within the sentence in which *dilapidated* appears. Rather, before *dilapidated* is encountered in the text, the following information has appeared: "The bridge was about to collapse, tourists don't dare cross the bridge, it could cave in at any moment." Then later the word *dilapidated* is used in a new description of the bridge. At that time, our lesson plan asks, "Given what you know about the condition of the bridge, what does *dilapidated* mean?"

Although we don't know, it is likely that naturally occurring text includes more context clues to a target word that are distant from the target word than we might have thought. But to the best of our knowledge, we know of no instruction that has brought distant context clues into learning word meanings from context. When a distant informative word meaning context is present, students should be asked to use it, as is shown in the lesson plan for *dilapidated*. In that case, students had to bring previous information forward, but it also happens that context clues may need to be brought backward. In any case, identifying and using distant information that enables word meaning is an exemplary activity. Students need to learn that context clues may not appear in the sentence in which a target word appeared, nor will useful context necessarily be found in text adjacent to a word. They also need to be aware that in many cases there are no context clues to a word's meaning. But when they are present, they are gems to which the teacher needs to bring attention.

Another vocabulary instructional question is "What does it take for students to really own a word?" That is, being able to use a word flexibly in reading, speaking, and writing. And the evidence is clear that many repetitions in various contexts are needed (Beck & McKeown, 2007b). When that is the goal, we address it after the text has been read and discussed. We take up after reading next.

# After Reading

There is both theoretical and empirical evidence that learning the meanings of words is incremental. This is not a problem for words that are common to everyday speech. It is because they are found in everyday speech and thus repeated often that they don't usually need to be taught. But words that are common to written language are not common in speech. As such, there is a need to provide opportunities for students to engage with Tier Two words—which by definition are words that are useful beyond the current context—often and over time. Thus we designated After Reading for working with new words as a permanent section of a text-based lesson.

The reason we want the work to occur after the text has been read and discussed is because there are different goals involved. The initial goal is to encourage and support comprehension of a text. The second is to help students learn new vocabulary well. Especially since part of that learning is to understand a word's uses beyond a single context, such instruction needs to come after a text has been completed.

There are two components of robust vocabulary instruction that take place after the text has been read and discussed: reintroduction of the set of words that will receive attention over subsequent days, and engaging with those words on several subsequent days. Of the five Tier Two words identified from "The Bridge on the River Clarinette" we will use *dilapidated, inhabitants,* and *uncanny* to discuss and provide activities for after reading. Were this a lesson to be carried out with students, we would provide after-reading instruction for all five Tier Two words identified.

## Reintroducing Words

Given that there is some delay from completing the reading and discussing a text to initial after-reading word activity, we begin after-reading work by reintroducing the set of Tier Two words for the lesson at hand:

- Provide the text context in which the word appeared.
- Provide a student-friendly explanation.
- Present an example of context other than text context.
- Ask students to explain why the example is an appropriate use of the word.
- Ask students to provide an example of something that is uncanny. (Depending on the students' ages, this is a good place to turn and talk with a partner.)

In relation to text reading and discussion, after-reading activities can occur the next day or several days later. The words should be the focus of activities after reading and discussion at least two different times and preferably three (depending on how many words in a set). It is best that the after-reading activities occur over several days with a day, or some time, between the activities for one set of words in keeping with the usefulness of distributed practice. For the most part, after-reading activities should take about 10 minutes and no more than 15 minutes.

## Activities that Require Students to Engage with the Words

Over the years we have developed a number of formats that require students to engage with the meanings of target words. Eventually, we developed a *Menu of Instructional Activities* that teachers can use to engage students in interacting with the words they are learning. Our use of *engage* implies attention, or directing one's mind to something. The *Menu* is extensive and includes seven categories of activities, with two to five variations within some categories, and can be found in the second edition of *Bringing Words to Life* (Beck et al., 2013). We draw on some of those formats in the activities below for each of the three words that were targeted. We present one activity for each word, but it is essential to be aware that one example of an activity for a word is very far from enough.

In virtually all the activities that follow, each item (question or statement) is really "bait" for students to use language to explain their responses. Most students can answer questions like "Which would you rather inhabit, a palace or a cabin?" It's what needs to come after—an explanation for their choices—that is the most useful for vocabulary, and indeed, language development. If a student chooses the less likely response and can justify it—such as choosing a cabin, "Because cabins are usually in the woods, and I love to be there." Then, by all means, accept that response. The important caveat here is *if they can justify it.*

We intend that the activities be teacher led. Also, sometimes activities can be used by assigning students to groups—the students in each group can do the same thing and then come together as a class and discuss the similarities and differences between different groups' responses. Or, different activities can be assigned to groups and then shared with the whole class. Although some activities may be somewhat beyond the youngest students, most activities are appropriate for all levels, with the difference being in the words and contexts that are used.

### Example/Non-Example Using *Dilapidated*

"If what I describe sounds dilapidated, say 'dilapidated.' If not, shake your head back and forth indicating no." Students should be asked why they responded as they did.

- "A car with two broken windows and two flat tires."
- "A post office building that had to be torn down."
- "A red car with a couple of light scratches."

- "A tall new school building."
- "A tall ladder with several missing rungs and broken hinges."
- "Your backpack."
- "A new sweater with holes and a rip."

Notice that the last item above starts as though it is not going to be a description of something dilapidated. These kinds of change-ups are useful and students seem to enjoy them. Relatedly, we learned early in our implementations of robust vocabulary that students, well into the middle grades, enjoy silly examples. And teachers working with robust vocabulary continue to reinforce that fact. Our advice is to try to include silly examples often enough that students look for them but not so often that they lose their value.

Also notice that in the format above students are asked to say the target word, which supports building a strong phonological representation of the words they are learning. That's important for helping to plant the words in students' memories.

## Questions/Statements Using *Inhabitant* or *Inhabit*

"If the answer to a question I ask is 'yes,' say 'yes.' If it is not an example, put a frown on your face. Also, when I tell you to do something, please do it." When appropriate for an item ask students why they responded as they did.

- "Are horses usually inhabitants of a barn?"
- "Do wasps inhabit a beehive?"
- "Name an inhabitant of the ocean."
- "Why could you not inhabit the ocean?"

Questions that extend the parameters of *inhabitants*:

- "Are you an inhabitant of a movie theater when you go to see a movie?"
- "Are you an inhabitant of the earth?"
- "Are you an inhabitant of your school?"
- "What would you have to do to inhabit your school?"

## Generating Contexts, Situations, and Examples Using *Uncanny*

Formats within this category are good for small-group collaborative work. For example, you might divide the class into four groups and have each group respond with several examples to the different portions of the following: "What might you see or hear that would make you say 'This is uncanny . . . '?"

- When you walk into your classroom

- When you walk into your house

- When you get out of bed in the morning

- When you turn on your TV

(Note: Students have a tendency to describe things that are just weird as *uncanny,* so they should be reminded that when something is uncanny, it can't be explained.)

## What about Vocabulary for Primary Grades Students?

Young children love "big words" and when taught them, they use them. We have been kept amused and delighted with teachers' reports of incidents of young students spontaneously using taught words in speech. A favorite example occurred in a kindergarten when students were working independently at their seats. A student signaled for the teacher and said, "I can't concentrate because Noah is being a nuisance. *Concentrate* and *nuisance* had been taught some weeks earlier."

An issue with young students' ability to learn vocabulary is where big words will be available to them. The problem is that because they are learning to read, the words they read in text are and should be words whose meanings they know. But we cannot, indeed we dare not, hold up children's oral/aural growth by not feeding their speaking and listening capabilities, which are ahead of their reading competence. So, at school and at home, adults are encouraged to read aloud. Thus we turn to trade books that we read aloud to primary grades students. There is a plethora of narrative books available to be read aloud to kindergarten, first-, and second-grade children, many of which include rich vocabulary.

In Chapter 6, we provided lesson plans for two texts for primary grades students, a narrative story and an expository article. In the lessons for both texts, we use Text Talk (Beck & McKeown, 2001, 2004a), our primary grades version of QtA, and we bring attention to useful Tier Two words.

For the narrative "A Donkey for Fifty Cents," which is a fairly simple story, we identified two Tier Two words in the text—*impressed* and *creature*—that would be useful entries in young students' vocabulary repertoires. We would bring those words to students' attention during after-reading instruction in the same ways we discussed for older students. For starters:

- "In the story it said that the man who was leading three donkeys was impressed that Pablo wanted a donkey to help his parents. If you are *impressed* by someone you are kind of amazed and think that something they are doing is pretty special."

- "The man liked the idea that a young boy wanted to take care of another creature. *Creature* is another word for any living thing—humans are creatures, and so are animals."

If a teacher would like to have more than two words to engage with during after-reading instruction, which makes for more interesting activities, or for any other reason, there are ways to bring additional Tier Two words onto the scene. Identify something in the story and use a word that describes or fits the text, even though the word does not appear in the story. For instance:

- "Pablo was really bothered by people asking him about the price of the donkey. Another way to say that is that Pablo was *annoyed*. If you are *annoyed*, you are bothered and upset by something."

The above example offered a simple synonym. But there are additional ways to link text material to good Tier Two words. For the story at hand, we saw opportunity to introduce words that describe Pablo's personality. For example:

- "I think we could describe Pablo as *feisty*. Someone who is feisty gets bothered easily and needs to do things his or her own way. How does this apply to Pablo?"
- "Another way I would describe Pablo is that he was *brazen*. If someone acts brazen, what they do is a little bit brave and a little bit rude. What did Pablo do that could be called brazen?"

The same formats for after-reading activities mentioned for "The Bridge on the River Clarinette" are appropriate for young students. What changes is the content of the example in terms of descriptions that would be within young students' experiences. Additionally, some of the ways in which students are asked to respond would include thumbs up/down, yays/boos, and the like.

## Vocabulary in Expository Text

Tier Three words are mostly found in expository text, often called informational text, and we will use the terms interchangeably. In contrast to narrative texts, which tell a story, often using new and different versions of well-known themes such as friendship, courage, good versus evil, and the like, the purpose of expository text is to inform and explain. "Polar Bears, the Giants of the Arctic" is an informational text, the kind of text that you might find in good magazines for school-age students. We intend it to serve as a microcosm of a chapter in a content area textbook, in which there will be Tier Three words as well as Tier Two words, as it would be impossible to explain a phenomenon without them.

In the first column of Table 8.2, there are 11 words designated for attention. But there is a difference between the first seven words and the remaining four words. That difference, which is quite important, is that the first seven words are Tier Three words and the remaining four words are Tier Two words. Additionally, no after reading is suggested for the seven Tier Three words. Given that we are strong proponents for after-reading attention, why?

To explain, we first comment on the last four words, the Tier Two words: *congregate, stealth, scavenge,* and *sauntering.* Those words are sophisticated labels for concepts with which students who would read the polar bears text are familiar. Such students would be of an age to understand *come together* and *join,* so *congregate* is not a new concept. But it is a more sophisticated way of expressing the concept. We make the same claim for *stealth.* Given that students understand "sneak up, don't let anyone see you," stealth is a new label for concepts already known. Similarly, *scavenge* is associated with looking for and collecting stuff that others have discarded for the scavenger's use. Finally, *sauntering* means walking in an unhurried way. Again, our claim is that the students who will read "Polar Bears" have enough control of different ways of walking, the concept underlying sauntering, to learn an additional kind of walking.

Now let's consider the Tier Three words. As we go through these words we will discuss a position we have held for some time that Tier Three words belong in content

**TABLE 8.2.** Words Identified for Attention in an Informational Text: Why Selected and When Instruction Is Provided

| Words selected | Important to comprehension in content areas | Quality Tier Two word | During reading | After reading |
|---|---|---|---|---|
| *predator* | × | | × | |
| *prey* | × | | × | |
| *ice floes* | × | | × | |
| *Alcatraz* | × | | × | |
| *indigenous* | × | | × | |
| *subsistence* | × | | × | |
| *global warming* | × | | × | |
| *congregate* | | × | × | × |
| *stealth* | | × | × | × |
| *scavenge* | | × | × | × |
| *sauntering* | | × | × | × |

*Note.* × = yes.

area classrooms as they are not sophisticated labels for known concepts, but rather concepts often not known to students.

There are seven Tier Three words, so we will think about four of them, just as we discussed four Tier Two words. The most important words for the text content are *ice floes, indigenous, subsistence,* and *global warming.* Ice floes are huge masses of floating ice sometimes miles long, but they are not attached to the shore. Ice floes are important to the polar bear article because polar bears spend much of their time on ice floes hunting for seals, their favorite food. There is not another way to say ice floes, and there is not another context beyond places where sea water forms ice floes. Thus anything more that can be provided to students about ice floes would come from additional content materials. Ice floes, then, is a new concept.

*Indigenous* people are the first people to ever live on a land. *Subsistence* level means having only enough food and necessities to live. There is an enormous amount of content material about indigenous people, as there is about living at a subsistence level, but there is no more to learn about the label for the first people to live on a land. The same is the case for subsistence level. But there is much to learn about those topics.

*Global warming* is a huge concept—most students will know or at least have heard that our planet is warming. It is to some extent the setting or the background for the article. The four Tier Three words were used because the concepts are relevant to the topic of the article, polar bears. There is much to learn about these potentially new concepts, but nothing more to learn about the labels for the concepts. Had the article been part of a content area unit, there likely would be additional content material available. Let us also make explicit that the kinds of after-reading activities that we have discussed for Tier Two words are not appropriate for Tier Three words. Finally, when complaints arise that students have difficulty with content area vocabulary, it is important to consider that the difficulty may be with understanding the new concepts in content areas.

Now let's briefly consider the vocabulary in the read-aloud expository text "Let's Explore Caves." There are two Tier Three words, *spelunking* and *bioluminescent,* and four Tier Two words. The lesson was designed so that all six of those words are briefly explained at the point of use in the lesson plan. For example, "The author tells us that the word for exploring caves is spelunking."

The other four words, *hollow, dissolve, ceremonies,* and *ruins,* are also explained at the point of use in the lesson. The four words are classified as Tier Two because they occur across domains and do not describe new concepts. However, they are rather limited in application, with only a few prototypical uses coming to mind for each. A key to the value of Tier Two words is that they have what we think of as "mileage." Students encounter them in a wide variety of contexts, which allows them to be a useful part of their vocabulary repertoires. Since the four words are not in that Tier Two sweet spot, we would choose not to provide further instruction for them beyond the story context.

Thus the intention was that both types of words be attended to during reading so that they did not inhibit comprehension. And we leave it at that—a brief appetizer for young students of an amazing geological phenomenon.

## One Final Way to Extend Vocabulary

Finally, we mention one more way to extend the attention to vocabulary, which can occur as texts are read and discussed. Words that have already been introduced can be brought forth as part of the present discussion. For example, a teacher might offer the following questions to prompt students to use new words:

- "Did anything in the story annoy you?"
- "What just happened seemed uncanny to me! Why might I think that?"
- "What creatures did the author introduce us to?"

We acknowledge that we got this idea from a first-grade class that we worked with in implementing Text Talk. We noticed that students started to spontaneously bring along words they had learned into the next story to describe new characters and events!

### ENDING NOTES

- The relationship between vocabulary knowledge and comprehension is called symbiotic because each enhances the other.

- Attending to vocabulary around texts read in the classroom is an effective and efficient way to address vocabulary learning because there may be words in texts that students do not know, and the context of text in which words occur offers a great start for word learning.

- The three-tiers framework narrows the choice of which words to teach by making the point that the meanings of words common to everyday speech, in Tier One, do not need to be taught. And the words associated with subjects that are common to content areas, Tier Three, should be taught in subject matter instruction when those topics are the focus of instruction. Tier Two words should be the words upon which instruction should focus. This is because Tier Two words are the words found in literate written language.

- Keep in mind that the Tier Two words selected for instruction should be those that can range across various topics. Additionally, it is important to recognize that Tier Two words are usually new labels for concepts that are under control by most young students—for example, students know the concepts of "being in favor of some-thing," so *endorse* is not a new concept, rather it is another label for a concept most students are aware of.

- Our suggestions for when to teach is two-fold. The teacher should clarify words, in a brief way, that are necessary for comprehension during reading and engage in robust instruction for Tier Two words after reading.

- Instructional steps for dealing with words after reading:
    - Provide the context in which the word appeared in the text.
    - Explain the word's meaning through a student-friendly explanation rather than dictionary definitions.
    - Provide another context in which the word is used.
    - Ask students to provide a context in which the word can be used. (This is a good place for students to turn and talk with a partner.)
    - The nature of word learning is that words are learned incrementally. Thus it is essential that after words have been introduced as noted above, practice and reinforcement be provided over several days in ways that engage students in thinking about and using the words in interesting and active ways.

# CHAPTER 9

## Approaching Writing with a Questioning the Author Perspective

We admit to a bias toward reading ability as the key ingredient for academic success, but we also acknowledge that writing is an important part of literacy. Seriously, the ability to write has a tremendous impact on students' future success and is an essential part of the school curriculum. However, writing ability seems to be lagging, with nearly 75% of U.S. students unable to reach grade-level expectations in writing (National Center for Education Statistics, 2012).

One likely root of lack of success in writing may be the lack of sufficient time devoted to instruction in and practice of writing in classrooms. Troia et al. (2015) present discouraging evidence gathered from studies in classrooms and surveys of teachers. For example, they report teachers' infrequent focus on writing activities such as instruction in planning, revising, and editing, and few assignments that require analysis or actual composing. Often student writing is limited to abbreviated responses or worksheets.

Of course this infrequency for writing can be viewed against a backdrop of limited classroom time in general and specifically the fact that writing is a time-consuming process, and improvement in writing requires practice and diligence. We can't offer a solution to all of that here. But we can demonstrate how QtA is aligned with the process of writing and how writing can be rather seamlessly integrated into QtA-directed reading and thinking.

As with many aspects of our becoming "smarter" over the years of working with QtA, our appreciation for the QtA/writing connection grew out of our interactions with teachers. In our work implementing QtA with local teachers, we met often with teachers and had wide-ranging conversations about what they saw in the interactions that took place during reading. During these conversations, teachers at several schools began to draw connections to writing. Some teachers saw similarities between QtA interactions and prompting students to think about writing. Other teachers who had noticed how QtA Queries helped students respond effectively in their reading asked us if there was a way to adapt QtA interactions for writing. Teachers' observations and questions helped us to formulate our thoughts about writing.

## QtA and Writing: Similarities of Process

The starting point is that writing, like reading, is a process of sense-making using language. Both processes include gathering information, culling it for importance, and establishing connections among ideas to build a coherent whole. In reading, we access printed language to form a meaningful representation of what an author has presented. In writing, we access and organize our own ideas to put them forward for others to access. Both reading and writing processes require substantial mental effort. Indeed, Graham, Gillespie, and McKeown (2013) suggest that the central role of thinking in writing must become more prominent. Just as no good reader simply zips through a text without mental effort, no writer just sits down and writes out a finished product.

The view of writing as a process can be traced to Donald Murray (1972), who admonished teachers to turn away from teaching writing as a product and to understand it as a process. This view had clearly taken hold by 1982, when Hairston (1982) referred to the change in focus from product to process as a paradigm shift. The writing process is generally seen to involve at least three distinct stages: (1) prewriting activities of gathering ideas and planning, (2) drafting ideas into connected sentences and paragraphs, and (3) evaluating the draft and revising. This is not a truly linear process, however, as, for example, revising might send a writer back to gathering further ideas and redrafting. Recognition of these stages makes it clear that writing is not a simple activity of setting words on a page but involves manipulating words and ideas.

QtA similarly highlights reading as a process, prompting the reader to make thinking about text visible, literally giving voice to what students are thinking about the text. Thus responding to text in QtA has a similar feel to the early steps in a writing process, when a writer begins to examine his or her ideas on a topic. QtA helps move readers away from the notion of taking on a complete text and toward building the text's message piece by piece. Similarly, writing is a process of building a text, beginning by consciously gathering one's ideas on a topic, organizing them, then stating, connecting, and polishing them. First, viewing writing as a process with a sequence of stages helps students see that you don't just pick up your pen and write out a finished paper, but you take it bit by bit. Second, actually engaging in writing as a process helps students accomplish writing tasks. Taking it a step at a time makes the whole enterprise of writing more accessible.

In describing the writing process, Graham et al. (2013) characterize writing as also a social activity involving a dialogue between writer(s) and reader(s). This notion of a dialogue or a conversation also applies to reading when a reader approaches text by questioning the author.

# Applying QtA to Writing

A QtA perspective provides access to writing and encourages awareness of audience. *Access* is finding a way into the process of writing, and *audience* is a writer's taking care to let the reader in. Access is promoted chiefly through prompting written responses to text from students, and audience is promoted through feedback to student writing.

## Access to Writing: Responding to Text

Think of access as helping students view the process of writing as more approachable and more doable. One way that a QtA perspective can make writing more approachable is by helping writers develop their own voice. Often students come to believe that they need to respond to questions, both in reading and writing, in a school voice. Certainly we do want students to become able to use academic language. But trying to phrase their responses in an academic way can also short-circuit students' ability to put voice to their thoughts. Thus in QtA, the interaction with text acquires the tone of conversation. What we ask of students is not to generate formal statements of an author's message, but provide something more like a "thinking aloud" of what they are getting from a text.

For example, compare the following responses to the appearance of the stranger in "The Bridge on the River Clarinette":

- "A stranger came across the dilapidated bridge and they were all very surprised that he was not afraid to cross it."

- "Everybody's saying like this guy's like pretty weird and all, but he seemed like he was kinda brave, coming over their rickety old bridge."

Our preference is for the second one, as it is obviously stated in student language and feels like a natural response to text that has arisen from a processing of ideas rather than recall alone.

Applying this kind of response to writing helps students to get in touch with what they understand and want to express about a topic. That is a strong starting point for writing what you mean. In later stages of a writing process, of course, more precise word choice can come into play.

The second and fundamental piece of access is using the QtA process and enacted discussions as a foundation for written responses. The QtA approach of digging into a text in a collaborative, constructive way lays the groundwork for students to be able to produce responses that are both well motivated and genuine. Embedding writing within QtA can allow the writing to be more grounded and better informed.

One way this can be implemented is that, within a QtA text discussion lesson, students can be asked to respond to one or more of the Queries in writing rather than responding orally. Writing can also be elicited after a text has been discussed and major ideas have been laid out. Writing following a QtA discussion relieves some of the initial effort of writing because the major ideas of the text have been articulated and are quite accessible for students to use in writing tasks. So in essence some of the early planning stages have already been accomplished.

The QtA process can be used as a basis for an integrated, reciprocal, cumulative approach to reading and writing in the classroom. You might begin making such an approach a regular part of the classroom literacy routine by having students write their responses to one Query at least once per text. Students' written responses might then be revisited at the end of the text, giving students opportunities to rethink or expand on their initial ideas about the text and characters. This reinforces the reciprocal processes of reading and writing, and, especially, the availability and importance of revision.

As an example, let us consider Segment 5 from the text on polar bears in Chapter 4. This segment provides a lot of grist for students to write about because it depicts key information about how polar bears' diminishing food sources send them wandering into towns, and the effects of the intersection between people and the bears. The stop after this segment might be a good place to ask students to write in response to the Query "How does this text segment deal with the bears' problem that the author has been describing?"

Time allotted for this writing should be brief, as it is in the midst of the text. But it can be briefly followed up with some sharing of responses. Students who are hesitant to share their responses might be coaxed by, for example, eliciting a response and then asking, "Does anyone else have something similar?" A show of hands might then be used to survey how many students focused on the same issues in their responses. Or the discussion might prompt and model connections if you ask, "Did anyone connect this segment to things we read earlier?" and then have a student read a response containing a connection.

Another piece of a QtA/writing routine could involve asking students to simply jot down their thoughts following a text discussion: "What are you thinking?"; "What will stay in your mind about this text?"; "Do you have any questions about the text?" This can be a very informal type of writing, more like a self-brainstorm. A next step could be a group discussion of the text or some aspect of it, in which students are invited to use their written reactions as they respond. Such an activity is very low-stakes for students; they have no requirement to use what they wrote or to submit it to evaluation, but for students reluctant to participate in discussions, they have a response already prepared to share.

At a later stage, students' brief writings can be incorporated into more formal writing assignments. For example, one assignment might ask students to choose one of their responses to a Query and develop their ideas further into a piece they submit for evaluation. Staging students' writing processes by starting small with ways of putting words on paper that are readily within reach and then expanding those responses into full written pieces gives students opportunities to explore and grow their capabilities as writers.

Teachers have shared with us some of the writing set-ups that they found to work well for eliciting writing about a text that has been read with QtA. Admittedly, these examples are not atypical of what teachers tend to use anyway to prompt writing. But when they are used for a text that has been well examined through QtA, they can lead students to create more informed and natural responses. The set-ups we have seen teachers use with QtA include:

- *Extending the text.* Ask students to go beyond a story ending or to write a kind of detour, filling in information about some event or character from the story. Or for an expository text, ask students to write an explanation of why they agree or disagree with an argument made in the text.

- *Letter writing.* Ask students to write a letter to one of the characters in the text, for example, telling a character how they felt about some event the character was involved in, or evaluating a decision the character made, possibly suggesting other options.

- *Connecting experiences.* Ask students to write about something reminiscent of a story event that occurred in their lives, or for an expository text, about similar problems or situations they have encountered or read about.

- *What's the mood/theme?* Ask students to write about the mood they felt as they read, or about what big ideas they saw that also occur in other stories or in real life.

- *Taking action.* For expository texts that address problematic issues, have students write about how to take action to address the problem.

## Considering Audience: Feedback on Writing

Teacher feedback on student writing and feedback from peers are cited by Graham et al. (2013) as an evidence-based practice for writing instruction. But according to Troia et al.'s (2015) observations, such activities occur infrequently. Without effective routines for feedback, it is less likely that meaningful revision will occur. Lack of a strong revision process severely restricts the development of young writers. Revising and understanding how to examine writing for revision are essential to becoming an effective writer.

Providing and receiving feedback can be a sensitive situation. Most classroom readers (teachers and peers) do not want to be put in the position of criticizing the writers in front of them, and novice writers do not relish being critiqued. However, using QtA to frame and examine writing can shift the perspective from "Is this writing good?" to "What are you (the author) trying to say?"

The notion of using QtA in the feedback and revision loop in writing can be introduced by prompting students to think about writing as connecting with an audience. Although the notion of audience is usually a part of how the writing process is introduced to students, simply stating the connection may not make it very real for students. To enliven the notion of audience, the teacher can remind students that they do the flip side—connect to an author as the audience reacting to an author's text—during QtA discussions.

General questions such as the following can initiate the QtA focus for writing:

- "What does the reader have to know?"

- "What do you want to leave the reader with?"

- "What are you trying to say to the reader?"

The language of QtA Queries can readily be directed to students as authors and used by the teacher or students in responding to student writing. See Table 9.1 on the next page for examples of how QtA Queries for reading can be used, or in some cases reframed, to help students think about their own writing.

The following is a brief example of a student's piece of writing about a story she read and the teacher's comments about it.

| Student's writing | Teacher feedback |
|---|---|
| The story told about a whale and his mother and how they got separated and almost never found each other again. | "What do you want your reader to know when you say they 'almost never found each other'?" |
| They searched and searched and then there he was. So now they are very careful about going into big waves. | "What do you mean by 'there he was'? How does going into big waves connect to their getting separated?" |

Teacher feedback to students about their writing is an obvious way to use a QtA frame in responding to writing. But QtA can also be used to help students develop peer feedback skills and to help students evaluate their own writing and develop their revision skills.

Despite the fact that evidence supports the effectiveness of peer feedback (Graham et al., 2013), many teachers have difficulty implementing and using it. We have had many conversations with teachers who say that they have tried to use peer feedback but run into issues they cannot overcome. In particular, they say that students don't know what to say to their peers or that the time that peers confer is not well

**TABLE 9.1.** QtA Queries for Reading and Writing

| QtA Queries for reading | QtA Queries for writing |
| --- | --- |
| "What do you think about all this?" | "What do you want your reader to think about all this?" |
| "What does the author want us to know?" | "What do you want your reader to know?" |
| "Where is this going?" | "Where is this going?" |
| "How does this connect?" | "How does this connect?" |
| | "How did you get here?" |
| "What's that all about?" | "What's that all about?" |
| "How has the author started us off?" | "What do you want your reader to think right here at the beginning?" |
| "What did we learn from this conversation?" | "How can you *show* your reader instead of *telling* your reader?" |
| "Why is the author telling us that?" | "Why are you telling the reader that?" |
| "What does the author mean by that?" | "What do you mean by that? What will your reader understand from that?" |
| "What picture has the author created for us?" | "What picture are you trying to create for the reader?" |
| "What did the author say to make you think that?" | "What can you say to make the reader see your point?" |

used. These are legitimate concerns that are challenging to address. However, taking advantage of QtA framing may help to ease students into providing and receiving feedback.

As QtA is used in a classroom for interacting with text, students become familiar with ways to query text, which prepares them to understand the idea of reading and writing as interactive processes. Experiencing this relationship may help them see that delving into and examining an author's work is an inherent part of literacy.

The task of providing feedback for a peer can be introduced as helping their classmate, as an author, see his or her text from the outside, as a reader meeting it for the first time. Students can be encouraged to make comments to their peers explicitly as their reader, for example, "As a reader, I didn't understand how these two connect."

## Readers Becoming Writers: Samples from a QtA Lesson

In the following section we offer a sample of the reading and writing interactions from a QtA lesson that a teacher conducted with a group of middle school students. The text for the QtA lesson was "Thank You Ma'am" by Langston Hughes (1958). The story begins with an encounter between Roger, a teenage boy, and Mrs. Jones, an older woman. As she is walking home from work late one night, Roger attempts to steal her purse, but Mrs. Jones is able to prevent that and grab Roger.

Mrs. Jones notices that his face is dirty and his hair is uncombed, and he admits that no one is looking after him. She drags him home with her, gives him supper, and learns that he wanted her money to buy a pair of blue suede shoes. Mrs. Jones explains to Roger that when she was young, she also couldn't afford things she wanted, and that she did some things she was not proud of.

At the end of the story, Mrs. Jones gives Roger 10 dollars to buy the blue suede shoes and tells him not to steal her purse or anyone else's for that matter, as shoes purchased with stolen money cause more trouble than they're worth. When he leaves, Roger wants to say something other than "Thank you, ma'am," but can barely get the words *thank you* out of his mouth before she shuts the door behind him.

The story lines that the teacher identified as key are as follows:

- "Ain't you got nobody home to tell you to wash your face?"
- "You ought to be my son. I would teach you right from wrong. Least I can do right now is to wash your face. Are you hungry?"
- "Maybe you ain't been to your supper either, late as it be. Have you?"
- "I were young once and I wanted things I could not get."
- "I have done things, too, which I would not tell you, son."
- "The woman did not ask the boy anything about where he lived, or his folks, or anything else that would embarrass him."
- "Now here, take this ten dollars and buy yourself some blue suede shoes. And next time, do not make the mistake of latching onto my pocketbook nor nobody else's—because shoes got by devilish ways will burn your feet."

As reading and discussion proceeded, students focused on Mrs. Jones's admission that she had done things that she was not proud of. They recognized both that she felt sympathy for the boy because he was not well cared for, and that she saw something of her young self in him.

After the conclusion of text reading and discussion, the teacher presented the following prompt for students to respond to in writing: "Why do you think Mrs. Jones helps Roger, a boy who just tried to steal her purse?" Support your ideas with evidence from the text.

The following are responses from three students in the group that typify what students wrote, followed by the teacher's feedback to each student. Notice that all three were successful in focusing on the big idea that Mrs. Jones related to the young boy because she had been in similar situations in her past. But none of the students explore the depth of that connection, specifically that her past motivates her to help because she believes that he can change and that he deserves a chance to make better decisions in life. DeMeter gets closest to this fuller notion by saying that she "wanted to impact the kid's life in a positive way." With her feedback the teacher is trying to nudge the students to go deeper, to stretch their interpretations of the story.

### Kenny

In the story "Thank You Ma'am," by Langston Hughes, a boy named Roger attempted to steal Mrs. Jones's pocketbook. Although Roger tried to steal Mrs. Jones's purse, she decides to help the boy. I believe she reacts in this way because his actions are almost similar to hers when she was a child. This shows she can relate to him. The evidence that persuades me to believe this is "I were young once and wanted things I could not get. . . . I have done things too which I would not tell you son—neither tell you or God if he didn't know already." Therefore she helped the boy because she sees herself in him and understands why he would try to steal it.

### Teacher Feedback

- "Can you make your readers understand more about what Mrs. Jones meant by 'wanted things I could not get'? What do you think she understands now, as an adult, about those kinds of 'things' or about wanting things?"

- "What do you want your readers to know about the things she did to help Roger?"

### Destiny

I think Mrs. Jones helped Roger because she relates to him and he might be homeless and it is always nice to help. Roger tried to take Mrs. Jones's pocketbook. Well, he tried but the strap broke and she started dragging him to her home. Then Mrs. Jones takes him home and washes up his face and gives him some food. Then when he is going to give him some money for blue suede shoes. Then when he walked out the door he was in shock. He couldn't believe it. She relates to him because they both wanted stuff but couldn't get it. I think that because she said when she was little she used to do the same things but didn't steal.

### Teacher Feedback

- "Do you think her giving him money for shoes connects to 'wanting things I could not get'? How could you show your readers that?"

- "How does her giving him money for shoes connect to his being in shock as he left?"

- "What do you want your readers to think about Roger at the end?"

*DeMeter*

*Mrs. Jones helped the boy who just tried to steal her purse because she use to be just like the young kid. She once did steal as well. In the text it states, "You thought I was going to say 'but I didn't snatch people's pocketbooks.' Well I wasn't going to say that." She is inferring that she stole stuff off people. The kid reminded her of herself and she wanted to impact the kid's life in a positive way.*

*Teacher Feedback*

- "What's Mrs. Jones saying about the consequences of wanting things and not being able to have them? Are you saying that she thinks it is okay to steal?"

- "What do you mean that she wanted to impact the kid's life in a positive way? How does that connect to her feeding him but also to her giving him money for the shoes? How does it connect to her not calling the police?"

The teacher's feedback for all three of these students was intended to provide a further goal for the student writers to strive for in revising their responses by opening up some questions that were not clearly answered in the text. Thus she nudges the students both as writers and as readers to consider circumstances beyond what an author provides, to explore possibilities and not be limited to definitive statements.

In addition, the teacher made several other comments to each student. Below we spotlight one particular kind of response. In the following feedback to Kenny and Destiny, the teacher comments on positive things the young writers do to inform their readers. Notice that she frames her response in terms of readers' reactions. This continues the focus on the interaction between reader and writer rather than on evaluating aspects of writing.

KENNY: In the story "Thank You Ma'am," by Langston Hughes, a boy named Roger attempted to steal Mrs. Jones's pocketbook.

TEACHER: Your readers will appreciate having this information about the story.

DESTINY: Roger tried to take Mrs. Jones's pocketbook. Well, he tried but the strap broke and she started dragging him to her home. Then Mrs. Jones takes him home and washes up his face and gives him some food.

TEACHER: Your readers will enjoy feeling like part of the story with these details that you provide.

## Concluding Thoughts

In this chapter we have discussed the benefits of using a QtA perspective for students' writing. Highlighting the QtA/writing connection transmits to students that reading and writing are two sides of the same coin, and that insight can enhance both processes. Too often students see reading as a task of getting through a text so that they can claim completion. Similarly with writing, students often see the main goal as completing an assignment and turning it in—done! It may help to acknowledge to students that both reading and writing take effort. They are both attempts to transfer to others the contents of one's thoughts. This takes an open mind on both sides of the process. We should be trying to hear what others are saying and trying to say things in ways that help others hear.

Considering the intersection of reading and writing, we want to encourage students, as readers, to "pull apart" a piece of text in order to identify the information it offers and build that into a coherent, memorable mental representation. And in writing, encourage students to pull apart their own ideas so that they can be ordered, explained, and developed into a coherent form for readers.

## ENDING NOTES

- QtA is aligned with the process of writing, and writing can be readily integrated into QtA-directed reading and thinking.

- Reading and writing are both processes of sense-making using language. Both include gathering information, culling it for importance, and establishing connections among ideas to build a coherent whole.

- Both reading and writing require effort. Reading is building the text's message piece by piece, and writing is building a text by gathering one's ideas on a topic, organizing them, stating, connecting, and polishing them.

- Responding to text in QtA has a similar feel to the early steps in a writing process, when a writer begins to examine ideas on a topic.

- The QtA approach of digging into a text in a collaborative, constructive way lays the groundwork for students to be able to produce well-motivated and genuine responses.

- Integrating writing and QtA could begin with asking students to respond to a Query in writing rather than orally during discussion.

- A QtA/writing routine could include asking students to jot down their thoughts following a text discussion. A next step could be a group discussion of the text in which students are invited to use their written reactions as they respond.

- Feedback on student writing from teachers and peers is an evidence-based practice for writing instruction, although such activities occur infrequently.

- Without effective routines for feedback, little meaningful revision will occur, and lack of a revision process restricts the development of young writers.

- The language of Queries can readily be directed to students as author and used by the teacher or students in responding to student writing.

- A QtA perspective provides access to writing and encourages awareness of audience. Access is promoted chiefly through prompting written responses to text from students and audience is promoted through feedback on student writing.

# Inside the Classroom

# CHAPTER 10

# Moves to Keep Discussion Productive

As we observed teachers in their classrooms and examined transcripts of our own lessons when we tried out QtA with students ourselves, we began to notice that certain moves made in discussion seemed to keep the talk productive. In this chapter we introduce those moves and present classroom transcripts that illustrate those moves in action.

One way to conceptualize the unfolding of a QtA discussion is to imagine that when students engage in reading and talking about a text, they enter a kind of maze. The ideas in a text make up the maze, and the goal for working through it is understanding. To reach understanding, students must follow any unexpected twists and turns the text maze presents and use strategic maneuvers to get through. The QtA teacher has already been through the maze, so he or she knows what students are facing. However, the QtA teacher's job is not to show students the path through the maze, but rather to prompt them to figure out their own way through.

In Chapter 3 we noted that in planning, teachers need to read the text while thinking about how the ideas in the text might be encountered by their students. Similarly, during a QtA discussion, teachers simultaneously balance two perspectives of the maze: one is the student's perspective (a ground-level view) and the other is their own perspective (a bird's-eye view). They have to keep in mind that, to students, a text may first appear confusing, dense, and ambiguous. At the same time, teachers have to keep in mind the major understandings they want students to construct and the actions they can take to focus student contributions toward building those ideas.

## Discussion Moves

Discussion Moves are actions that teachers take to assist in orchestrating student ideas and making on-the-spot decisions toward the goal of building meaning. We have identified six QtA Discussion Moves: Marking, Turning Back (to students or to text), Revoicing, Recapping, Modeling, and Annotating. Table 10.1 provides a brief introduction to the Moves.

**TABLE 10.1.** Introduction to QtA Moves

| Move | Description |
| --- | --- |
| Marking | Signaling key ideas in student responses |
| Turning Back to students | Turning responsibility for meaning-building back to students |
| Turning Back to text | Turning students' attention back to the text |
| Revoicing | Restating student contributions for clarification or emphasis |
| Recapping | Summarizing key ideas from the discussion |
| Modeling | Teacher sharing reaction to text or demonstrating processing of text |
| Annotating | Teacher adding information to the discussion beyond what was in the text |

## Marking

Marking is a way of responding to student comments that signals to students that an idea is of particular importance to the discussion. An example is a student comment that was made during discussion of the story *Ben and Me* (Lawson, 1939), told by a mouse that went up in Ben Franklin's kite. The students were discussing a segment about why the friendship between Ben and the mouse had broken up. A student commented, "It says 'deceit,' umm, that's an act of lying, so it means a lie broke up their friendship." The teacher marked the student's idea, saying, "Oh, interesting. Jamie said *lying* caused a rift in their friendship." By Marking the student's comment in this way, the teacher attempted to underscore the connections between the friendship breaking up and lying and to set students up for building that idea.

## Turning Back

The Turning-Back Discussion Move is associated with two kinds of actions. First, Turning Back refers to the teacher's turning the discussion back to students. Second, Turning Back refers to turning students' attention back to the text to clarify or focus their thinking.

### Turning Back to Students

With this Move, a teacher turns responsibility back to students for thinking through and figuring out ideas. The most basic Turning-Back Move is used when a student's contribution does not fully respond to the issue at hand, which can occur frequently, as Queries ask students to share in-process thinking. So teachers simply turn back to the students to fill out the information provided. This is usually accomplished by directing a Follow-Up Query to their response, for example asking a student, "What did you mean by . . . ?"

Turning back to students can also function in concert with Marking. So, continuing the *Ben and Me* (Lawson, 1939) example from earlier, after the teacher marked Jamie's response targeting lying, he or she might then ask, "How did Ben's lying play a role here?" The question invites students to continue that line of thinking about how lying disrupted the friendship of Ben and the mouse.

Another situation that calls for turning back is when student comments are related but the students have not seen fit to connect them. Here, turning back takes the form of a connection follow-up, when a teacher asks, for example, "So, Jennifer, how does your comment connect to what Deanna told us?" The importance of this function of turning back is to encourage interactive talk rather than serial responses. Being prompted to connect reminds students that they are part of an interactive discussion in collaboration with others, and that the goal is building meaning together.

The Turning Back to Students Move is very productive, as it helps teachers avoid the tendency to simply accept sparse responses and then fill in the rest of the information themselves. The teacher fill-in is a kind of occupational hazard. As teachers, we do it almost reflexively, because, after all, we are there to teach. It is so easy to lose sight of the effectiveness of prompting students to do the thinking on their own. And most often, teachers find that students can, indeed, do the thinking.

To sum up, Turning Back to students puts the ball back in the students' court, by inviting them to either continue an incomplete line of thinking or to explicitly connect their ideas to those of another student.

## Turning Back to Text

Turning Back also refers to turning students' attention back to the text to clarify or focus their thinking. Turning back to the text is an action taken toward having students take account of the text and use it as their focus in building meaning. The issue here is twofold. One is that at times students misunderstand the text, and the other is that students sometimes get caught up in their own and others' responses and lose track of the text as the focus for building meaning.

The simplest turn-to-text move is used when a student has clearly misread or misinterpreted something in the text. When this occurs, the QtA teacher asks simply, "Is that what the author said?" and encourages the student to check the text. More often than not, this results in the student's making a self-correction. This scenario seems far preferable to telling a student he or she has the "wrong answer." It frames the situation as a temporary misstep rather than flagging it as an outright error, and is a quick way to clear up confusion.

A turn-to-text move is also called upon when students debate an issue that could be easily clarified by what the author has explicitly presented. In such situations, discussion has taken on a life of its own, away from the text. Although a goal in discussions is to have students interact with each other, sometimes students get so caught up in the discussion that they seem to almost forget that the text is there. For example, in the discussion about *Ben and Me* (Lawson, 1939), a text segment describes the mouse flying in Franklin's kite, and ends, "Enabled to ascend and descend at will, I spent many happy hours at this thrilling sport." But students discussed the mouse's feelings with comments such as "I don't think he liked it" and "It sounds like fun, but I don't know if he was happy." The teacher then intervened, asking, "Does the author tell us if he is happy?" A student checked the text and read, "'I spent many happy hours at this thrilling sport.'" The class was then able to agree that the mouse was, indeed, happy flying in the kite.

Another variation on turning to text is rereading a portion of the text when students are having difficulty grasping a major idea in a text segment. Rereading provides the students another chance to consider the text and reflect on the ideas. Students often need a second take. Adults, as mature readers, can tend to forget that the material we give young students to read is unfamiliar to them, and it may take more than one pass for it to "sink in."

The Turning Back to Text Move helps prevent students from going off on tangents and introducing irrelevant information into a discussion. When students are reminded to take account of the author's words and ideas, the discussion returns to more productive construction of meaning.

Whether directed to students for elaboration of their comments or to text for students to take better account of what an author has said, the Turning-Back Discussion Move encourages students to take responsibility for figuring out ideas and resolving issues in contrast to having the teacher explain information to them.

## Revoicing

Revoicing means interpreting what students are struggling to express and rephrasing the ideas so that they can become part of the discussion. Revoicing is applying a kind of "in other words" mechanism when students need assistance in expressing their own ideas.

Using this Move, the teacher distills from student comments the most important information or implicit ideas. Revoicing also raises the level of language, giving more articulate expression to students' ideas. The use of Revoicing is most common with younger students, as they are still developing language and figuring out how to express their thoughts with words.

Let's consider an example from a discussion in which a student was trying to describe reasons behind workers' early efforts to organize for better working conditions in factories. The student commented, "Work was really dirty and stuff in the factories, and so people wanted to pass laws for health and safety and no children." The teacher recognized that the student had the key ideas, but the comment was not phrased clearly. So the teacher revoiced the comment: "So you're pointing out that the working conditions could be unsafe or unhealthy, and that people wanted laws made so that conditions were better, and also that they didn't want children working in the factories." This kind of Revoicing clarifies and captures the essence of an idea and thus allows a student's unwieldy ideas to become part of the discussion. When student comments are made clearer and more concise through Revoicing, other students can more easily respond to and build on the comments toward developing meaning.

The Revoicing Move has a similar function to Marking. In both cases the "thinking" work has already been done by students, and the Moves are used to emphasize and set up ideas so they can become a part of a productive discussion. The difference is that in Revoicing, the teacher is doing some revising of a student's comment rather than just giving emphasis to it. In either case, Revoicing or Marking, these Moves make it easier for students to incorporate peers' ideas into their developing representation of the text.

## Recapping

Recapping is a kind of summary of discussion so far, and is used when students have grasped the essential meaning and are ready to move on in the text. But it is needed only occasionally. Recapping ideas is not necessary for each text segment. Rather, the Move is called for when discussion has been wide-ranging or extended. This might occur, for example, when building the idea of a segment has been difficult for students or when many students have contributed to the discussion. Recapping reminds students of where they are in the text and of the major ideas that they have developed so far.

Recapping can also signal students that they have accomplished something and reinforces the understanding they have built together. For example, here is how a teacher recapped a segment of social studies text about the French and Indian War:

> "So now we know that Washington gave the French leader's message to the Governor that they didn't plan to leave Pennsylvania. And then together we figured out that Washington counted the canoes at the fort and made the drawing so he could give the Governor information about plans the French had and maybe how strong their forces were. Good work, class!"

Recapping does not have to be the sole responsibility of the teacher. We have found that inviting students to recap is an effective way of having them engage in the task of reinforcing what has been built. Recapping encourages a mental organization of the ideas that students have been grappling with and signals that the grappling has indeed produced understanding.

## Modeling and Annotating

In these final two Moves, teachers bring themselves into the interaction more directly than with the previous Moves. Modeling and Annotating can be viewed as "rescue moves" to the extent that they are used when it appears that students have reached the extent of what they can do on their own. Viewing them as rescue moves reminds the teacher that they should be used sparingly; students should be at the center of the thinking and grappling. Students may struggle sometimes to articulate their ideas or connect ideas together to build meaning, but this is not necessarily a bad thing. Struggling to express ideas is an ingredient in the growth of students' thinking.

## Modeling

Various forms of modeling of cognitive tasks have been around for a long time. The motivation for modeling is that in a cognitive context, the major activity of thinking is invisible, and thus modeling is an attempt to "make public" some of the processes in which experts or mature thinkers engage. For example, in an algebra class, many of us have heard teachers say something like "Okay I looked at each side of the equal sign and saw that I could get rid of this $x$ by subtracting it from both sides, so that is what I will do next."

There have been many recommendations to extend modeling to other content domains, including reading (see, e.g., Duffy, Roehler, & Hermann, 1988; Harbour, Evanovich, Sweigart, & Hughes, 2015). But what is modeling in reading? When teachers model some of the things they do as they read, they are trying to reveal the processes by which they interact with the ideas in the text.

Although there are many examples of modeling that work well, there are also some tendencies that reduce the potential impact of modeling as a teaching strategy. For example, attempts at predicting an obvious event, such as "I think the wolf is going to blow the third little pig's house down," do little to illustrate what is involved in figuring out ideas. This example points to a common problem in examples of modeling that we have seen, which is that what gets modeled tends to be the obvious. It also highlights the contrived nature of some kinds of modeling.

In contrast, modeling when done well can help students "see" things in texts they might not have noticed and can allow students to observe or "overhear" how an expert thinks through a complicated idea. Which parts or ideas in a text that a teacher chooses to model are determined by the text ideas that the teacher thinks students might need help with, as well as by the teacher's spontaneous reactions to text—yes, modeling should be reserved for what one has authentically noticed as a reader. Modeling should be as natural in character as possible. It should also be as brief as possible; a long soliloquy by the teacher is unlikely to effectively communicate key ideas to students.

Below, we provide some examples of how teachers have used the Modeling Move. The examples represent general categories of what teachers chose to model. The first shows how Modeling was used to communicate a teacher's affective responses to text. The second example presents an instance of a teacher's modeling the process of building an understanding of a confusing portion of the text.

This first example shows how a teacher brought attention to some exquisitely presented material to encourage appreciation of what the author did and how it affected her as a reader. In the course of a ninth-grade class discussion of the beginning of *Great Expectations* (1861) in which Dickens described the escaped convict, the teacher said:

> "*What a frightening man*! Mmm, every time I read Dickens I find myself in awe of the effect his use of language has on me. Those sentence fragments, how effective. . . . *A man soaked in water, and smothered in mud, and lamed by stones, and cut by flints, and stung by nettles, and torn by briars, who limped and shivered and glared and growled. . . .*"

The teacher's repetition of text phrases emphasized their cumulative effect on her as a reader. It also provided an opportunity for students to see how that effect was created. The example shows how a teacher exposed her own reactions to what an author said. It is not particularly long or pedantic, but rather a natural attempt to share a response to the text.

Another way in which Modeling can be used effectively is in demonstrating how one might work through confusing portions of text. Calling attention to text that is not clear is also an opportunity to reinforce the notion that an author is fallible, someone who is trying to communicate a message and who is sometimes not successful.

The following example comes from a fifth-grade discussion of a story about Native American children who have run away from school, and the principal has gone after them. The students seem to think the boys are in a lot of trouble, but the teacher notices that the principal is expressing sympathy for them. So she shares her thoughts, saying,

> "What I was thinking as we read that is it sounded as if the principal was making excuses for the boys. I mean, he's telling the teacher that 'yeah, they're just used to open spaces where they've heard the howl of coyotes at night.' So it sounded like even though the principal knew he had to punish these two boys, he really couldn't blame them too much."

In our view, the most effective kind of modeling is not only natural and brief, but it ends by turning issues under discussion back to students. For example, the teacher in the previous example could have worded her comments as follows:

> "This is a little confusing, because it sounded like the principal knew he had to punish these two boys, but then he tells the teacher that 'they're just used to open spaces.' So what do you think he's thinking?"

We have observed many cases in which teachers shared their confusion with students. In some cases, it seemed like genuine confusion on the part of the teacher, and in other cases, recognition that a portion of text could well cause confusion for students. We noted that these instances seemed to work very well to energize students to try to figure out what was happening. So the "I'm confused" tactic can engage students as well as acknowledge that text can be confusing, and that the reader's role is to figure it out.

## Annotating

The Discussion Move of Annotating involves those instances during a discussion when a teacher provides information to fill in gaps in the text. This is needed—on occasion—because sometimes authors simply do not provide enough information for students to be able to construct meaning from the text alone. There are gaps in information, holes in lines of reasoning, and assumptions about background knowledge that young readers don't have. To deal with such problems, teachers annotate the text.

To elaborate the Annotating Move, let's look at an example from a class of fourth-grade students who had been studying about the drafting of the U.S. Constitution to replace the Articles of Confederation. The text provided sparse information about the new Constitution, saying simply, "The Constitution was finally finished. Now it was up to the states to ratify, or approve it. Ratify means approve. If nine states ratified the Constitution, it would become law" (Macmillan/McGraw-Hill, 1997). So the teacher annotated by adding information to the discussion that was important if students were to construct a deeper understanding of what made this new Constitutional provision so important and such a departure from what had gone before:

> "What happened in this new Constitution? This is not all in the book, but I want you to understand what actually happened. In the new Constitution, three-fourths of the states have to approve for something to change. But in the old Articles of Confederation, the way these rules were written up, all states had to agree before there would be a change. Look at the contrast. Tell me about the contrast. Tell us about what would happen."

Notice that the teacher ends by turning back to students for their responses to the situation based on the information he or she has added. Annotating is a way for teachers to step into the discussion and keep it going by providing necessary information that students cannot generate or discover on their own.

## Discussion in Action

In this section, we go inside classrooms to observe the Discussion Moves in action. The following excerpts are taken from transcripts of classrooms in which we partnered with teachers to implement QtA. In both cases we have selected discussion around certain text segments to demonstrate how Moves were used. Since we are not presenting the entire lesson, we summarize each segment of text being read. The students, of course, read the entire story, in QtA fashion. Each student had the book open at his or her desk, and each segment was read aloud by the teacher or a student, followed by discussion. For both excerpt sequences all names used are pseudonyms.

## Ms. Daly's Third Grade

The first classroom we enter is Ms. Daly's. Ms. Daly taught third graders in an urban public school. The class is reading an excerpt from the book *A Gift for Tia Rosa* (Taha, 1991), about an older woman, Tia Rosa, and a young girl, Carmela, who lives next door. In the excerpt, Tia Rosa has just returned from two weeks in the hospital and is apparently very ill.

### Excerpt 1

As the story opens, Carmela is at home, knitting, when she sees Tia Rosa's car turn into the driveway. She is excited and wants to visit, but her mother tells her that Tia Rosa has just returned from the hospital and needs to rest.

MS. DALY: So what's going on here in the beginning of the story? Set up the story for us, Anthony.

ANTHONY: Carmela um [saw] Tia Maria. She wants to visit. Her mother said um she know that Carmela want to see Tia Rosa but that Tia Rosa had a long trip and Tia Rosa must be tired after 2 weeks in the hospital.

Anthony has given a respectable but literal summary, which Ms. Daly **marks** and then **turns the discussion back to a student,** asking for "your own words." Connor gets to the main issue very succinctly.

MS. DALY: Okay, so Anthony pulled out important information from the story. Actually right, he read the text and he pulled it out. So what is he telling us? Set up in your own words what is going on in the story. Connor?

CONNOR: Carmela was happy because now Tia Rosa is home and she really wanted to see Tia Rosa.

### Excerpt 2

At this point in the text, Carmela's mother has told her that she can't visit or even call Tia Rosa now, since she has just gotten home. Then the phone rings, and it is Tia Rosa inviting Carmela to visit and saying that she has a gift for her, which makes Carmela's eyes sparkle.

MS. DALY: So now what's going on in the story?

SIENNA: Tia, um, Carmela answered the phone and at first she didn't even know who it was. But it was Tia Rosa, and she said to come over and that she, she had a surprise for her.

MS. DALY: That's right, Tia Rosa invited her to come over. And what does it mean that Carmela's eyes sparkled?

A student applies a personal interpretation to the "sparkling eyes" image, which the teacher **revoices:**

BRENDEN: When people like, sometimes 'cause my mama walk down the street and she sees her best friend she hasn't seen in a long time, she'll like say long time no see or something like that. So maybe that would like make my mama eyes sparkle 'cause like she's happy to see her friend.

MS. DALY: Right, so she kind of has the same thing as your mom, you could kind of make a connection with your mom and her friend how Carmela is with Tia Rosa. Exactly, she gets excited. She has a sparkle in her eye. Now let's connect back to the story, why were Carmela's eyes sparkling?

ANTOINE: Because she didn't see Tia Rosa for a while and now she's home and she can't even go over there to say hi. So when Tia Rosa called, she's thinking now she could see her, like Tia Rosa asked her to come over. So, she is all happy.

In the interchange above, Ms. Daly pivoted back to the story with a Follow-Up that **turned back to a student** and implicitly **back to the text.**

## Excerpt 3

In a later segment of text, Carmela is at Tia Rosa's house and Tia Rosa gives her a small box. Carmela opens it and finds, under some cotton, a silver rose on a chain. Tia Rosa tells her that this is so Carmela will remember her. Notice below that Ms. Daly's Query brings a literal recounting that kind of buries the main point. After Ms. Daly **marks** the response and **turns back to students,** Jaquan's response hits on the key inference, that Tia Rosa may be dying.

MS. DALY: What's going on? What's going on, Veronique?

VERONIQUE: That when she opened the box and there was a, um, a cotton ball and um she pulled it out and there was a flower chain and then she, Tia Rosa said it is for you just in case you forget.

MS. DALY: That's right. Says she got the surprise, this beautiful silver rose. And she said something very important. So what's all this mean? Jaquan?

JAQUAN: I think that she said 'cause she when she opened the box she said cotton, she thought it was all cotton, then she pulled out a silver, a tiny silver rose and she said uh that uh, the rose is so you'll remember your old Tia Rosa and then I think she is about to die because she's really sick.

Ms. Daly then **marks** Jaquan's response and presses for evidence—**turning back** again **to students and to the text** for evidence to support the idea that Tia Rosa may die. Curtell then offers the evidence.

> Ms. DALY: Okay, so you think she is about ready to die? Curtis, is that what you were going to say? What clues gave you that, gave you that idea?
>
> CURTELL: So, she will remember, she said you will remember your old Tia Rosa.

The discussion seems headed on the right path at that point when a student voices a comment indicating a mistaken interpretation of Tia Rosa's not wanting to be forgotten. Ms. Daly **turns back** the comment and students weigh in to clarify and reinforce the initial interpretation.

> ALINA: She thinks that, um, Carmela thought she um, forgot all about her 'cause she hasn't seen her in like 2 weeks.
>
> Ms. DALY: Okay, but is she giving her the gift because she hasn't seen her in 2 weeks?
>
> JAYDEN: No.
>
> Ms. DALY: Why is she giving her the gift? Monica, what were you going to say?
>
> MONICA: She is about to die.

Notice below that Ms. Daly **recaps** the point, but as she does a student takes over spontaneously!

> Ms. DALY: So Tia Rosa is about to die so she gave Carmela this little . . .
>
> IMANI: Rose. And a chain so she wouldn't forget her when she dies.

## Excerpt 4

A later text segment describes Carmela not quite coming to terms with the situation of Tia Rosa's condition. In a conversation with her father, Carmela reminds him about times that Tia Rosa cared for her when she was sick and declares she will care for her friend until she is better. The first student gives a somewhat muddled account of that, and Ms. Daly then **revoices.**

> KAYLEEN: Um, the reason why, the reason why she don't hear from her dad that she is dying is because whenever Carmela, she has always been there when she was sick and always been there and they didn't think she was going to die. She never knew that she was so old and she was going to die.

MS. DALY: That's right. So, she just like, she loves the friendship so much and all the things that they have done. Now Carmela wants to take care of Tia Rosa because she doesn't have a clue. She doesn't realize that she is going to die.

In the excerpts presented, we see Ms. Daly's third-grade students actively engaged in discussing the story. Ms. Daly monitored comments, acknowledged students' contributions, and stepped in with various Discussion Moves to offer direction when needed. We also see students aptly able to play a role in keeping discussion productive.

## Mr. Stine's Fourth-Grade Classroom

The next classroom we visit is Mr. Stine's fourth grade, located in a different midsize urban public school. The class is reading a short story by Isaac Bashevis Singer, who won the Nobel Prize for literature. The story, "The Snow in Chelm" (Singer, 1966), is about an incident in the village of Chelm, a town in Jewish folklore that is populated by fools—only fools.

Excerpt 1

The story begins one night when someone saw the moon reflected in a barrel of water and shouted out that the moon was in their water barrel. People gathered to see it and imagined it had fallen in. So that no one would take the moon, they put the top on the barrel securely. When the barrel was opened in the morning and the moon was not there, the villagers decided it had been stolen. They sent for the police, and when the thief couldn't be found, the fools of Chelm were dismayed.

MR. STINE: So what's going on?

PATTY: Those people are fools.

MR. STINE: Okay, can someone tell us more?

JAMARA: They, they think that the moon is gone, they think it's stolen.

RASHEEN: They are fools and the sun—I mean the moon—the moon's really not stolen.

As shown above, three students responded, each with one piece of information. Below note that Mr. Stine's response **revoices** each comment, **turns back to students** and importantly asks how the pieces of information connect.

MR. STINE: Okay, so let's connect what has been said. They're fools. They think the moon's been stolen. But it's really not stolen. What do those things have to do with each other?

The next response from Charelle is incomplete, so Mr. Stine **turns back to students** to elaborate, and Dawson's response is right on.

> CHARELLE: Um that, they don't think right.
>
> MR. STINE: So what does their thinking the moon's been stolen have to do with them being fools. In your own mind what does that mean?
>
> DAWSON: 'Cause the moon. . . . The moon hasn't really been stolen. It can't be stolen, but they think it has been stolen because they are fools. They just don't know what they are talking about.
>
> MR. STINE: That's the connection. Only fools would think the moon had been stolen.

Notice that when Mr. Stine said, "That's the connection," he **marked** Dawson's statement and then **revoiced** it to an apt short comment, and reinforced the importance of making connections across the ideas in a text.

## Excerpt 2

This part of the story introduces the town's seven elders, who are the oldest and most foolish people. One night the elders met and worriedly discussed that the village was out of money. That same night snow began to fall, and the moon's soft light made the landscape sparkle like silver. The elders believed it *was* silver, shouting out things like "The snow is silver!"; "I see pearls in the snow!"; and "And I see diamonds."

> MR. STINE: What's going on?
>
> JESSIE: They are thinking there is diamonds in the snow. And pearls too.
>
> ETHAN: Oh, one more thing. They think the snow is silver.
>
> LASHAWN: The village don't have no money, so now they think they can get some money.
>
> ROBERTA: They thought . . . they thought there was good stuff. They thought there was pearls and diamonds so they could give it to the poor people in the village.

Two students stick to literal descriptions of what was said and the third student goes to the consequences of the treasure, "now they think they can get some money." Roberta suggested that the money will go to the poor. (Her inference appears to be from background knowledge that it is a good thing to give to the poor, but not connected to the thread of the story about fools.) So Mr. Stine spontaneously changes his question to what the elders thought and **marks,** by emphasizing the word *thought,* and then **turns back to the students.**

MR. STINE: When you guys are talking about what the people of Chelm are doing or saying, you mostly use words such as *they think, they thought.*

 Why do you always use those words? "They aren't thinking right." Why don't you say, "They said," "They explained," "They knew"?

CHARLENE: Because they don't know. They don't even know. They are just saying what they want to say um . . . they are just making it up.

LaSHAWN: Because it's not possible.

ERIN: They are fools.

## Excerpt 3

Soon the elders began to worry that when the villagers walked on the snow they would break the diamonds and pearls. The youngest elder suggested getting someone to go to all the houses and tell people that they couldn't go out of their houses until all the silver, pearls, and diamonds had been collected. But when Dopey Lekisch, one of the citizens of Chelm, pointed out that the messenger himself would step on the treasure, the elders were horrified.

MR. STINE: What does Dopey's comment tell us about Dopey?

DESMOND: He's thinking right.

JAMARA: That Dopey person is thinking right. But wait, um this guy is not dopey, the others are dopey. Why is he called Dopey?

MR. STINE: Good question.

Mr. Stine **revoices** and **turns** the question **back to students** several times:

MR. STINE: Why did fools call someone who is not a fool Dopey?

ERIN: Maybe because they are jealous.

DESMOND: Maybe because he thinks right.

MR. STINE: Okay, so based on what we know about the villagers, what does Dopey "thinking right," as Desmond says, have to do with the villagers calling him Dopey?

MALEEK: Wait, wait, I get it. The villagers are like so foolish that they, um, like I don't know how to say it, but like, they can't even see that this Dopey guy is kinda, like, he's kinda like smart. Um, so like they call him Dopey 'cause he thinks different, but like, but his different kind of thinking is smart, and the way they think isn't.

RASHEED: Yeah, like, they are the dopey ones.

DESMOND: Yep. He's a minority.

MR. STINE: That is an interesting hypothesis. Remember what hypothesis means? Let's come back to that when we finish the story. . . . Let's be sure to discuss why fools might call a person who is not a fool Dopey.

(Note that it turned out the class didn't have time to go back to the matter right after the story, but they did the next day. We were not recording that day, but Mr. Stine said the students brought up interesting ideas with a major idea being that they call him Dopey because he has different ideas. And since the elders think they are so smart, Dopey's different ideas are viewed as not being smart. Thus the name Dopey.)

## Excerpt 4

At this place in the story, the elders are crying in misery. But their tears stop when another citizen of Chelm, whose name is Shmerel, suggests that since the messenger can't put his feet on the snow, he can be carried on a table so that his feet will not touch the snow.

Notice below that Mr. Stine **turns back to students** a number of times in the rest of this lesson requiring them to think through the issues and use more language when explaining what is going on. In the following discussion, we italicize the words he uses for those turn-backs.

MR. STINE: Hmm. How about that? *What do you think of that idea?*

TALIQUE: It's bad.

MR. STINE: Talique, *why is it bad?*

TALIQUE: Because how is the table going to move?

MR. STINE: Good question. *Is the table plan a better or worse idea than the messenger plan?*

STUDENTS: Worse!

MR. STINE: Please *explain why* you think it is worse.

STUDENT: Because the elder people don't want anyone to walk on the snow.

MR. STINE: Yes, we know that. But *the question is why* is putting a messenger on a table a worse idea. Think about a table, *what's the problem* with that idea?

DARNELL: They might have to set it down on the snow. So the legs would make four holes in the snow.

MR. STINE: Darnell said, "They might need to set it down. . . . " *Who's the "They"?*

DARNELL: The people carrying the table.

Several clarification questions that lay out the foundation for the next part of the discussion follow below.

MR. STINE: So how many footprints might there be if four people carry the table? *How many sets of footprints?* Wait a minute, let's make sure we all know what a set of footprints is. *What is a set of footprints?*

CONNER: Two.

MR. STINE: *How did you get two?*

CONNER: One for each foot. A right foot and a left foot.

MR. STINE: Okay, let's say one foot followed by the other foot is one step.

## Excerpt 5

With Shmerel's idea to put the messenger on a table, the elders smiled and smiled, thinking how wise they were. They immediately called for the kitchen boy and stood him on a table.

MR. STINE: *Do you think* the elders realize the implication?

STUDENTS: No. Yes. No.

MR. STINE: This is a good place to turn to a partner to discuss the implications.

Mr. Stine suggests partner discussion because he wants to provide opportunity for students to dig into the issue. The partners talk to each other for about 3 or 4 minutes.

MR. STINE: So *what are the implications?*

TERRELL/JAKE: Four people are going to have to carry the table, so instead of one set of foot prints, there will be four.

MR. STINE: *Do you think* the elders realize that? And whatever your response is, *tell us the reason for it.*

CODY/EMILY: No. And the reason is they don't think about anything. They are fools.

JAMARA: Mr. Stine, why would they say a table? Why wouldn't they get something to carry it from the roofs or something?

STUDENTS: (*shouting out*) "Because they don't think," "Because they are fools."

MR. STINE: Yes. We don't think they realize what they are doing because they are so foolish.

As we have tried to illustrate with the two sets of classroom discussion excerpts, Discussion Moves are actions that can help a teacher manage and facilitate a discussion. The Moves are used as needed and relevant for what is happening in a discussion. There is no recipe for using the Moves, or requirement that all the Moves be used. Rather the various situations that arise during a discussion determine the specific Moves that can help maintain focus and keep the discussion meaningful.

## ENDING NOTES

- Dynamic discussion in which students and teacher work together to build meaning from text is at the heart of QtA.

- A QtA discussion is not a situation of a teacher posing Queries and students simply responding to them, or of students going off on their own and getting further and further away from the text.

- During discussion, the teacher prompts student thinking about text and students reveal and share their thinking, and through further teacher prompting connect and integrate ideas to build a coherent representation from a text.

- Because the events of a QtA discussion can be unpredictable, teachers rely on some tools to manage discussion and make improvisational decisions. We call these Discussion Moves and have identified six: Marking, Turning Back, Revoicing, Recapping, Modeling, and Annotating.

- Marking involves drawing attention to an idea that a student has contributed to emphasize its importance and to use it as a basis for further discussion.

- Turning Back can involve turning back to students the responsibility to think through and figure out ideas or turning back to text as a source for clarifying thinking and keeping discussion on track.

- In Revoicing, a teacher interprets what students are struggling to express so their ideas can become part of the discussion. Marking, Turning Back, and Revoicing represent different ways to make productive use of what students have offered in a discussion.

- When Recapping, a teacher reviews or highlights major ideas and understandings learned so far. Over time, students can assume more responsibility for Recapping.

- The Modeling and Annotating Moves involve greater teacher input in the discussion, and can be seen as rescue moves. The teacher steps in, in a more direct way. Modeling is making public the processes in which readers engage in the course of reading, and is most effective when it is kept short and is folded into discussions to emphasize an authentic response to text. Annotating involves providing information to fill in gaps in a text.

# CHAPTER 11

## One Teacher's Journey with Questioning the Author

In Chapter 10, we provided examples of the kinds of Moves teachers use to keep the discussion focused and to provide students with opportunities to build meaning from the ideas presented in the text. As many teachers recognize, becoming skilled at using these Discussion Moves doesn't happen overnight. In this chapter we share transcript examples that answer a question most often asked by teachers: "But what does QtA look like when a teacher is just beginning?" In the first sections of this chapter, we share transcripts from one fourth-grade teacher's early lessons and talk about common patterns we see when teachers first begin implementing QtA lessons.

Ms. Tantello, our teacher new to QtA, is a fourth-grade teacher in an urban charter school and has 2 years' teaching experience. She began working with QtA in her third year of teaching. As we share examples from her lessons, we also will suggest which of the Discussion Moves she could have implemented in order to move the discussion and keep the talk productive. Then, we will examine excerpts from Ms. Tantello's QtA lessons as the year progressed and she became more skilled at the Discussion Moves and on following up student responses. Finally, we will share our favorite example of one of her students who became a QtA "expert."

## Queries: Early Patterns

One of the first patterns we noticed when working with teachers new to QtA is that they tend to give away too much information in their Initiating Queries. Because they are used to asking more closed questions, their initial attempts at designing open Queries tend to be somewhat leading. This pattern was reflected in Ms. Tantello's early lessons.

In the segments below we provide the text and the Queries that Ms. Tantello planned for the first two segments of one of her early lessons, for the text *Alice in Wonderland* (Carroll, 1865). We then share our thinking about her Queries.

## Analysis of Ms. Tantello's Planned Queries

<table>
<tr><td align="center">TEXT SEGMENT 1</td></tr>
</table>

Alice was beginning to get very tired of sitting by her sister on the bank, and of having nothing to do: once or twice she had peeped into the book her sister was reading, but it had no pictures or conversations in it, "and what is the use of a book," thought Alice, "without pictures or conversations?"

So she was considering in her own mind (as well as she could, for the hot day made her feel very sleepy and stupid) whether the pleasure of making a daisy-chain would be worth the trouble of getting up and picking the daisies, when suddenly a White Rabbit with pink eyes ran close by her.

<table>
<tr><td align="center">Queries and Analysis</td></tr>
</table>

**Initiating Query: "Why is Alice tired of sitting by the bank?"**

Although this Query is open, consider the amount of information Ms. Tantello has already given the students. She has told them that Alice is sitting by a bank, and she is tired of that activity, two pieces of information we would want to get from the students. Students are left with little to construct other than "Because she has nothing to do." A Query such as "What's going on in our story?" would have given students the opportunity to provide all of the key details, not just one element.

**Follow-Up Query: "What happened in that last sentence that might make things better for Alice?"**

The Follow-Up Query targets the Rabbit's visit, but again, gives away too much information. First, Ms. Tantello lets the students know to look at the last sentence and plants the seed that things might be looking up for Alice.

If students do not mention the Rabbit's visit and discuss only Alice's boredom, a Follow-Up Query such as "Is that all that happened? Someone want to tell us more?" would allow students to go back into the text and find the additional information. We suggest also adding an "if needed" Follow-Up Query that targets Alice's character. She is such a fascinating character that we want to begin to draw students' attention to her. A Follow-Up such as "So what do Alice's actions tell us about her character?" provides students with an opportunity to share their initial impressions of Alice.

<table>
<tr><td align="center">TEXT SEGMENT 2</td></tr>
</table>

There was nothing so *very* remarkable in that; nor did Alice think it so *very* much out of the way to hear the Rabbit say to itself, "Oh dear! Oh dear! I shall be too late!" (when she thought it over afterwards, it occurred to her that she ought to have wondered at this, but at the time it all seemed quite natural); but when the Rabbit actually *took a watch out of its waistcoat-pocket*, and looked at it, and then hurried on, Alice started to her feet, for it flashed across her mind that she had never before seen a rabbit with either a waistcoat-pocket, or a watch to take out of it, and burning with curiosity, she ran across the field after it, and was just in time to see it pop down

| TEXT SEGMENT 2 (*continued*) |
|---|
| a large rabbit-hole under the hedge. In another moment down went Alice after it, never once considering how in the world she was to get out again. |
| **Queries and Analysis** |
| **Initiating Query:** "So Alice wasn't surprised that the Rabbit could talk but was surprised he had a watch. What's that about?" |
| Although the Query "What's that about?" works, it's the lead-in to the Query that is problematic. Ms. Tantello has already told them what Alice thinks of the Rabbit's behavior. A simple "What happened in this section?" would have allowed the students to provide the key pieces of information already given to them. |
| **Follow-up Query:** "What happened to the Rabbit and Alice?" |
| Although we think a Follow-Up Query is needed, Ms. Tantello's Query will yield the literal response "They both went down the hole." Since we suggested asking, "What happened in this section?" (see our Initiating Query above), we think what happened to the Rabbit and Alice would be discussed when dealing with the Initiating Query. We think a more interesting topic would be to address what more we're learning about Alice from her actions. We would add a Follow-Up Query to address that topic and would ask, "Okay, so student X told us that the Rabbit went down the rabbit-hole, and Alice followed. How does that information add to what we already know about Alice?" |

After working with Ms. Tantello on several plans, we were able to support her in understanding that an open Query can still be leading. We had her review her plans and for each Query ask, "What information have I already given the students?" If she was able to identify key pieces, we had her revise the Query. Once we tackled the issues with planning, we moved on to providing support with implementing her plans.

## Implementing Discussions: Early Patterns

When analyzing Ms. Tantello's transcripts from her early lessons, we also saw some of the common patterns we see when teachers are new to QtA. One of the biggest issues is handling student responses. As mentioned in Chapter 5, often Follow-Up Queries need to be spontaneously created, and that's one place where many teachers, including Ms. Tantello, struggle initially. As you can see in the transcript excerpt below, Ms. Tantello had a planned connection Query but ran into trouble when she didn't get the targeted response. Rather than continue to ask open Follow-Up Queries that pushed students to elaborate and explain, or turn back to the text, Ms. Tantello asked questions that encouraged students to provide one- or two-word responses.

## Transcript Example 1: Narrow Follow-Ups

In this segment, students were reading a short text about how elephants have excellent memories, and the big idea from this section was that their incredible memories allow them to remember people regardless of the amount of time that has passed between meetings (Carboni, n.d.). The author provides evidence for this theory by sharing a story about a zoologist who had a special friendship with an elephant. After the two were separated for years, upon being reunited they rekindled their friendship immediately.

MS. TANTELLO: So what did we learn in this section?

MAYA: Ian Douglas-Hamilton developed a special friendship with the elephant.

MS. TANTELLO: Exactly. How does that connect with the main idea of our story?

JAKE: Their brain.

MS. TANTELLO: Their brain and their . . . ?

AMARI: Memory.

MS. TANTELLO: What about their memory?

MAYA: They are good.

MS. TANTELLO: They have good memories, and they remember what?

QUINTON: People.

MS. TANTELLO: Yes, they remember people.

Notice how the students never fully grasped the important idea, and instead, restated meaning they already established—that elephants have good memories. The only point they added was to supply the word *people*. There are several places in the discussion where Ms. Tantello could have turned back to the students or to the text. After Jake's initial response, she could have asked, "So what about their brain?" to spark a discussion about their memories rather than her closed query that allowed for a one-word response. Another option would be to turn back to the text after Amari's response. Ms. Tantello could have asked, "So, let's go back into the text. What are they saying about elephants' memories in this section?" That Query would have allowed students to address the idea that there was a long lapse between the meetings, yet the elephant's exceptional memory allowed her to remember him.

## Transcript Example 2: Collecting Comments

Another common pattern that surfaced from Ms. Tantello's early transcripts was the issue of "collecting comments." In this pattern, Ms. Tantello, typical of teachers new to QtA, tends to ask an open Query and then allow multiple students to respond until someone is able to supply the targeted response. The following excerpt from an early lesson demonstrates this pattern.

In this excerpt the students were reading a passage from *The Tale of Despereaux* (DiCamillo, 2003), a fantasy tale about Despereaux, a mouse that lives in a castle; Roscuro, a jealous rat; Mig, a poorly treated servant; and Princess Pea, a human princess. In a previous segment, students learned about the plan to kill the princess. In this segment, the teacher wants them to connect Despereaux's desire to save the princess with how he knew she was in danger in the first place. It's a rather confusing section where students have to infer that Despereaux learned of the plan because he overheard a conversation between Roscuro and Mig about kidnapping Princess Pea. Despereaux was hidden under a napkin on a tray of leftovers that was being taken back to the kitchen, and the characters felt free to discuss the plan within Despereaux's hearing. Instead of building that meaning, students simply took turns guessing which characters they thought might have told Despereaux of the plan.

MS. TANTELLO: What did we learn in this section?

CHLOE: Despereaux has to save the princess.

MS. TANTELLO: But how did he know she needed to be saved?

TEVIN: Because, I think, like Mig told him.

LUCIA: Roscuro told him.

SARA: Nah, the Cook told him.

DRAKE: It was Gregory.

MAYA: No, nobody told him. He was under that napkin and um heard that, um, heard them talking about like how they was gonna kill the princess.

MS. TANTELLO: Okay, I think Maya remembered how he knew. Despereaux knows the plan because he was under the napkin and overheard it, and now he has to do something to save the princess.

Students began to guess which character told him, rather than connect to the previous section, which gave them the information. This would have been a great place for the teacher to ask students to turn back to the segment where Despereaux was hidden under the napkin. Revisiting that portion of the text would have allowed students to make the connection between Despereaux's plan to save the princess and how he knew he needed a plan.

## Transcript Example 3: (Overly) Helpful Teacher

Another pattern that emerged in Ms. Tantello's early lessons was what we call "helpful teacher syndrome." Because teachers don't like to see students struggle, they tend to supply the important information or elaborate for them instead of turning back to the students and asking additional Follow-Up Queries that allow students to do the work. The following example shows Ms. Tantello building meaning for students.

From the beginning of the novel, Despereaux spends a lot of time reading. He learns from his books about knights in shining armor who save princesses and truly believes in happily ever after. In this segment, everything Despereaux has believed in comes crashing down on this gentle soul, and he feels defeated after learning that there really is no knight in shining armor.

MS. TANTELLO: What just happened?

DERRICK: He's given up.

MARA: He's sayin' like there ain't no hope.

MS. TANTELLO: Okay, so Derrick and Mara are saying that now that he's realized there really is no knight in shining armor, and there's really no happily after, he might as well give up because there is no hope. His dreams are being crashed. Anybody agree with that?

Notice that the students are on the right track, and this would have been a great opportunity to turn back to the students and ask a Follow-Up Query such as "Okay, so Derrick says that he's given up and Mara adds that he's saying there isn't any hope, so who can explain why he's feeling this way?" Instead, the teacher provides the elaboration and connections for them.

## Experiencing Progress

### Transcript Example 4: Encouraging Student Responses

As the year progressed, Ms. Tantello became more skilled at asking Follow-Up Queries that encouraged students to carry the cognitive load and build on others' responses; however, in the early stages of this progress, many students were stuck in the "I agree" or "I'd like to add on" stage without really adding anything to the discussion. In the following excerpt, students are reading a passage from *Ninth Ward* (Rhodes, 2010), a fascinating novel about a young girl named Lanesha who has the power to see the dead, and her grandmother, Mama Ya-Ya, who has visions. The story follows Lanesha's and the town's struggles as they battle Hurricane Katrina. In this segment, Mama Ya-Ya is having visions about the danger coming to their town. Although she "sees" the storms, there is far more to her visions than just the impending storm. She "sees" the rain, the sun, happy people, but also everything going black. Usually, Mama Ya-Ya is able to interpret the meanings of her visions, but this time, the meaning is unclear, and it scares her. Ms. Tantello is working hard to encourage students to build on others' responses, but she can't seem to move beyond the initial stage of "I agree/I disagree."

Ms. Tantello: What did we learn in this section?

Jalil: Mama Ya-Ya is having dreams about the storm.

Seira: I agree with Jalil. It's like about Mama Ya-Ya's dreams and the storms that are coming.

Jaymir: Oh, um, and I want to add on to what Seira said 'cause like the weather people were saying it was going to be a really bad storm, and, so um, her dreams are like saying the same thing.

In this example, students quickly became stuck in the "I agree" and "I want to add on" pattern. Although talk stems such as these are something teachers and students often use when engaging in discussion, and can be very useful, sometimes, as in this case, students get stuck in the stem and don't address the content. It is important when using stems to remind students that the stem has a purpose, and it's to serve as a vehicle for the comment that follows it. The focus should be on what comes after the stem and not the stem itself.

Notice that students are working only with the idea in the first line, that the dreams are about storms, and just restating that point. They aren't dealing with the important idea that Lanesha is afraid because Mama Ya-Ya isn't able to understand her dreams. It would have been a good idea to step in after the initial comment, to encourage students to focus on the deeper ideas. However, Ms. Tantello does step in after the third comment, taking an opportunity to point out the purpose of using stems and then turning students back to the text.

Ms. Tantello: Okay, I see that you've picked up on the idea that part of her dream is about a storm, and I like that you are commenting on other students' comments, but remember it's not only about using the talk stems. What's important is what comes after the stem. If you are going to agree or add to a comment, include evidence or an explanation for why you are agreeing or what you want to add. You're all talking about what Mama Ya-Ya's dreams are about, but is that all there is to this section? Let's reread and think about it. (Student rereads.)

Now, what's the big deal with Mama Ya-Ya's dreams?

Lauren: Oh, okay, so, um, that, um Lanesha is kinda afraid of Mama Ya-Ya's dreams.

Ms. Tantello: Okay, Lauren brings up a good point. But why is Lanesha afraid?

Notice that by addressing the "I agree" pattern, and her decision to revisit the text, Ms. Tantello was able to move students beyond the idea that Mama Ya-Ya's dreams were only about the storm. Ms. Tantello also reminds students that unless the talk stem is followed by important content, it isn't really productive. Notice also that

Ms. Tantello then pushes students to dig deeper about Lanesha's fears by marking an important idea and then turning back to students with the following, "Okay, Lauren brings up a good point. But why is Lanesha afraid?"

## Transcript Example 5: Teacher and Student Roles in More Productive Discussion

By the end of the year, Ms. Tantello was able to make better use of student responses and spontaneously turn back to students and design Follow-Up Queries that allowed students to do the work and move the discussion forward. Note also the growth shown by the students in Ms. Tantello's class. They were building on other students' responses and challenging their peers' comments in meaningful ways.

The following excerpt is from a class discussion of a segment from *Charlotte's Web* (White, 1952). In the text, Charlotte and Wilbur are having a pleasant conversation about where Wilbur would like to be that evening when the lamb interrupts and hurts Wilbur's feelings by telling him that he is the "smelliest creature in the place." Although one student recognized that one of the animals hurt Wilbur's feelings, there was a misunderstanding as to which animal actually made the hurtful comment.

MS. TANTELLO: So what just happened?

KIMBERLYN: Wilbur got interrupted.

MS. TANTELLO: Can anyone take that idea further?

KENDALL: Wilbur got interrupted and then started crying 'cause he felt bad.

MS. TANTELLO: Why was he crying?

DEVONTE: 'Cause he got interrupted.

MARIAH: I'd like to build on Kendall's idea 'cause he was crying 'cause he felt bad 'cause Charlotte said he was the worst smelling in the barn.

JAMIR: I respect your answer but I'm not sure it's right. I don't think Charlotte said it. They just became friends, and that comment would ruin their friendship, so I think it was someone else, but I don't remember who.

MS. TANTELLO: That's okay, go back and see who it was.

JAMIR: I think it was, it says it was the lamb that said Wilbur was the smelliest creature in the barn.

MS. TANTELLO: (*"air high-five" to Jamir*) I love how you went back in the book and read the quote that lets us know who it was that said it.

Notice that Ms. Tantello used both turning back to students and turning back to the text in order to prompt students to explain why Wilbur was crying and to clear up the misconception about which character caused Wilbur to cry. It also was clear that students were now understanding the purpose of the Discussion Moves and talk stems and the role they play in QtA discussions. They understood that responding to QtA Queries provided them with opportunities to work with the ideas in the text in order to make sense of what they were reading.

## Transcript Example 6: Class Discussion at the End of the Year

In order to better capture Ms. Tantello's growth throughout the year, we thought it would be helpful to provide a longer sequence of excerpts from discussions of a novel students read at the end of the year. *My Father's Dragon* (Gannett, 1948) is a captivating story of a young boy who takes it upon himself to travel to an island to save a baby dragon who is being selfishly used by the inhabitants to carry their goods across the river. Notice how Ms. Tantello skillfully incorporates the various Discussion Moves in order to provide students with opportunities to build meaning and keep the talk productive.

Prior to the parts of the text in the excerpts provided below, students already have learned from the boy narrating the story that his father befriended an alley cat, much to the chagrin of his mother, who threw the cat out of their house. At this point in the story, the cat is telling the boy about Wild Island, a place he discovered on his travels.

Excerpt 1

"Wild Island is practically cut in two by a very wide and muddy river," continued the cat. "This river begins near one end of the island and flows into the ocean at the other. Now the animals there are very lazy, and they used to hate having to go all the way around the beginning of this river to get to the other side of the island. It made visiting inconvenient and mail deliveries slow, particularly during the Christmas rush. Crocodiles could have carried passengers and mail across the river, but crocodiles are very moody, and not the least bit dependable, and are always looking for something to eat. They don't care if the animals have to walk around the river, so that's just what the animals did for many years."

MS. TANTELLO: So what did we learn in this section?

ANTONIO: The, um, the cat is telling him about Wild Island and the animals that, like, that like, they're lazy.

MS. TANTELLO: Okay, and what does being lazy have to do with the island?

Ms. Tantello recognizes that Antonio brought up an important point, that the animals are lazy, but there's more to it than that. The animals being lazy creates a problem, so she turned back to the students in order for them to make that connection.

RICO: It's a problem 'cause, like, there's like, something weird about like how the island is made.

MS. TANTELLO: What about the island? Go back to the text and explain what you mean.

Rico is on the right track but needs to clarify his thinking that there is something weird about the island, so Ms. Tantello suggested that he turn back to the text to explain what he means.

RICO: Okay, so it says "Now the animals there are very lazy, and they used to hate having to go all the way around the beginning of this river to get to the other side of the island."

MS. TANTELLO: Yes, that's exactly what the text says. Can someone put that information in your own words?

Ms. Tantello used the "go to" Query for whenever students restate the exact language in the text and turned back to the students to put the information in their own words.

BROOKLYN: Yeah, so, there's this big river that they have to go around to get to the other side, and um, but they're too lazy, so they don't want to like, so they're so lazy that they don't, like, they don't want to walk all the way around, so it's like a problem being lazy.

MS. TANTELLO: Okay, so Brooklyn explained that because they have to walk around the river to get to the other side, being lazy is a problem. Did we find out anything else in this section?

Ms. Tantello marked the important idea students have established but now wants them to turn their attention to another important idea, so she turned back to the students with a Follow-Up Query.

JAZIR: Yeah, the crocodiles have a attitude problem. (*Other students laugh.*)

MS. TANTELLO: Okay, so Jazir says the crocodiles have an attitude problem. Can someone explain why he thinks that?

In great kid language, Jazir hits on the targeted topic, so Ms. Tantello turns back to students to allow them to elaborate and explain his comment.

TRACEY: Yeah, like if they wanted, they could like carry everyone across the river but they don't want to.

JAZIR: Yeah, and I want to add on to what Tracey said. 'Cause like the reason that um, like the reason they won't do it is 'cause it says, it says that they don't care like they don't care if um if um the other animals have to walk around. 'Cause that's what make me say they got a attitude problem. That's like wrong. They could help, but like they don't care.

MS. TANTELLO: Okay, thank you, Jazir, for explaining your thinking. I like your description that they have an attitude problem and could help but don't, simply because they don't want to. So, we dealt with a lot in this section, so before we move on, can someone quickly recap the important points we discussed?

Ms. Tantello recognized that there was a lot of discussion in this exchange and wants to make sure students recognize the important meaning constructed, so she asked students for a recap of those ideas.

MELANI: So, like there's this island called Wild Island, and like the animals are lazy and um, and ah, don't want to walk around the river.

KATIE: And so I want to add on to what Melani said, 'cause like the crocodiles could help, but um, but they don't care, so like, they don't help.

MS. TANTELLO: Okay, I think you two did a nice job of recapping the important ideas in that section, so let's move on and see what happens next.

## Excerpt 2

"But what does all this have to do with airplanes?" asked my father, who thought the cat was taking an awfully long time to explain.

"Be patient, Elmer," said the cat, and she went on with the story. "One day about four months before I arrived on Wild Island a baby dragon fell from a low-flying cloud onto the bank of the river. He was too young to fly very well, and besides, he had bruised one wing quite badly, so he couldn't get back to his cloud. The animals found him soon afterwards and everybody said, 'Why, this is just exactly what we've needed all these years!' They tied a big rope around his neck and waited for the wing to get well. This was going to end all their crossing-the-river troubles."

MS. TANTELLO: Now what did we find out?

SHAWR: A baby dragon fell onto the island.

DRAVON: I agree with Shawr that like a dragon fell on the island, and like I want to add something. Like after it fell, and like the animals said it was going to solve all their problems.

MS. TANTELLO: Hmm, it's going to solve their problems. How is the dragon going to solve their problems?

This part is a bit tricky as students must draw an inference as to how the dragon is going to solve their problems, but the first two students have not yet done so. Ms. Tantello asked a Follow-Up Query that pushed students to expand on the thinking of the first two students and provide the explanation.

SHAYLA: It says, "This was going to end all their crossing-the-river troubles."

Ms. TANTELLO: So what was going to end all their crossing-the-river troubles?

SEIRA: The dragon that fell.

Ms. TANTELLO: How can that be? Can someone make the connection for us? Based on what we know about the island and the animals on it, how can the dragon put an end to their crossing-the-river troubles?

LASHAWN: Aww, man, are they gonna fly on the baby dragon to get across the river?

Students are in the right space but are not quite making the connection between the baby dragon and solving the island's problems, so Ms. Tantello asked another Follow-Up Query that provided them with the opportunity to think specifically about that connection. The student, LaShawn, responded, "Aww, man, are they gonna fly on the baby dragon to get across the river?" His genuine reaction to the realization that the baby dragon probably is going to be used to carry everyone across the river is priceless!

Ms. TANTELLO: So LaShawn thinks that they are going to use the dragon as their means to get across the river. What do the rest of you think about that idea?

BRAYA: I agree with LaShawn. 'Cause like dragons can fly so like that baby gonna have to fly them across the river.

Ms. TANTELLO: Okay, so let's read on to see if we are right.

As you can see by the transcript excerpts, Ms. Tantello was able to use the various Discussion Moves in order to provide students with the opportunity to build meaning and draw connections across the ideas, but it is a process that takes time. Ms. Tantello's growth was a result of careful planning and regular reflection on her QtA lessons.

What was most impressive about Ms. Tantello's growth was how much the students picked up on her new style of teaching. At the end of the year, Ms. Tantello asked her students to read to a first-grade classroom. When the students returned to the classroom, one student told Ms. Tantello that she asked her first-grade partner, "What just happened?"; "What did you learn?" She told Ms. Tantello that she also asked her partner to think about what she read from the book to find her evidence while answering her QtA questions. She said, "I was being a teacher just like you, and I wanted her to understand the story." Ms. Tantello said, "I laughed and smiled so big; it was a proud teacher moment."

## ENDING NOTES

- Becoming more comfortable with and more skilled at facilitating QtA discussions is a process that takes time.

- A common pattern we see when teachers are new to the QtA planning process is designing Initiating Queries that tend to be too leading.

- Other common patterns we see when teachers are new to facilitating QtA discussions include providing too much information, collecting comments, and the "helpful teacher syndrome."

- As teachers progress, they become more skilled at asking Follow-Up Queries that encourage students to carry the cognitive load and build on others' responses.

- As students gain more experience participating in QtA discussions, they understand the purpose of the Queries and Discussion Moves and use both by directly questioning their peers and elaborating on their responses.

# CHAPTER 12

# Students Take the Wheel

We've talked about the important role QtA instruction plays in laying the foundation for students to successfully comprehend a text in teacher-led, whole-class instruction. It is, however, essential to move whole-class QtA to independent QtA. In fact, the ultimate goal of engaging in QtA is that students transfer what they have learned about building meaning when engaging with text during teacher-led whole-class QtA lessons to their independent reading. Easier said than done! There is evidence reaching back to Thorndike (Thorndike & Woodworth, 1901) that shows clearly that *transfer does not just happen, rather one must teach for transfer* (Bransford, Brown, & Cocking, 2000).

Teachers have asked whether there is a process for teaching for transfer: How does it work? Are there specific steps involved in making it happen? How to begin? In this chapter we will describe a process to move from whole-class, teacher-led QtA to independent QtA.

## Beginning a Process for Transferring QtA Responsibility to Students

The process for moving students to independence can begin once teachers and students have established a successful whole-class routine. Typically we have seen teachers have success with this process after having conducted whole-class QtA over several months of the school year. The process begins with moving some of the responsibility for QtA components to students through a systematic gradual release approach. To initiate our discussion of the transfer process, we present in Table 12.1 an overview of steps in gradually releasing responsibility to student control.

As shown in the table, in Teacher-Led Whole-Class Instruction, the original and initial form of QtA, it is the teacher's responsibility to prepare the lesson by identifying text segments, developing Queries, and initiating discussion through Queries. Students are expected to be active participants, however, even posing their

**TABLE 12.1.** Releases of Responsibilities from Teacher to Students

| Teacher responsibilities | Student responsibilities |
|---|---|
| **Teacher-Led Whole-Class QtA** | |
| • Identifies segments. | • Participates in lesson. |
| • Prepares Queries and follow-ups. | • Collaborates with and responds to classmates. |
| • Poses Queries and follow-ups. | |
| • Conducts interspersed discussion. | |
| **Release 1** | |
| • Identifies segments. | • Participates in lesson. |
| • Prepares Queries and follow-ups. | • Collaborates with and responds to classmates. |
| • Poses Queries and follow-ups. | • **Conducts interspersed discussion.** |
| **Release 2** | |
| • Identifies segments. | • Participates in lesson. |
| • Prepares Queries and follow-ups. | • Collaborates and responds to classmates. |
| | • **Poses Queries and follow-ups.** |
| | • **Conducts interspersed discussion.** |

*Note.* Released components are shown in **bold.**

own questions as needed to build their understanding. The transfer process begins in Release 1, where one component of QtA, the responsibility for Interspersed Discussion, is released to students. In Release 2, the students now pose the Queries in addition to managing Interspersed Discussion. Thus the teacher prepares the lesson and the students conduct the lesson. Ideally, a text for early forays into this process would be fairly brief, with accessible content that has clear opportunities for interactive discussion.

Releases 1 and 2 employ small groups of students conducting their lesson responsibilities. If there is already a small-group structure in place in the classroom, that structure can be adapted for QtA lessons. If you have not worked with small groups before, you will need some time to plan the assignment of students to groups and develop a clear set of instructions about how the groups will conduct their part of the QtA lesson. Because responsibility is released to groups for only portions of the lesson at this point, monitoring group success should be relatively manageable. There is a wealth of resources available online about myriad aspects of organizing and conducting small groups. Resources that may be relevant for using small groups with QtA include the following:

- *www.teachthought.com/pedagogy/use-flexible-grouping-classroom*
  This site includes group warm-ups to get students used to working in groups.

- *www.insidehighered.com/advice/2018/12/11/how-effectively-organize-small-groups-classes-opinion*

    This site mentions that "the most common mistake in organizing small-group work is to give students a topic and simply ask them to discuss it. That leaves students confused about what they are supposed to do." This issue should not arise with QtA, as groups are being tasked with responding to posed Queries.

Whether adapting or creating small-group structures, identifying students to take on the roles of Facilitator and Reporter is important. The Facilitator asks the Queries and keeps the interspersed discussion moving along. The Reporter provides comments about his or her group's discussion when reporting back to the whole class at the end of the group sessions.

## Release Step 1: Interspersed Discussion Released to Small Groups

For this initial release step, the teacher plans the text with segments, Queries, and Follow-Up Queries as with any QtA lesson and then conducts the lesson as follows:

- Assemble students into their small groups and explain the responsibility of the Facilitator and Reporter in each group.

- Provide each group facilitator with a copy of the segmented text. The other students should have a copy of the text without segments identified.

- After students are in their groups, the teacher pauses at the first stopping point and asks the Query. Students respond to the Query within their groups. Each group's facilitator conducts the discussion as the students in each group respond to the issue or topic targeted by the Query.

- The teacher circulates, getting a sense of the groups' discussion and poses follow-ups as appropriate either to a group or to the entire class.

- After a short time, each group's Reporter provides short comments about the group's responses to the whole class. The teacher tells the reporting students that they should give a kind of recap as is often done within QtA discussions to explain what their group's discussion was about.

- If needed, teacher and students can then pose additional Follow-Up Queries as appropriate to the whole class.

If groups are operating well, continue the procedure with the teacher posing Queries at selected stopping points and students discussing within their groups until the text is complete. But if needed, or if time becomes an issue, conduct the remainder of the lesson with the whole class. In either case after the text is read, guide some concluding discussion as appropriate to the understanding students have built in their groups.

### Release Step 2: Teacher-Prepared Queries and Interspersed Discussion Released to Small Groups

For this step, the lesson takes place entirely within the small groups, using teacher-prepared segments and Queries. The lesson proceeds as follows:

- Assemble students into their small groups and remind them of the responsibility of the Facilitator and Reporter in each group.

- Provide each group Facilitator with a copy of the segmented text and Queries, and other students with a copy of the text without segments or Queries identified.

- Each group reads the text as in a regular QtA lesson, with the Facilitator stopping the group at each stopping point.

- At each stopping point, the Facilitator poses the Query and students respond within their groups.

- While students are discussing in their groups, listen in on their conversations and encourage them to ask Follow-Up Queries and work together to develop meaning. The process can continue for the entire text if groups are operating well and discussions are meaningful.

- When the groups have completed their discussions of the text, bring the groups together to give the Reporters an opportunity to share what they discussed in their groups.

- As in Release 1, teacher and students can then engage in final discussion to conclude the lesson.


## Moving toward Independence

To this point we have focused on students assuming responsibility for conducting discussions on their own, in small groups, using the teacher's planned segments and Queries. The last two elements of the process toward independence are the requirements to identify segments and provide Queries. We recommend that the activity structure for these two components be teacher-led whole class.

Helping students decide where to stop reading in a text is key to enabling them to build successful comprehension skills. This is because comprehension, as we have discussed in earlier chapters, is built as the reader moves through a text, deciding what is important and how to connect important information to subsequent text to make sense of a text as a whole.

What about Queries? In helping students to use QtA processes on their own, is it important to teach them to develop Queries? Not exactly. The Query is a vehicle that the teacher uses to guide students to examine ideas and information in a text. As we discussed in Chapter 5, the purpose of Queries comes down to two categories: to prompt students to figure out what a text segment is about, and to connect ideas. As far as students are concerned, the goal is for them to enact the purposes underlying Queries; that is, to figure out what a text segment is about and to connect ideas across segments.

So in the next sections we focus on guiding students to identify the text information needed to help build comprehension, using the Query in a kind of supporting role. That is, students have become accustomed to responding to Queries, so those still may be helpful in communicating to students what they need to do on their own. But the goal is not for them to become expert Query-makers. Rather, having students engage with identifying specific Queries for specific texts serves as an underpinning for students to deal with text content in ways that promote attending to important ideas and establishing connections between them. Identifying Queries can function mostly through students' selecting Queries from the QtA Queries by Category handout (Table 12.2). But students are also welcome to create their own wording if that seems useful in directing them to what they need to understand.

If you have not shared with students the idea that Queries have two main purposes, we suggest that you do so. Perhaps tell students that a teacher asks Queries in different ways to help students think about different things in a text, but that the main purpose of Queries is nearly always to prompt them to pay attention to the important information in a section of text or to connect ideas from segment to segment. This would be a good time to provide each student a QtA Queries handout (Table 12.2) and a Rescue Routine handout (Table 12.3). (Copies of these handouts formatted for ease in making multiple copies for the classroom appear on the book's companion website;

**TABLE 12.2.** QtA Queries by Category

| Category | Queries |
|---|---|
| To figure out what the segment is about | "What's this all about?" |
| | "What's going on in this section?" |
| | "What's the author talking about?" |
| | "What did we learn in this part?" |
| To make connections | "How does this connect with what I already read about this?" |
| | "How does this new information fit with what we already know?" |
| | "How does this new information help me better understand X?" |
| | "Does this make sense with what happened before?" |

**TABLE 12.3.** Rescue Routine

---

What to do when I don't understand:

- Read the text again.

- Read a few sentences in the paragraph that follows the confusing segment. Does it help you understand the first part?

- Get help from . . . [a classmate/the teacher]

---

see the box at the end of the table of contents.) On the Queries handout point out how the sample Queries incorporate the two purposes. On the Rescue Routine handout comment that sometimes figuring out the important information in a text is difficult because the text is confusing or your mind wanders away from the text for a few seconds. Tell students that the Rescue Routine handout lists actions they can take that might help when they are confused.

Then remind students that the whole reason for learning to participate in QtA is to improve their ability to build comprehension as they read independently. Even though you have been doing that mostly as a whole class, the reason behind QtA is to use what they have learned about reading from QtA lessons as they read on their own. Remind them that in their groups they have run the discussion on their own, and that next you will do some activities to guide them to deal with Queries and stopping points on their own as well. The following sections on identifying Queries and segmenting the text are the precursor supports for the last section of this chapter—individual QtA.

## Queries Released to Students

QtA asks students to use language to express ideas that are represented in print. Print is not alive until the ideas in print become represented by language—oral or written—or conscious thought. We ask students to create or select Queries for a given text as part of a transition to asking and responding to their own Queries in the course of reading.

At this point in our transition process, keep in mind that students are far from blank slates about Queries, as our process specifies that students need to have been engaged with QtA for at least a number of months in teacher-led whole-class instruction and then in small-group structures, as we have described at the beginning of this chapter. Thus students come to the task with a lot of knowledge about how Queries work.

For this step, plan text segments as you usually would and plan Queries to use as needed if students falter. This lesson is conducted in whole-class format. As usual, students have the text in front of them with no segments identified, and a copy of the Queries handout (Table 12.2). The lesson proceeds as follows:

- Read the first planned segment and then say something like "This is a good place to stop and ask a Query."
- Ask students, "Why do you think this is a good place to stop?"
- After students have provided their reasons for stopping, ask, "What Query could you ask to get at that information?" Asking this Query will reinforce for students that there are valid reasons for stopping points and will discourage them from random decisions.

Continue with the rest of the text, reading each segment, and stopping and asking students to provide the key information for that segment and any connections that need to be made. You might share the Query you had prepared for each segment if it seems to support students' transition to processing text on their own.

## Segmenting Text Released to Students

For this activity, plan text segments and Queries as you usually would so you have them available if you need to refer to them during the discussion of students' stopping points. Provide each student with a copy of the text to be read, with no stops marked. Ask them to have their QtA Queries handout available as well. The lesson proceeds as follows:

- Explain to students that you are going to begin by reading the text aloud as they follow along, and they are to raise their hand when they think it's a good place to stop and talk about what's going on.
- Read the text, and as you see several hands raised, pause. If a majority of the class has not indicated a stop, you might say that it is fine if not everyone agrees on the same place, but let's see why some people wanted to stop.
- Ask why they wanted to stop. If students' responses capture the essential content of the segment, acknowledge that, perhaps by telling them how it matches what you identified as the important information—some revoicing may be useful here. You also might share which Query you might have used to prompt them to contribute that information.
- If their responses are not on target, you could model your thinking or offer your stopping point and the Query you would have used and guide them to attend to the text segment's key information.
- It might also be helpful to occasionally ask students if there were any places in the text where they thought the Rescue Routine might have been useful. You might even want to take an opportunity to stop at a place of potential confusion,

identify it as such, and ask students what they could do to help clear up the confusion.

Proceed with the rest of the text this way, asking students where they might stop and why. At some points it might be helpful to ask what the important information is that they need to pay attention to and if there is anything that needs to be connected. If students' responses imply, but do not state, connections, you might revoice to make the connection explicit (e.g., "so you are connecting this with what she seemed to be planning earlier . . . ").

# Individual QtA

Once students have found success with small-group QtA and the segment and Query release work described above, the next step is to transition the work to their independent reading. We suggest that you begin the process with students reading independently during class to provide "at-elbow" support.

## Independent QtA in the Classroom

A logical place to start is to build on the work students did in the previous activity, when they stopped at places they wanted to query and shared their reasons for those stopping points. They can follow the same format when reading independently, proceeding as follows:

- Assign a portion of text for students to read independently.
- In addition to the text, each student should have available a QtA Queries handout (Table 12.2) and a Rescue Routine handout (Table 12.3).
- Provide students with Post-It notes and tell them to stop at places in the text where they are working to figure out what's going on or trying to make connections.
- When they encounter such places, tell them to jot down a Query they might want to ask themselves or to jot down what was important or confusing that led them to choose the stopping point. The key is taking on responsibility for working through the ideas in the text. Whether students direct that process for themselves by using a Query or by describing what's important as they read is not the issue.
- Of course a student's response to a portion of text may be "I'm confused"; "This makes no sense." Remind them that if that occurs, they can turn to the Rescue Routine discussed earlier.

As students are working, circulate and take note of where they stopped and the key text information they have noted or Queries they have selected. Use this information as a way to formatively assess their understanding of the text. Note where students have similar stopping points but also identify "outliers" that might indicate potential obstacles. Give students a designated amount of time, say 15–20 minutes, to work through the text and identify places where they would stop. Then, bring students together and begin by asking a student to share a stopping point. You might ask certain students ahead of time to share a particular stopping point, a Query, or information identified as important, especially if you notice that it is a place that appeared on a number of Post-Its.

Since students have identified their own stopping points and some may have created their own Queries, allow them to lead the discussion and encourage them to ask Follow-Up Queries. Depending on the extent to which you have introduced QtA terminology in your classroom, the term Follow-Up Queries may or may not be familiar to students, and it need not be. The point is to encourage students to engage in follow-up questioning as needed to clarify or connect information or fill out their understanding. Interject when necessary, as it keeps the discussion focused and continues to serve as a model for students. Encourage students to share why they stopped at particular places in the text. This "thinking aloud" serves as a student model for others who might struggle to identify places to stop.

Something to consider when moving students to engage in QtA work independently is whether they might have difficulty getting through the words of the text on their own. Students who struggle with decoding or EL students might need additional support when reading independently. One option is to have students listen to that segment of the text on tape, as a number of reading programs provide books on tape, and others can be found on various Internet sites. If a particular text is not available on a site, another option is to record the section of the text they will be reading. In any of these options, it is important that students have access to the text and follow along with the recording. If either of those is not an option, another alternative is to sit with students in small groups and read the text while allowing time for them to identify stopping points. Whichever method you choose, the goal remains the same. You want students to transfer what they learned about constructing meaning during their whole-class QtA discussions to their independent reading.

## Independence: Homework

Now that students have engaged in small-group and independent QtA discussions during class with teacher support, a logical next step is to provide them with opportunities to engage in QtA work during homework. We suggest two ways to move students to this step.

### Option 1

The first option is to assign a section of text and provide students with stopping points and Queries for part of that section. Tell students that as they read that section for homework, they should jot notes in response to the Queries. Then for the rest of the section, they should identify stopping points, and at each stop explain why they would stop or provide a Query they would ask. The initial stopping points and Queries serve as a model to support students when identifying their own places to stop. For example, if working with "The Bridge on the River Clarinette," your first "model" stopping point might be after the town's problem is identified and your accompanying Query, "What have we learned so far?," targets that issue.

To help students understand what they should do for each of their stopping points, explain to them that good readers ask themselves questions as they read, but the point of those questions is to help direct their attention to important information or recognize what they need to be on the lookout for. For example, if a new character suddenly starts speaking in a text, they might ask themselves, "Who is this person?," but the point would be alerting themselves to be on the lookout for clues to the character's identity. Therefore, if students choose to frame Queries, we want them to understand that the Query is a means to help direct their understanding; it is not an end point. To support students to complete the QtA homework task, remind them to have their QtA Queries handout (Table 12.2) and their Rescue Routine handout (Table 12.3) close by.

Begin the next day by addressing your model stopping points and Queries first. For example, referencing again "The Bridge on the River Clarinette," you would begin with your Query, "What have we learned so far?" Once you have worked through the model stopping points and Queries, move to student-initiated stopping points. Allow students to take the lead when discussing their stopping points. If students contribute Queries, ask how they'd respond to the Query or simply why they chose to stop there. Queries should be part of the discussion only to the extent that their role is useful in guiding meaning-building. Encourage students to ask Follow-Up Queries as the discussions at each stopping point unfold. Having students take the lead allows them to take ownership of their learning.

## Option 2

The second option is for students who no longer need the teacher model for support. Assign students the text and have them identify stopping points without providing the model for the first part of the text. As with Option 1, for each stopping point they select, they should also note their reasons for stopping or design a Query if useful for guiding their understanding. It still would be a good idea to have students use the Queries handout as they work through the text for homework. Begin the next day by asking students to share their stopping points and reasoning. As was the case with Option 1, allow students to take the lead and encourage them to ask Follow-Up Queries.

## QtA with Novels

Another question we often hear from teachers is "How does QtA work with novels?" We recognize that if you engage students in whole-class discussions for entire novels, you won't get anything else done during your English/Language Arts block, so we suggest incorporating the small-group and independent options described above.

Before moving students to small-group and independent work with novels, we suggest that you engage them in a whole-class QtA discussion of the first section of the novel. Depending upon the length of the novel and chapters, you might choose to design Queries for the entire first chapter or just part of the chapter and engage students in a whole-class discussion. It is important that students develop a basic understanding of the characters and events that initiate the story before turning the reins over to them. We suggest that you follow the gradual release of moving from small-group QtA to in-class independent QtA, and finally, to independent QtA for homework. Engaging students in the small-group work first allows you to monitor how much of the text they can handle independently and provides information about whether they are developing an understanding of the characters and what is happening in the text.

As we have emphasized in this chapter, our goal is for students to transfer what they learn about constructing meaning during whole-class QtA discussions to their independent reading. In this chapter, we described a gradual release model to support that process. However, we don't want you to think that once you've taken students through the process they have to engage in only independent QtA. Once students have engaged in the various steps in the gradual release process, we suggest that you continue to vary the routine in order to keep students engaged and excited about texts and the discussions around them. It can be particularly beneficial to conduct a group discussion, for example, around some key point in a novel that has potential to be difficult to understand or where the turn of events is surprising. Such discussions not only support comprehension but also support students' developing enjoyment in reading. Teachers have told us that after students are working successfully in small groups, and even when they have moved to independent work, they sometimes ask to occasionally have whole-class reading and discussion, like in the "old times," "like we used to do."

## ENDING NOTES

- It is essential that students are able to transfer what they have learned about building meaning through whole-class QtA to independent reading.

- Research has made clear that transfer does not just happen, but it must be intentionally developed.

- After a teacher and students have become successful engaging in QtA through whole-class teacher-led instruction, there is a set of steps that provide systematic gradual release from teacher-led instruction to students' independent reading and comprehension.

- The process begins with moving to small-group instruction. If there is not an ongoing system for small-group instruction, it is important to set one up carefully prior to engaging in small-group QtA.

- For the first step in the gradual release of responsibility, arrange students in small groups, appointing a Facilitator and a Reporter, and begin reading the text as usual. Ask the Query planned for the first stopping point, but rather than discussing with the whole class, have students discuss with their small groups. Continue with subsequent text segments and conclude with a whole-class discussion in which the Reporters recap their groups' discussions.

- For the next release step, provide each group Facilitator with a copy of the text that includes stopping points, Queries, and Follow-Up Queries. The group reads the text on its own, as in a regular QtA lesson, and Facilitators are responsible for asking the Queries at the stopping points and conducting discussion.

- Moving toward greater independence, begin as in a whole-class lesson, but at each stopping point ask students to decide why it is a good place to stop and what Query might be useful.

- For the next step, again begin as in a whole-class lesson, but ask students to raise their hands when they think it is a good stopping point. Ask why it was a good place to stop and possibly what Query might be useful there.

- The next transition is to students' independent reading, beginning with "at-elbow" support. Here assign students to read a text in class independently and indicate stopping points and Queries as you circulate and offer support as requested.

- The final options in the transition process are for students to use QtA in independent reading that they do for homework. For an assigned text, students should identify stopping points and jot notes about the important information in that section of text. This step can begin with teacher-provided stopping points and Queries for a portion of the text.

- QtA can be used with novels. It is best to begin by engaging students in a whole-class QtA discussion of the first section of the novel. Then you can follow the gradual release from small-group QtA to in-class independent QtA, and finally, to independent QtA for homework for the rest of the book.

- It is important to help students keep in mind that the purpose of engaging in QtA, whether together or on their own, is to build understanding from what they read by identifying important information and making connections.

# Appendix

## Lesson Texts from Chapters 4 and 6

# The Bridge on the River Clarinette

## by Pierre Gamarra

*Translated from the French by Paulette Henderson*

The inhabitants of the little town of Framboisy-sur-Clarinette were worried. The bridge that spanned the River Clarinette was about to collapse. And if the bridge did collapse, the citizens of Framboisy would lose touch with the rest of France. There would be no more trade, no more traffic, no more tourists.

It was therefore necessary to reconstruct the bridge. But Framboisy was poor, and the town council was deeply troubled.

Just the other morning—on Framboisy's large central plaza—Monsieur Leopold, the owner of the Green Swan Inn, greeted Madame Barbette, the grocer. "How are things with you this morning, Madame Barbette?"

"Very bad, Monsieur Leopold. Business is falling off. I did not sell more than one package of macaroni last week. People just don't have money anymore."

Monsieur Leopold sighed. "As for me, I don't have customers either. The tourists don't dare cross the bridge nowadays."

"Did it split last night?"

"Yes, it did; I heard it. It's a disgrace. It could cave in at any moment."

"What's to become of us? What we need is a new bridge."

At that moment Monsieur Leopold and Madame Barbette saw the mayor and the teacher coming out of the town hall.

"Well, well, gentlemen," said Monsieur Leopold, "how are town matters going? Are we going to rebuild the bridge?"

The mayor shook his head with infinite sadness. "The council has examined various bridge plans. But it's an outrageously expensive undertaking. We'll never be able to pay for it."

"Nevertheless, you must make a decision," insisted Madame Barbette, nearly stabbing the mayor with her long, pointed nose. "Without a bridge we're ruined. No one dares to venture across our dilapidated old bridge."

The teacher shaded his eyes and gazed in the direction of the bridge. "Someone is coming!" he called.

" Stranger! Impossible! He wasn't afraid to cross," cried Monsieur Leopold.

"Amazing!" agreed the teacher. "But what an odd sort of person, all dressed in red and black and hopping from side to side. Look at his strange, uncanny smile, and the glint in his eyes."

The stranger approached the group and bowed to each of the citizens with great respect. His eyes glowed like deep red rubies. "I am very honored," he said, "to be visiting the distinguished inhabitants of Framboisy-sur-Clarinette."

"Monsieur is travelling?" the innkeeper asked politely.

"I'm going about the land on business."

"Monsieur is a businessman, then?" queried the teacher.

"Yes, I buy and I sell."

"And what is it that you sell?"

"Anything and everything."

"Anything and everything?"

"Yes, anything at all. Sausages, cars, houses, shirts, bridges . . ."

The mayor stepped forward. "Did you say bridges? You sell bridges?"

"But of course. Bridges. All sorts of bridges. Big ones, small ones, medium-sized ones. Made of wood, iron, even concrete."

The mayor scratched his head. "It just so happens that, at this time, we are in need of a bridge. A solid bridge with two or three arches."

"Easy!" said the stranger with a soft little laugh.

"And what is the price of a bridge?" demanded Madame Barbette defiantly.

"Nothing at all."

The four inhabitants of Framboisy jumped for joy, but the teacher said, "that can't be true. If you build us a new bridge, certainly you will ask us for something in exchange."

"Almost nothing," said the stranger.

"What would you ask of us?"

"Your words."

To the astonishment of his audience, the stranger explained, "You give me your words, and I will build you a beautiful bridge in five seconds. Note that I am not asking for all your words; I will leave you a few for your daily needs . . . drink, eat, sleep, bread, butter, coffee . . ."

"I don't understand," murmured the teacher. "What are you going to do with our words?"

"That's my business," said the stranger. "Promise that you will give me your words, and I will build you a bridge—a magnificent concrete and steel bridge, guaranteed for ten centuries!"

"It's a bad joke," muttered the mayor. "And furthermore, if you take our words, we shall find it very difficult to converse."

"No, no, no. I will leave you enough to satisfy you. Do you really have to talk so much? I'll leave you the most important words. And you shall have an extraordinary bridge in five seconds."

"So you're a magician, then?" asked the innkeeper.

"I have a very advanced technique at my disposal," the stranger replied modestly.

"We could at least give it a try," said Monsieur Leopold.

"All right," said Madame Barbette. "Let him have our words, and we shall have our bridge."

"I object!" cried the teacher. "We should never give up our words. At any rate, it's a crazy joke. Do you really think that a bridge can be built in five seconds?"

"Let us try, anyway," said the innkeeper.

"You agree, then?" concluded the stranger with a somewhat malicious swiftness.

"I leave you a few words—as I said before: bread, milk, eat, drink, sleep, house, chair—and I build you an extraordinary bridge?"

"Agreed," said the mayor, the innkeeper, and the grocer.

The teacher shook his head in refusal. Too late. The stranger was already turning toward the dilapidated bridge, pointing his index finger. And all of a sudden there arose a beautiful three-arched bridge, silhouetted against the sky.

The mayor nudged the innkeeper and said, "Bread, butter, eat, drink."

The innkeeper looked at him and replied, "Drink, sleep, house, chair."

# Polar Bears, the Giants of the Arctic
## by Nancy Curry

Polar bears, the most powerful carnivores on land, live in the Arctic portions of Norway, Greenland, Russia, the United States (Alaska), and Canada (Manitoba). They can be as tall as 10 feet and weigh over a ton (1,400 pounds). That is equivalent to about ten men. Polar bears are exceedingly dangerous animals as they are predators who are not prey to any other animal. Moreover they have no fear of human beings.

For many thousands of years, polar bears have been important to the indigenous peoples around the Arctic. Most of those people have been called Eskimos, but the term Eskimo includes six groupings of people, each of which has its own culture and language, and they prefer to be known by their own names, such as Inuit and Yupak. Indigenous people still hunt polar bears as they are essential to living at a subsistence level. And, much of a polar bear's remains are used. For example the hide is made into clothing, the meat is eaten, the bones are carved into tools and used to make crafts.

Seals are as important to polar bears as polar bears are to the indigenous people. The bears hunt their favorite food by remaining on sea ice floes for long periods. These huge bears have three characteristics—stealth, patience, and excellent sense of smell—that they put to good use to hunt seals. And seals "help" to the extent that they need to carve out breathing holes in the thick polar ice. A polar bear with its outstanding sense of smell locates a breathing hole and stealthily moves on the ice floe as close to the hole as possible, biding its time until a seal raises its head through the hole for a breath. POW! The bear zooms to the hole and catches his favorite prey. Well, not all the time. Seals are fast and many get away, so the polar bear will have to use its patience and await another opportunity.

When the sea ice melts in the spring, some polar bears go north to find hardened ice, but others go onto land. On land they do not hibernate like other bears, but they do rest and are not very active. During that time, polar bears live off the blubber that their bodies have accumulated from their fat rich diet of seals, and they will scavenge for food. These great animals will eat any vegetation they can find and anything else— including human garbage. They have been seen eating tin cans, broken furniture, batteries and other such debris, as well as left over human garbage.

In late fall before the ice has hardened, in Manitoba, Canada, polar bears begin to congregate near the small town of Churchill, waiting for the sea ice to harden. It has been said that about 1,000 bears may congregate in October and November. It is at that time when visitors go to Churchill to see the bears. Tourist agencies in Churchill, and countries other than Canada that are near the Arctic Ocean, have the expertise and equipment to get tourists close to the bears safely.

The fall is also the time when the hungry bears—whose diet is very reduced during the summer—may wander close to where people live. In the early 2000s Churchill had serious invasions of bears that with their excellent sense of smell found feasts at the town dump. Since people dump garbage close to where they live, the bears wandered near to residential housing. Churchill tried scaring the bears with lights and trucks and noisemakers, but they came back to their feasts.

Eventually officials in Churchill rounded up troublemaker bears and put them in "polar bear jail" until the ice had hardened. To get them back to the ice or far away from town, they tranquilized them and helicoptered them out. But that was only a short-term solution. They tried to secure the dumps by installing fences and light fires to burn the trash, but the bears were stubborn and there are images from videos that show fires burning behind polar bears eating. In 2005, the town opened what became known as the "Alcatraz of garbage," a secure building with concrete floors and bars on windows, where garbage could be securely stored until taken to a place where it could be buried deeply. The following year, there were fewer reports of bears near the town.

On the other side of the Arctic Ocean, some 15 years later, in 2019, several small towns in the Arctic area of Russia declared states of emergency because polar bears had "invaded" their communities. Tass, a Russian news agency, reported that about 50 polar bears, had visited the small town of Belushya Guba. In fact, at any one time there were from six to ten bears partaking of what the dump had to offer. The people in Belushya Guba were on edge, and who wouldn't be. Not only had the bears come near to where people lived, some had actually entered houses and other buildings. There is a photo from a video of a bear walking down a hall in an apartment building and another of a female bear and her two cubs sauntering in the courtyard of a residential area.

Polar bears have come closer to human communities to solve a problem that has arisen because of rapidly melting ice in the Arctic caused by global warming. Melting ice means that there are fewer ice floes near shore where the bears can hunt their food. The bears need to go further out from the shore to find breathing holes or attack seals in the open sea. That can be dangerous for the bears. Although they are mighty swimmers, they are not as fast as their favorite prey. Instead of going out further on the ice floes, some bears have chosen to find food by migrating north where the ice is still hard. That means they have to be on land longer than in the past, but on land they cannot find the prey that are so important for their well-being. This makes for hungry polar bears. So when they encounter the attractive odors from human garbage dumps, they go off to the banquet.

It has been estimated that these magnificent animals have been on this planet from about 400,000 to 600,000 years. Now with global warming, many people are worried that if the ice continues to melt at the present rate, polar bears will become extinct. The hope is that scientists who study global warming and those who study polar bear behavior will provide solutions that the people of the earth will embrace.

## A Donkey for Fifty Cents

### Puerto Rican folktale adapted by Jean Acosta

This is the story of a boy named Pablo who lived in a small village in Puerto Rico. Is it a true story? Who knows! But the people in Puerto Rico have told this tale for many years. Pablo wanted a donkey. He told his parents that if he had a donkey of his own, he could help them out by carrying things from the store and back and forth from his family's fields. They told him he could get a donkey if he paid for it himself.

Since he was just a boy, Pablo did not have much money. He scraped together the few coins he had and went out to look for a donkey. After walking a little ways, Pablo ran into an old man who was leading three donkeys. He called to him, "Kind sir, are you interested in selling one of your donkeys?" The man looked at Pablo and smiled, for he was quite surprised to have a young boy wanting to buy a donkey.

"Now, what are you going to do with a donkey, son?" the man said, with kindness in his eyes.

"I want to have something of my own to take care of," replied Pablo. "And if I have a donkey then I can be of more help to my parents. With a donkey I can carry things so my mother and father don't need to make so many trips to the store and in and out from their fields."

The man was very pleased with Pablo's answer. He liked the idea that a young boy wanted to take care of another creature. And he was very impressed that Pablo wanted to help his parents. So he said to the boy, "Yes, I will sell you a donkey."

Pablo smiled broadly. Then his face changed and he said, "Sir, I have only fifty cents."

The man said, "Well, what luck! That is exactly the price of this donkey" as he pointed to the smallest animal.

Pablo was so excited! He dug the fifty cents out of his pocket, handed it to the man, and took the reins of the donkey. As he walked back home with his donkey, a man called to him from the side of the road, "How much did you pay for that donkey?"

"Fifty cents," he called.

Before he got home, three more people stopped him to ask about the cost of the donkey. "Fifty cents," he said each time.

The next day Pablo was so excited to go out with his new donkey. He asked his mother if he could get anything from the store and she gave him a list. He set out, proudly leading his donkey. And it began to happen again. Everyone kept asking him how much he paid for the donkey. "Fifty cents," he would say, again and again.

Day after day as he walked about with his donkey people kept asking him how much he paid for it. "Fifty cents," he would say, again and again. But he got very tired of this. Then one night an idea crept into his mind.

The next day Pablo ran into the old Town Hall. In the back of the hall stood a marble statue of the town's first mayor, Mateo Bonilla, who everyone in town said had magical powers. Pablo went behind the statue and called out, "Go and tell all the

177

people of the town to gather here." The town clerk came out of his office when he heard the voice. He thought that it was the voice of the magical Mayor Bonilla with an important message for the town!

The town clerk did what he was told. He ran and got everyone to come to the town hall and stand in front of the statue. The clerk said to the statue, "I have done what you have asked. All are gathered here now." Then the boy came out from behind the statue. He said, "I'm glad that you are all here. Now let me tell you all—the donkey cost fifty cents. Please do not ask me again."

# Let's Explore Caves
## by Chloe Davis

On days when it was rainy or too cold to go outside, my mother let my sister and me build a little hiding place under the kitchen table. We would put a long tablecloth over the table and pull in the chairs. It felt like a secret place where we could play and hide. We used to call it our home cave. It probably felt like a cave to us because we felt cozy and protected where no one could see us. But what is a cave?

Real caves are big openings in the ground. They can extend deep underground, even for miles. Or they can look like big hollow places on the side of a rocky cliff.

Caves are created when water begins to drip onto rock. Natural chemicals that are in the water dissolve, or wear away, the rock. Over time so much rock dissolves that only large hollow places are left. These large hollow places are caves.

Caves have been useful to people for a very long time. People who lived long, long ago used them for shelter from bad weather or to store food. Sometimes people even used caves as their homes or as a special place for ceremonies.

Caves have always seemed kind of mysterious. Maybe that is because caves are dark inside and when you go into one, you don't know how deep it is. And you never know what you are going to find inside.

There are many, many caves of all different types around the world. And because humans are curious, they like to explore caves. There is a special name for that activity—exploring caves is called spelunking. Would you want to be a spelunker?

We can do some pretend spelunking and find out about interesting caves all over the world!

The largest cave in the world is five and a half miles long! It would take a normal adult nearly 2 hours to walk that distance. This cave is underneath a forest in the country of Vietnam. The cave is called Son Doong Cave, which means "cave of the mountain river" in the Vietnamese language. It is so big that it has a jungle and a river inside it! It is so big that it could hold a 40-story skyscraper inside it!

But this cave was a secret of Nature until 6 years ago. A man who lives near the cave discovered it. Maybe the most surprising thing about Son Doong Cave is that scientists say that it is still growing!

Another amazing cave is Waitomo Glowworm Cave in New Zealand. New Zealand is a country all the way on the other side of the world, near Australia. Tiny glow-worms, just a quarter-inch long, hang from the cave ceiling. Glowworms are biolumi-nescent, which means they are a type of living thing that gives off its own light. The glowworms in Waitomo Cave give off a blue light. There are so many of them along the ceiling that the whole cave looks blue!

Let's talk about one more cave. This one is called Spruce Tree House. It is in the state of Colorado in a park called Mesa Verde. What is special about this cave is that there are ruins of a village where ancient people lived, centuries ago. It has 130 rooms that were built into a cliff in the hillside, and the remains of them are still there for everyone to see. Scientists have figured out that groups of 60 to 80 people lived in the cave and farmed corn, beans, and squash. The cave got its name because it was discovered behind a giant spruce tree. Two ranchers discovered the cave when they were looking for stray cattle.

So we have a cave that has a jungle and a river in it, a cave that has glowworms hanging from the ceiling, and a cave that has ruins of long-ago cliff dwellers. Which cave would you want to go spelunking in?

# References

Acosta, J. (2019). *A donkey for fifty cents*. Unpublished manuscript.

Adams, M. J. (1990). *Beginning to read: Thinking and learning about print*. Cambridge, MA: MIT Press.

Alvermann, D. E., O'Brien, D. G., & Dillon, D. R. (1990). What teachers do when they say they're having discussions of content area reading assignments: A qualitative analysis. *Reading Research Quarterly, 24*(4), 296–322.

Anderson, R. C., Chin, C., Commeyras, M., Stallman, A., Waggoner, M., & Wilkinson, I. (1992, December). The reflective thinking project. In K. Jongsma (Chair), *Understanding and enhancing literature discussion in elementary classrooms*. Symposium conducted at the meeting of the National Reading Conference, San Antonio, TX.

Anglin, J. M. (1993). Vocabulary development: A morphological analysis. *Monographs of the Society for Research in Child Development, 58* (Serial No. 238).

Applebee, A. N., Langer, J. A., Nystrand, M., & Gamoran, A. (2003). Discussion-based approaches to developing understanding: Classroom instruction and student performance in middle and high school English. *American Educational Research Journal, 40*(3), 685–730.

Apthorp, H., Randel, B., Cherasaro, T., Clark, T., McKeown, M., & Beck, I. L. (2012). Effects of a supplemental vocabulary program on word knowledge and passage comprehension. *Journal of Research on Educational Effectiveness, 5*(2), 160–188.

August, D., & Shanahan, T. (2006). *Developing literacy in second-language learners: Report of the National Literacy Panel on Language-Minority Children and Youth*. New York: Routledge.

Babbitt, N. (1975). *Tuck everlasting*. New York: Scholastic.

Barrett, T. C. (1967). Goals of the reading program: The basis for evaluation. In T. C. Barrett (Ed.), *The evaluation of children's reading achievement* (pp. 13–26). Newark, DE: International Reading Association.

Beck, I. L., & Beck, M. E. (2013). *Making sense of phonics: The hows and whys* (2nd ed.). New York: Guilford Press.

Beck, I. L., & McKeown, M. G. (1981). Developing questions that promote comprehension: The story map. *Language Arts, 58*(8), 913–918.

Beck, I. L., & McKeown, M. G. (2001). Text Talk: Capturing the benefits of reading aloud for young children. *The Reading Teacher, 55*(1), 10–19.

Beck, I. L., & McKeown, M. G. (2004a). *Text Talk* (Vocabulary supplemental program for kindergarten through grade 2). New York: Scholastic.

Beck, I. L., & McKeown, M. G. (2004b). *Elements of reading: Vocabulary* (Vocabulary supplemental program for kindergarten through grade 5). Austin, TX: Harcourt Achieve.

Beck, I. L., & McKeown, M. G. (2006). *Improving comprehension with Questioning the Author.* New York: Scholastic.

Beck, I. L., & McKeown, M. G. (2007a). Different ways for different goals, but keep your eye on the higher verbal goals. In R. K. Wagner, A. Muse, & K. Tannenbaum (Eds.), *Vocabulary and reading* (pp. 182–204). New York: Guilford Press.

Beck, I. L., & McKeown, M. G. (2007b). Increasing young low income children's oral vocabulary repertoires through rich and focused instruction. *Elementary School Journal, 107*(3), 251–271.

Beck, I. L., McKeown, M. G., & Gromoll, E. W. (1989). Learning from social studies texts. *Cognition and Instruction, 6*(2), 99–158.

Beck, I. L., McKeown, M. G., & Kucan, L. (2002). *Bringing words to life: Robust vocabulary instruction.* New York: Guilford Press.

Beck, I. L., McKeown, M. G., & Kucan, L. (2013). *Bringing words to life: Robust vocabulary instruction* (2nd ed). New York: Guilford Press.

Beck, I. L., McKeown, M. G., McCaslin, E. S., & Burkes, A. M. (1979). *Instructional dimensions that may affect reading comprehension: Examples from two commercial reading programs* (LRDC Pub. No. 1979/20). Pittsburgh: University of Pittsburgh, Learning Research and Development Center.

Beck, I. L., McKeown, M. G., Omanson, R. C., & Pople, M. T. (1984). Improving the comprehensibility of stories: The effects of revisions that improve coherence. *Reading Research Quarterly, 19*(3), 263–277.

Beck, I. L., Omanson, R. C., & McKeown, M. G. (1982). An instructional redesign of reading lessons: Effects on comprehension. *Reading Research Quarterly, 17*(4), 462–481.

Beck, I. L., Perfetti, C. A., & McKeown, M. G. (1982). The effects of long-term vocabulary instruction on lexical access and reading comprehension. *Journal of Educational Psychology, 74*(4), 506–521.

Bellack, A. A., Kliebard, H. M., Hyman, R. T., & Smith, F. L., Jr. (1966). *The language in the classroom.* New York: Teachers College Press.

Black, J. B. (1985). An exposition on understanding expository text. In B. K. Britton & J. B. Black (Eds.), *Understanding expository text: A theoretical and practical handbook for analyzing explanatory text* (pp. 249–267). Hillsdale, NJ: Erlbaum.

Bloom, B. S. (1956). *Taxonomy of educational objectives: The classification of educational goals.* New York: David McKay.

Bransford, J., Brown, A. L., & Cocking, R. R. (2000). *How people learn: Brain, mind, experience, and school.* New York: National Academy Press.

Brown, A. L. (1981). Metacognition and reading and writing: The development and facilitation of selective attention strategies for learning from texts. In M. L. Kamil (Ed.), *Directions in reading: Research and instruction* (pp. 21–43). Washington, DC: National Reading Conference.

Brown, A. L. (1982). Learning and development: The problem of compatibility, access, and induction. *Human Development, 25,* 89–115.

Brown, A. L., Bransford, J. D., Ferrara, R. A., & Campione, J. C. (1983). Learning, remembering, and understanding. In J. H. Flavell & E. M. Markman (Eds.), *Handbook of child psychology* (4th ed., pp. 77–166). New York: Wiley.

Brown, A. L., & Smiley, S. S. (1977). Rating the importance of structural units of prose passages: A problem of metacognitive development. *Child Development, 48*(1), 1–8.

Brown, A. L., & Smiley, S. S. (1978). The development of strategies for studying texts. *Child Development, 49*(4), 1076–1088.

Byrnes, J. P., & Wasik, B. A. (2019). *Language and literacy development* (2nd ed.). New York: Guilford Press.

Caccamise, D., Friend, A., Littrell-Baez, M. K., & Kintsch, E. (2015). Constructivist theory as a framework for instruction and assessment of reading comprehension. In S. R. Parris & K. Headley (Eds.), *Comprehension instruction: Research-based best practices* (3rd ed., pp. 88–104). New York: Guilford Press.

Carboni, R. (n.d.). *Does an elephant never forget?* Unpublished article.

Carlo, M. S., August, D., McLaughlin, B., Snow, C. E., Dressler, C., Lippman, D. N., et al. (2004). Closing the gap: Addressing the vocabulary needs of English language learners in bilingual and mainstream classrooms. *Reading Research Quarterly, 39*(2), 188–215.

Carroll, L. (1865). *Alice in Wonderland*. London: Macmillan.

Carver, R. P. (1987). Should reading comprehension skills be taught? In J. E. Readance & R. S. Baldwin (Eds.), *Research in literacy: Merging perspectives* (Thirty-sixth yearbook of the National Reading Conference, pp. 115–126). Rochester, New York: National Reading Conference.

Chi, M. T. H., Bassok, M., Lewis, M. Reimann, P., & Glaser, R. (1989). Self-explanations: How students study and use examples in learning to solve problems. *Cognitive Science, 13*(2), 45–182.

Chi, M. T. H., de Leeuw, N., Chiu, M., & LaVancher, C. (1994). Eliciting self-explanations improves understanding. *Cognitive Science, 18*(3), 439–477.

Cho, B. Y., & Afflerbach, P. (2015). Reading on the Internet: Realizing and constructing potential texts. *Journal of Adolescent and Adult Literacy, 58*(6), 504–517.

Coiro, J., & Dobler, E. (2007). Exploring the online reading comprehension strategies used by sixth-grade skilled readers to search for and locate information on the Internet. *Reading Research Quarterly, 42*(2), 214–257.

Coyne, M. D., Capozzoli, A., Ware, S., & Loftus, S. (2010, Spring). Beyond RTI for decoding: Supporting early vocabulary development within a multitier approach to instruction and intervention. *Perspectives on Language and Literacy, 36*(2), 18–21.

Curry, N. (2019). *Polar bears, the giants of the arctic*. Unpublished manuscript.

Davis, C. (2019). *Let's explore caves*. Unpublished manuscript.

Davis, F. B. (1944). Fundamental factors in reading comprehension. *Psychometrika, 9,* 185–197.

de la Peña, M. (2015). *Last stop on Market Street*. New York: Penguin Books.

Dennis, R., & Moldof, G. (1983). *A handbook on interpretive reading and discussion*. Chicago: Great Books Foundation.

DiCamillo, K. (2003). *The tale of Despereaux*. Somerville, MA: Candlewick Press.

Dickens, C. (1861). *Great expectations*. London: Chapman & Hall.

Dole, J. A., Duffy, G. G., Roehler, L. R., & Pearson, P. D. (1991). Moving from the old to the new: Research on reading comprehension instruction. *Review of Educational Research, 61*(2), 239–264.

Dowds, S. J. P., Haverback, H. R., & Parkinson, M. M. (2016). Classifying the context clues in children's text. *Journal of Experimental Education, 84*(1), 1–22.

Duffy, G. G., Roehler, L. R., & Hermann, B. A. (1988). Modeling mental processes helps poor readers become strategic readers. *The Reading Teacher, 41*(8), 762–767.

Duffy, G. G., Roehler, L., Sivan, E., Rackliffe, G., Book, C., Meloth, M., et al. (1987). Effects of explaining the reasoning associated with using reading strategies. *Reading Research Quarterly, 22*(3), 347–368.

Duke, N. K. (2000). 3.6 minutes per day: The scarcity of informational texts in first grade. *Reading Research Quarterly, 35*(2), 202–224.

Elleman, A. M., Lindo, E. J., Morphy, P., & Compton, D. L. (2009). The impact of vocabulary instruction on passage-level comprehension of school-age children: A meta-analysis. *Journal of Research on Educational Effectiveness, 2*(1), 1–44.

Fletcher, C. R., van den Broek, P. W., & Arthur, E. (1996). A model of narrative comprehension and recall. In B. K. Britton & A. C. Graesser (Eds.), *Models of understanding text* (pp. 141–163). Mahwah, NJ: Erlbaum.

Gamarra, P. (1993). The bridge on the river Clarinette. In J. Barry, S. Siamon, & G. Huser (Eds.), *Just fantastic!* (pp. 100–104). Calgary, Alberta, Canada: Nelson Canada.

Gannett, R. S. (1948). *My father's dragon.* New York: Random House.

Gaskins, I. W., Anderson, R. C., Pressley, M., Cunicelli, E. A., & Satlow, E. (1993). Six teachers' dialogue during cognitive process instruction. *The Elementary School Journal, 93*(3), 277–304.

Goldenberg, C. (1992). Instructional conversations: Promoting comprehension through discussion. *The Reading Teacher, 46*(4), 316–326.

Goldenberg, C. (2006). Improving achievement for English-learners: What the research tells us. *Education Week, 25*(43), 34–36.

Graesser, A. G., Singer, M., & Trabasso, T. (1994). Constructing inferences during narrative text comprehension. *Psychological Review, 101*(3), 371–395.

Graham, S., Gillespie, A., & McKeown, D. (2013). Writing: Importance, development, and instruction. *Reading and Writing, 26*(1), 1–15.

Hairston, M. (1982). The winds of change: Thomas Kuhn and the revolution in the teaching of writing. *College Composition and Communication, 33*(1), 76–88.

Harbour, K. E., Evanovich, L. L., Sweigart, C. A., & Hughes, L. E. (2015). A brief review of effective teaching practices that maximize student engagement. *Preventing School Failure: Alternative Education for Children and Youth, 59*(1), 5–13.

Hughes, L. (2014). *Thank you, m'am.* North Mankato, MN: Child's World. (Original work published 1958)

Kamil, M. L., Borman, G. D., Dole, J., Kral, C. C., Salinger, T., & Torgesen, J. (2008). Improving adolescent literacy: Effective classroom and intervention practices (IES Practice Guide; NCEE 2008-4027). Washington, DC: National Center for Education Evaluation and Regional Assistance.

Kieffer, M. J., & Lesaux, N. K. (2012). Effects of academic language on relational and syntactic aspects of morphological awareness for sixth graders from linguistically diverse backgrounds. *Elementary School Journal, 112*(3), 519–545.

Kim, J. S., Hemphill, L., Troyer, M. T., Thomson, J. M., Jones, S. J., LaRusso, M., et al. (2016). Engaging struggling adolescent readers to improve reading skills. *Reading Research Quarterly, 52*(3), 357–382.

Kintsch, W., & van Dijk, T. A. (1978). Toward a model of text comprehension and production. *Psychological Review, 85*(5), 363–394.

Lawson, R. (1939). *Ben and me.* New York: Little, Brown.

Linderholm, T., Virtue, S., Tzeng, Y., & van den Broek, P. (2004). Fluctuations in the availability of information during reading: Capturing cognitive processes using the landscape model. *Discourse Processes, 37*(2), 165–186.

MacDonald, A. (1998). *Beware of the bears.* Waukesha, WI: Little Tiger Press.

Macmillan/McGraw-Hill. (1997). *Our nation: Adventures in time and place.* New York: Author.

McIntyre, E. (2015). Comprehension instruction in culturally responsive classrooms. In K. Headley & S. R. Parris (Eds.), *Comprehension instruction: Research-based best practices* (pp. 136–146). New York: Guilford Press.

McKeown, M. G. (1993). Creating effective definitions for young word learners. *Reading Research Quarterly, 28*(1), 16–31.

McKeown, M. G., & Beck, I. L. (1988). Learning vocabulary: Different ways for different goals. *Remedial and Special Education, 9*(1), 42–46.

McKeown, M. G., & Beck, I. L. (2006). Encouraging young children's language interactions with stories. In D. K. Dickinson & S. B. Neuman (Eds.), *Handbook of early literacy research* (Vol. 2, 281–294). New York: Guilford Press.

McKeown, M. G., & Beck, I. L. (2014). Effects of vocabulary instruction on measures of language processing: Comparing two approaches. *Early Childhood Research Quarterly, 29*(4), 520–530.

McKeown, M. G., Beck, I. L., & Blake, R. G. K. (2009). Rethinking reading comprehension instruction: A comparison of instruction for strategies and content approaches. *Reading Research Quarterly, 44*(3), 218–253.

McKeown, M. G., Beck, I. L., Omanson, R. C., & Pople, M. T. (1985). Some effects of the nature and frequency of vocabulary instruction on the knowledge and use of words. *Reading Research Quarterly, 20*(5), 522–535.

McKeown, M. G., Beck, I. L., Sinatra, G. M. & Loxterman, J. A. (1992). The contribution of prior knowledge and coherent text to comprehension. *Reading Research Quarterly, 27*(1), 78–93.

McKeown, M. G., Crosson, A. C., Artz, N. J., Sandora, C., & Beck, I. L. (2013). In the media: Expanding students' experience with academic vocabulary. *The Reading Teacher, 67*(1), 45–53.

McMahon, S. I., Raphael, T. E., Goately, V.S., Boyd, F. B., & Pardo, L. S. (1992). The book club project. In K. Jongsma (Chair), *Understanding and enhancing literature discussion in elementary classrooms.* Symposium conducted at the meeting of the National Reading Conference, San Antonio, TX.

Mehan, H. (1979). *Learning lessons: Social organization in the classroom.* Cambridge, MA: Harvard University Press.

Murray, D. M. (1972, November). Teach writing as process not product. *The Leaflet,* pp. 11–14.

National Center for Education Statistics. (2012). *Vocabulary results from the 2009 and 2011 NAEP Reading Assessments* (NCES 2013-452). Washington, DC: Institute of Education Sciences, U.S. Department of Education.

National Governors Association Center for Best Practices & Council of Chief State School Officers. (2010). *Common Core Standards for English language arts and literacy in history/social studies, science, and technical subjects.* Washington, DC: Authors.

National Reading Panel. (2000). *Teaching children to read: An evidence-based assessment of the scientific literature on reading and its implications for reading instruction* (NIH Pub. No. 00-4754). Washington, DC: National Institutes of Health.

O'Flahavan, J. F., & Stein, C. (1992, December). The conversational discussion groups project. In K. Jongsma (Chair), *Understanding and enhancing literature discussion in elementary classrooms.* Symposium conducted at the meeting of the National Reading Conference, San Antonio, TX.

Palincsar, A. S., & Brown, A. L. (1984). Reciprocal teaching of comprehension-fostering and monitoring activities. *Cognition and Instruction, 1*(2), 117–175.

Paris, S. G., Cross, D. R., & Lipson, M. Y. (1984). Informed strategies for learning: A program to improve children's awareness and comprehension. *Journal of Educational Psychology, 76*(6), 1239–1252.

Pearson, P. D., & Fielding, L. (1991). Comprehension instruction. In R. Barr, M. Kamil, P. Mosenthal, & P. D. Pearson (Eds.), *Handbook of reading research* (Vol. 2, pp. 815–860). New York: Longman.

Perfetti, C., & Stafura, J. (2014). Word knowledge in a theory of reading comprehension. *Scientific Studies of Reading, 18*(1), 22–37.

Polacco, P. (1992). *Picnic at Mudsock Meadow.* New York: Putnam.

Polacco, P. (1998). *Thank you, Mr. Falker.* New York: Philomel Books.

Polacco, P. (2010). *The junkyard wonders.* New York: Philomel Books.

Pressley, M., El-Dinary, P. B., Gaskins, I., Schuder, T., Bergman, J. L., Almasi, J., et al. (1992). Beyond direct explanation: Transactional instruction of reading comprehension strategies. *Elementary School Journal, 92*(5), 513–555.

Rey, H. A. (1941). *Curious George.* Boston: Houghton Mifflin.

Reznitskaya, A., Kuo, L.-J., Glina, M., & Anderson, R. C. (2009). Measuring argumentative reasoning: What's behind the numbers. *Learning and Individual Differences, 19*(2), 219–224.

Rhodes, J. P. (2010). *Ninth ward.* New York: Little, Brown.

Rueda, R., Unrau, N. J., & Son, E. (2015). Comprehension instruction for English language learners. In K. Headley & S. R. Parris (Eds.), *Comprehension instruction: Research-based best practices* (pp. 193–208). New York: Guilford Press.

Sandora, C., Beck, I., & McKeown, M. (1999). A comparison of two discussion strategies on students' comprehension and interpretation of complex literature. *Reading Psychology, 20*(3), 177–212.

Shanahan, T., Callison, K., Carriere, C., Duke, N. K., Pearson, P. D., Schatschneider, C., et al. (2010). *Improving reading comprehension in kindergarten through 3rd grade* (IES Practice Guide; NCEE 2010-4038). Washington, DC: What Works Clearinghouse.

Singer, I. B. (1966). *The snow in Chelm.* New York: HarperCollins.

Snow, C. E., Burns, M. S., & Griffin, P. (Eds.). (1998). *Preventing reading difficulties in young children.* Washington, DC: National Academy Press.

Spearitt, D. (1972). Identification of subskills of reading comprehension by maximum likelihood factor analysis. *Reading Research Quarterly, 8*(1), 92–111.

Stahl, S. A., & Fairbanks, M. M. (1986). The effects of vocabulary instruction: A model-based meta-analysis. *Review of Educational Research, 56*(1), 72–110.

Symons, S., Snyder, B. L., Cariglia-Bull, T., & Pressley, M. (1989). Why be optimistic about cognitive strategy instruction? In C. McCormick, G. Miller, & M. Pressley (Eds.),

*Cognitive strategy research: From basic research to educational applications* (pp. 3–32). New York: Springer-Verlag.

Taha, K. (1991). *A gift for Tia Rosa*. New York: Yearling Books/Random House Children's Books.

Thorndike, E. L., & Woodworth, R. S. (1901). The influence of improvement in one mental function upon the efficiency of other functions (I). *Psychological Review, 8,* 247–261.

Torgerson, C., Brooks, G., Gascoine, L., & Higgins, S. (2019). Phonics: Reading policy and the evidence of effectiveness from a systematic 'tertiary' review. *Research Papers in Education, 34*(2), 208–238.

Troia, G. A., Olinghouse, N. G., Mo, Y., Hawkins, L., Kopke, R. A., Chen, A., et al. (2015). Academic standards for writing: To what degree do standards signpost evidence-based instructional practices and interventions? *Elementary School Journal, 116*(2), 291–321.

van den Broek, P. (1994). Comprehension and memory of narrative texts: Inferences and coherence. In M. A. Gernsbacher (Ed.), *Handbook of psycholinguistics* (pp. 539–588). New York: Academic Press.

van den Broek, P., & Kendeou, P. (2008). Cognitive processes in comprehension of science texts: The role of co-activation in confronting misconceptions. *Applied Cognitive Psychology, 22*(3), 335–351.

van den Broek, P., Young, M., Tzeng, Y., & Linderholm, T. (1998). The landscape model of reading: Inferences and the on-line construction of a memory representation. In H. van Oostendorp & S. R. Goldman (Eds.), *The construction of mental representations during reading* (pp. 71–98). Mahwah, NJ: Erlbaum.

Werner, H., & Kaplan, E. (1950). The acquisition of word meanings: A developmental study. *Monographs of the Society of Research in Child Development, 15*(1), 1–120.

White, E. B. (1952). *Charlotte's web*. New York: Harper & Row.

Wilkinson, I. A. G., Sotor, A. O., & Murphy, P. K. (2010). Developing a model of quality talk about literary text. In M. G. McKeown & L. Kucan (Eds.), *Bringing reading research to life* (pp. 142–169). New York: Guilford Press.

Wright, T., & Cervetti, G. (2017). A systematic review of research on vocabulary instruction that impacts text comprehension. *Reading Research Quarterly, 52*(2), 203–226.

# Index

Note. *f* or *t* following a page number indicates a figure or table.